BETWEEN PEN AND PIXEL

Comics, Materiality, and the Book of the Future

AARON KASHTAN

THE OHIO STATE UNIVERSITY PRESS | COLUMBUS

Library of Congress Cataloging-in-Publication Data

Names: Kashtan, Aaron, author.

Title: Between pen and pixel : comics, materiality, and the book of the future / Aaron Kashtan.

Other titles: Studies in comics and cartoons.

Description: Columbus : The Ohio State University Press, [2018] | Series: Studies in comics and cartoons | Includes bibliographical references and index.

Identifiers: LCCN 2017052754 | ISBN 9780814254707 (pbk. ; alk. paper) | ISBN 0814254705 (pbk. ; alk. paper) | ISBN 9780814213643 (hardcover ; alk. paper) | ISBN 0814213642 (hardcover ; alk. paper)

Subjects: LCSH: Comic books, strips, etc.—History and criticism. | Digital media. | Material culture. | Cartooning—Technique. | Webcomics. | Cartoonists—Comic books, strips, etc.

Classification: LCC PN6714 .K37 2018 | DDC 741.5/9—dc23

LC record available at https://lccn.loc.gov/2017052754

Cover design by Martyn Schmoll
Text design by Juliet Williams
Type set in Palatino Linotype

To my grandfather, Lionel Finkelstein,
a great lover of books

CONTENTS

ILLUSTRATIONS

ACKNOWLEDGMENTS

I WROTE this book while working in a series of nontenure track jobs that did not require me to publish. Therefore, the fact that this book exists at all is a credit to the many colleagues and friends who supported and encouraged my work, believing in me even when I didn't believe in myself. These include but are not limited to Roger Whitson, Rachel Dean-Ruzicka, Matt Ruzicka, Katy Hanggi, Brandon Bentley, Rebecca Weaver, Christine Hoffman, and Jon Kotchian, and, at Miami, Lilian Mina, Tess Evans, and Scott Wagar. I am also indebted to my current and former supervisors, particularly Rebecca Burnett, Robin Wharton, Joan Mullin, and Cat Mahaffey, for creating an environment where I felt comfortable pursuing my research. In addition, I thank the participants in my online writing group, including Lilian Mina (again), Tania Darlington, and Abra Gibson, for keeping me honest and helping me finish this book.

In a larger sense, this book is the product of a lifetime of reading comics and being involved in comics fandom. My father first took me to a comic book store when I was seven years old, but my active involvement in comics fandom began when I started posting at the comicbookresources.com forums. Mordechai Luchins, Rob Imes, Steven Pott, Jim and Terri MacQuarrie, and Christine and Mark Calise, among hundreds of others, taught me most of what I know about comics and helped me feel that my love of comics was not a solitary pastime. Jon B. Cooke gave me my first "official" job in comics fandom and made me feel like I could write about comics and be taken seriously.

As an academic in the field of comics studies, I have other debts that must be acknowledged. My mentors Ana Merino, Michael Chaney, Terry Harpold, and Don Ault helped me become a comics scholar. I also acknowledge the mentorship I received from Beatriz Pastor, Marsha Bryant, Kenneth Kidd, Anastasia Ulanowicz, and the late Scott Nygren. My graduate school friends, including Tof and Nikki Eklund, Stephanie Boluk, Lyndsay Brown, Phil Sandifer, and Zach Whalen, offered me invaluable support at the start of my career.

I have been involved in many academic communities and have presented work derived from this book in a variety of academic contexts, but my disciplinary home has always been comics studies. I am grateful to the many wonderful senior colleagues who have made me feel welcome in the field, including but not limited to Charles Hatfield, Corey Creekmur, Meg Worley, Rebecca Wanzo, Craig Fischer, Qiana Whitted, Derek Parker Royal, Andrew Kunka, Ernesto Priego, and Drew Morton, and also to junior colleagues like Maggie Galvan, Leah Misemer, and Osvaldo Oyola.

On a personal level, my greatest debt is to my parents, Judith and Clifford Kashtan. Besides being responsible for my very existence, they made my undergraduate education possible, and they have offered invaluable emotional and sometimes material support since then. They also showed a keen interest in the progress of this book, and I look forward to seeing how they react to it. This book is dedicated to my grandfather, Lionel Finkelstein, who sometimes wondered why I studied comics rather than serious literature, but whose intellectual curiosity and passion for learning have always been an inspiration to me. However, he and my grandmother, Florence Finkelstein, have always loved comic strips like *The Katzenjammer Kids*, and I hope this book demonstrates how my interests in comics and more "serious" topics can be reconciled. In addition to them, I thank my other grandmother, the late Doris Kashtan. I barely remember my great-grandfather Isaac Finkelstein, but I am inspired by the stories I've heard about his love for and active promotion of Yiddish literature. My babysitter, Leslie Watson, gave me my first composition book.

On a practical level, I am indebted to Chris Roberson, Allison Baker, and Jason Shiga for agreeing to be interviewed at length, and to Gene Ambaum, Alison Bechdel, Colleen Coover, the late Joe Dever, Nat Gertler, Jeet Heer,

Chip Kidd, Andrew Plotkin, Paul Tobin, and the anonymous author of *Cardboard Crack* for answering questions or permitting me to quote unpublished material. I thank Meg Worley (again) for sending me a scan of the cover of the *Fun Home* hardcover; Andrew Kunka (again) for sending me photos of the four-page spread from *MIND MGMT,* volume 3; and Nat Gertler (again) for generously supplying images of *Peanuts* strips in vertical and square format, although these ultimately couldn't be included. I also thank the staff at the University City, Charlotte, location of FedEx Office. I thank the people who have kindly granted image and text permissions, all of whom are individually acknowledged in the text. Besides people listed above, Kevin A. Boyd, Mollie Dezern, Franny Howes, Seth Johnson, and Jarrod Roselló gave me ideas that have made it into the book. This book and my general mental health have benefitted greatly from in-person and Facebook discussions with other people too numerous to name.

I thank my acquisitions editor, Lindsay Martin, for her professionalism, her generosity, her understanding of the field, and her patience with a first-time author. She is a credit to her profession. I also thank Jared Gardner and Lucy Caswell, editors of the OSU Press Studies in Comics and Cartoons series; in particular, not only has Jared's scholarship been an inspiration to me, but he offered me crucial encouragement at an early stage in this project and gave me the initial idea to submit it to OSU Press. I am grateful to two anonymous reviewers for valuable feedback.

Finally, I'd like to thank my cat, Princess Koriand'r of Tamaran. Most of this book was written before he was born, but he takes credit for it anyway.

INTRODUCTION

COMICS, MATERIALITY, AND THE FUTURE OF THE BOOK

LONG BELIEVED to have been terminally ill, the print medium finally died on July 25, 2013. *The Onion,* America's finest news source, reported: "Sources close to print, the method of applying ink to paper in order to convey information to a mass audience, have confirmed that the declining medium passed away early Thursday morning." The demise of print was the result of a long, drawn-out struggle in which "younger, more nimble channels such as the internet, email, and social media" chipped away at some of its most cherished manifestations, including the newspaper and the magazine ("Print Dead"). Yet perhaps the single event that dealt the death blow to print was the replacement of its oldest and most honored incarnation, the printed codex book, by e-books and mobile reading devices such as the iPad and the Kindle. Since its origins in the early Christian era, the printed book had been Western culture's most cherished means of conveying information. However, on January 27, 2011, Amazon.com reported that sales of e-books had outstripped sales of printed books for the first time in history (Adams n.p.), confirming that readers had begun to prefer the convenience and portability of the e-book over the insistent materiality of the printed book. Nostalgic attachment to the medium of the printed book remained a significant current in American culture but had little power to stop the inexorable progress of the digitization of books. It was thus only a matter of time before print finally gave up the ghost. When its funeral was held on July 26, the mourners included a small but deeply saddened group of comic book fans, who had been among the most faithful followers of the dead medium.

While the above account is satirical, it expresses a genuine and widely held anxiety about the future of print. Concerns over the death of print, and in particular the death of the book, are now widespread both in academia and in popular writing. For example, in January 2014, Jordan Weissmann wrote in the *Atlantic* that

> the Pew Research Center reported last week that nearly a quarter of American adults had not read a single book in the past year. As in, they hadn't cracked a paperback, fired up a Kindle, or even hit play on an audiobook while in the car. The number of non-book-readers has nearly tripled since 1978. If you are the sort of person who believes that TV and the Internet have turned American culture into a post-literate scrubland full of cat GIFs and reality TV spinoffs, then this news will probably reinforce your worst suspicions.

Academic works like Sven Birkerts's *The Gutenberg Elegies,* Andrew Piper's *Book Was There,* and Nicholas Carr's *The Shallows* forecast a similarly bleak future for the printed book, as well as for society in general. According to these authors, the death of the print book is inevitable and will result in the loss of the mode of sustained critical thought fostered by print.

Yet Weissman's *Atlantic* article goes on to add that the decline in reading among young people appeared to have stopped, suggesting a more optimistic future for reading. Over the course of 2013, the year of *The Onion*'s obituary for print, other news suggested that reports of print's death were greatly exaggerated. For example, a December 2013 *Wall Street Journal* article observed that "independent bookstores are opening and expanding in Brooklyn and elsewhere in the region, buoyed by the dual role many play as community gathering grounds" (Weiss n.p.). In a September 2014 *Buzzfeed* article, Lincoln Michel observed the curious persistence of print despite continuous reports of its death: "Most articles and nearly every comment thread are filled with declarations that e-book dominance is already here. . . . Anyone who reads print is a 'luddite' propping up a 'dying industry.' If they don't get on board [with e-books] soon, they're doomed! Strangely, you can read those same comments in articles from last year. Or five years ago. Or 10" (n.p.). As a result, a consensus seems to be emerging that print books and digital media are complementary rather than competitive. As Brandon Keim wrote in a 2014 *Wired* article: "Maybe it's time to start thinking of paper and screens another way: not as an old technology and its inevitable replacement, but as different and complementary interfaces, each stimulating particular modes of thinking. Maybe paper is a technology uniquely suited for imbibing novels and essays and complex narratives, just as screens are for browsing and scanning." According to this new consensus, print is capable of surviving the challenge of digital media because it has properties that digital media cannot replicate.[1]

One particular type of book has been even more curiously resistant to replacement by digital equivalents than other genres of books, despite its extreme marginality within the American book industry in general, and may therefore offer valuable lessons about the continuing role that printed books might play in a digital age. I am referring to comic books and graphic novels. This might seem a strange example considering that the comic book has often been seen as far closer to death than the printed book in general. In 2009, for example, Heather Massey observed that the price of comic books (i.e., monthly serialized pamphlets) had risen far more quickly than the inflation rate and that readers were increasingly choosing to consume comic books in the form of collected paperback volumes, imperiling the future of specialty comic book stores. Moreover, since the 1980s, comic books have primarily appealed to an aging audience of primarily white and male readers, leading to concerns about their continued viability. As Michael Chabon said in his 2004 Eisner Awards keynote address: "More adults are reading better comics than ever before; but far fewer people overall" (n.p.). Yet in an age of digitization, the comic book has not only survived but even thrived. According to John Jackson Miller's statistics, sales of printed comic books and graphic novels in May 2013 represented an increase of 90 percent relative to May 2003 (Macdonald 2013). On May 17, 2015, nine of the ten books on the *New York Times* bestseller list for Paperback Graphic Fiction had at least one female creator, and the top five books were YA or middle-grade titles targeted primarily at girls ("Best Sellers"). This statistic, unimaginable even five years before, suggests that comics are successfully expanding beyond their traditional niche audience. At a panel titled "Digital vs. Print: Friends or Foes" at the 2013 Comic-Con International San Diego, Jeff Webber, Vice President of Digital Publishing at

1. There is a clear analogy here to vinyl records, which have grown in popularity even as CDs have been replaced by digital music, thanks to vinyl's analog quality and the tactile, materially rich experience it provides.

IDW Publishing, observed that comics are the *only* sector of the publishing industry that has not been significantly hurt by the trend toward digitization (Parkin n.p.). Indeed, Hillary Chute and Patrick Jagoda have gone so far as to claim that "comics, a site-specific form that cannot be reflowed the way typeset prose can and is a boon in book publishing, is, in a sense, saving the concept of the book as object today" (6). The sales growth in comics has been driven by both the transformation of the comic book store and the integration of comics into the mainstream book industry. While the traditional comic book store has a notorious reputation as a sexist, unwelcoming space, at least some comic book stores have sought to overcome this reputation and to attract new readers.[2] Meanwhile, the adoption of graphic novels by Amazon and by traditional bookstores means that readers are able to purchase comics even if they are not able or willing to enter a comic book store.

Yet at the same time that print represents a vital distribution format for comics, digital comics also represent a significant and growing market. ComiXology, the most popular digital comics application, was the highest-grossing non-game iPad app of 2013 (McMillan n.p.). Webcomics like *xkcd* and *Saturday Morning Breakfast Cereal* have become firmly canonized in Internet culture. Thus, in comics, digital and print formats exist, at least for the moment, in a complementary rather than antagonistic relationship.

This book seeks to examine what it is about comics that makes them so readily adaptable to both digital and print culture and, therefore, what we can learn from comics about the future of the printed book more generally. Why have comics succeeded in maintaining their viability as a print medium, while also successfully transitioning to digital platforms? How might comics serve as a model for other types of books? These are the questions this book strives to answer. My basic contention is that if we want to know where the printed book is going and where it ought to go, we need to think about comics. This is true, moreover, because the debate over the future of the book is largely a question of materiality or material rhetoric. This debate asks what particular material properties of a reading technology are of most value to readers and which medium better promotes these material properties. Or, in a less adversarial framing, the debate asks how

---

2. Further discussion of this topic is outside the scope of the present book, but see my forthcoming book chapter with the working title "How the Comic Book Store Became Ecological," to appear in an anthology from McFarland Press. The transformation of the comics audience and the rise of new reader populations is a massively important development which I hope to discuss in my next major project.

one medium can remediate or draw upon the cherished material properties of the other.

Comics are a useful source of examples in this debate because in the first place, comics offer a model of how the printed book can survive despite competition for digital technology. Many recent works of literature, such as Anne Carson's *Nox* or the novels of Mark Z. Danielewski and Jonathan Safran Foer, have sought to compete with the superior convenience of digital technology by foregrounding their own material properties. In other words, these works of literature demand to be viewed from the viewpoint of *material rhetoric,* which Jack Selzer defines as follows: "Language and rhetoric have a persistent material aspect that demands acknowledgement, and material realities often (if not always) contain a rhetorical dimension that deserves attention; for language is not the only medium or material that speaks" (8). In terms of visible and deliberate exploitation of material rhetoric, however, print literature has lagged significantly behind comics, where the highly prominent and visible use of material rhetoric is the rule rather than the exception.

At the same time, comics also offer instructive examples of how digital texts can replicate the material properties of printed texts. Digital texts are often criticized for their excessive slickness and lack of material richness. Moreover, digital books have often lagged behind print books in terms of their exploitation of the material and tactile possibilities of typography and publication design. In a 2010 *Chronicle of Higher Education* article, the electronic literature scholar Mark Sample observed that "e-books are simply not interesting" because "the e-books you might read on it are much less experimental than any paper-and-glue book" (O'Donnell, et al. n.p.). He observed that the works of authors like Danielewski and Foer could not be adapted onto then-existing e-book devices, but that

> the real problem isn't so much that e-readers won't let me read books that experiment with form. The real problem is that most novelists are writing books that don't experiment with form. Generally people still think about e-books as, well, electronic books. And they imagine the only difference between books and e-books is the screen's replacing the page. . . . For me at least, e-books won't become compelling until writers and publishers begin taking advantage of the native capabilities of e-readers. (n.p.)

While comics don't always exploit the capabilities of digital platforms either, they do suggest ways in which electronic texts can mobilize their own material properties as signifying resources. They also offer a prototype of how existing experimental print texts can be adapted into digital form without sacrificing their experimental nature. Finally, comics also suggest interesting possibilities for print-digital integration and augmented reality, possibilities that have been inadequately explored by existing text-based literature.

My key contentions then are, first, that materiality and material rhetoric are at the heart of the debate between print and digital literature and, second, that comics help us understand this debate better because materiality is a central and constantly visible aspect of the comics reading experience, whereas it is much easier to ignore when reading print literature. In order to explain these two claims in order, let me begin by explaining what I mean by *materiality*.

THEORIES OF MATERIALITY

My understanding of materiality is based on Katherine Hayles's definition of materiality as "the interplay between a text's physical characteristics and its signifying strategies" (2004, 67). I understand materiality as the way in which the physical, technological, and sensuous components of a media artifact help to shape the reader's reception of that media artifact. Materiality is also, as Johanna Drucker has argued, a point of intersection between the physical, phenomenal substance of a text and its activation of codes of signification that operate via relationality and difference. For Drucker, materiality

> includes two major intertwined strands: that of a relational, insubstantial and nontranscendent difference and that of a phenomenological, apprehendable, immanent substance. . . . The material form of the trace, the embodied visual aspect which letters, words, inscriptions present as evidence, is always subject to the rules of linguistic usage and mechanical means which the culture has at its disposal. (1997, 43–44)

Thus materiality includes both the visual and material substrate of texts and the cultural connotations attached to such visual and material substrates. Understood in this sense, materiality is at work both when the physical and technological forms of a media text impact the reading experience and when the physical and technological forms of a media text are shaped by the desire to produce a specific type of reading experience.

Defining materiality in this way makes it clear that the contemporary debate between print and electronic books is a debate over the relative value of two alternative forms of materiality. As Kiene Brillenburg Wurth writes:

> Typically, digital screens have been placed in opposition to the book and paper page in the last two decades: either to defend the latter as the last trace of a material humanist tradition against the incursions of a network of digital distraction, or to promote digitization as liberation from the material constraints of paper and print (from an allegedly "fixed" to a dynamic page, from "static" to moving, dancing, illuminated letters). (2)

Advocates of printed books (e.g., Birkerts, Piper, Carr) argue that the material properties of the printed book are better suited than those of the digital book to keeping the "material humanist tradition" alive. Wurth's reference to "digital distraction" recalls Carr's claim that the visually cluttered and procedurally complicated environment of digital media produces excessive distraction, reducing the ability to contemplate what one reads (6). Technological skeptics like Sven Birkerts and Mark Bauerlein have expanded upon Carr's argument, contending that computers destroy traditional humanistic values such as critical reflection, personality, and authenticity. The opposite side to this debate is represented by first-generation hypertext theorists like George Landow, Jay Bolter, and Michael Joyce, who celebrate the freedom of digital texts from the fixity of the static page and the ability of electronic literature to achieve effects not possible with print. A more nuanced view is offered by scholars like Katherine Hayles (2008), Matthew Kirschenbaum, and Lori Emerson, who emphasize continuities rather than ruptures between print and digital, and this work seeks to follow in their tradition.

A simpler category of objections to digital books relates to their materially impoverished nature. For example, a classic complaint about e-reading devices is that a computer can't be brought into the bathtub. (At a November 2013 conference I heard a senior scholar say that the newspaper would never go away because computers can't be brought into the bathroom. I resisted the temptation to show him my iPhone.) Conversely, the key advantage of the e-reading device over the physical book is its portability and its ability to contain many texts within a single space.

The rise of digital media has changed materiality from a topic of primary interest to textual critics and book historians into a question of central importance in both academic and popular discourses. For much of the twentieth century, especially before the pioneering work of scholars like Jerome McGann and W. J. T. Mitchell, reading was imagined as a purely semiotic experience. The material experience of reading was either ignored or seen as an irrelevant accident of history, a factor that did not need to be taken into account in interpretative accounts of literature. The classic example of this neglect of materiality is W. W. Greg's distinction between "accidentals" and "substantives" in textual editing. For Greg, an editor needed to concern himself or herself only with the semantic content of the text. Issues such as punctuation and spelling were mere "accidental" features, and in reproducing these features, the editor was obliged to follow his or her copy-text exactly (21–22). The substantive/accidental distinction reflects Lessing's classical distinction between word and image, in which the intelligible word takes priority over the sensible image. It is thus congruent with Beatrice Warde's "crystal goblet" philosophy of typography, in which the physical form of the text acts merely as an invisible container for meaning. For Warde,

> if you have no feelings about wine one way or the other, you will want the sensation of drinking the stuff out of a vessel that may have cost thousands of pounds; but if you are a member of that vanishing tribe, the amateurs of fine vintages, you will choose the crystal, because everything about it is calculated to reveal rather than hide the beautiful thing which it was meant to contain. (n.p.)

Analogously, a true lover of typography will choose a font that transmits the semiotic meaning of the text with as little interference as possible. The crystal goblet is currently the normative model of typography for both literary and practical texts. Literary texts that violate the crystal goblet ethos, such as George Herbert's pattern poetry or Blake's illustrated books, have traditionally been viewed as one-of-a-kind experiments or as exceptions that prove the general rule of the unimportance of the physical form of the text. As Jonathan Safran Foer explains, lack of interest in the visual and tactile form of the text is the default attitude among contemporary American authors:

> I've never met an artist [*sic*][3] who wasn't interested in the visual arts, yet we've drawn a deep line in the sand around what we consider the novel to be, and what we're supposed to care about. So we're in the strange position

3. Presumably Foer meant "author," not "artist."

> of having much to say about what hangs on gallery walls and little about what hangs on the pages of our books. (qtd. in Heller n.p.)

While Foer believes that "literature doesn't need a visual component—my favorite books are all black words on white pages" (Heller n.p.), he observes that authors and literary critics have historically been hostile to the notion that the literary experience is visual rather than purely semiotic.

In textual studies, the substantive/accidental distinction was significantly challenged by the work of scholars like D. F. McKenzie and Jerome McGann, who called "attention to the text as a laced network of linguistic and bibliographical codes" (McGann 13). McGann observes that texts, like all other things human, are embodied phenomena, and the body of the text is not exclusively linguistic: "By studying texts through a distinction drawn between linguistic and bibliographical codes, we gain at once a more global and a more uniform view of texts and the processes of textual production. Body is not bruised to pleasure soul" (13–14). Citing Blake's illustrated books and Emily Dickinson's manuscripts as examples, McGann observes that "in these kinds of literary works the distinction between physical medium and conceptual message breaks down completely" (77). Accordingly, many contemporary American authors—including Foer himself as well as Mark Z. Danielewski, Jennifer Egan, Garth Risk Hallberg, and Salvador Plascencia—have deliberately sought to create works that employ the visual form of the text as a carrier of semantic meaning. (As I will discuss later, all of these works are motivated at some level by the contemporary need to differentiate print from digital literature.) Yet works like these are not the exception that proves the rule that a text's typography and publication design are irrelevant to its semiotic meaning. On the contrary, book historians have shown how even in texts whose physical layout is not obviously relevant to their meaning, typography can significantly condition the reader's experience of the text. For example, D. F. McKenzie's essay "Typography and Meaning: The Case of William Congreve" demonstrates how Congreve's 1710 collected works "deployed a variety of typographical, bibliographical, and textual resources—many of them so-called accidentals—to bridge the gap between the ephemeral, three-dimensional stage and the enduring, two-dimensional page," and also to "[confer] a more dignified cultural status on the text" than it had had in earlier quarto publications (McDonald and Suarez 198). In Congreve's collected works, the effect of materiality on the reader's perception of the text is all the more powerful precisely because the relevant material qualities of the text are invisible (figure I.1).

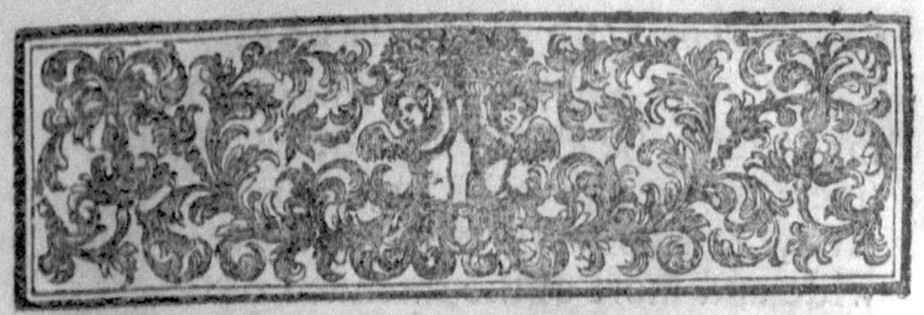

THE

OLD BATCHELOR.

ACT I. SCENE I.

SCENE, *The Street.*

Bellmour *and* Vainlove *meeting,*

BELLMOUR.

Ainlove, and abroad ſo early! good Morrow; I thought a Contemplative Lover could no more have parted with his Bed in a Morning, than he could have ſlept in't.

Vain. Bellmour, good Morrow—Why truth on't is, theſe early Sallies are not uſual to me; but Buſineſs, as you ſee, Sir—[*Shewing Letters.*] And Buſineſs muſt be follow'd, or be loſt.

B *Bell.*

FIGURE I.1. The first page of William Congreve's *The Old Bachelor*, from Jacob Tonson's 1710 edition of his collected works. Note the typographic ornaments and act and scene division, which are missing from the earlier quarto version of the play. Image courtesy of The Ohio State University Library.

One of the major contentions of this book, however, is that discussions of the impact of materiality on reading are often confused and indeterminate because such discussions have historically focused on text-based literary forms, such as novels and nonfictional prose. It is difficult to see how materiality affects the experience of reading a literary text when the verbal and semiotic content of a literary text is typically the same regardless of the material form in which it is encountered. To put it another way, in prose fiction, the importance of materiality tends to be obscured by the dominant crystal goblet ethos of book design and by the related fact that readers are typically socialized into reading transparently, without attention to materiality. In other words, largely *due* to the *standard* crystal *goblet* model of *typography, we as* readers are *unlikely* to pay attention *to* the physical *attributes* of the text we read—unless the *author or* typographer intentionally *calls* our attention to those attributes, as in the present sentence. When a text employs crystal goblet design and does not deliberately invite the reader to pay attention to its material properties, as is the case with the vast majority of prose literary works, then the reader notices its visual, physical, and tactile attributes only if he or she performs a deliberate act of attentional reorientation. For any professionally published book, publication designers and typographers spend a great amount of time and effort on shaping the physical appearance of the book so that it helps produce the desired reading experience. However, the work that goes into the physical design of the book is invisible to the reader, and the reader rarely notices how the book's design shapes his or her perceptions.[4] The act of reading a book is never purely a cognitive experience but is always also a material, embodied process—yet unless we deliberately redirect our attention, we typically see it as the former and not the latter.

This, I suggest, is why our discussions of the materiality of literature should focus not on textual literature but on another medium where the effect of materiality is much harder to ignore. If we want to know how the reading experience will be transformed by changes in its material context, we need to be looking at comics. However, the idea of studying comics for this reason is not immediately obvious because of the way that the field of comics studies has been constituted.

4. This is why I often show my students Gary Hustwit's 2007 independent documentary film *Helvetica*—because I want them to be aware that the visual design of a text is the result of deliberate rhetorical decisions.

THEORIES OF MATERIALITY IN COMICS STUDIES

Formerly dismissed as mere pop culture for children, comics have increasingly been recognized as one of the central literary and visual art forms of the twentieth and early twenty-first centuries. In the academy, texts such as Art Spiegelman's *Maus,* Alison Bechdel's *Fun Home,* and Marjane Satrapi's *Persepolis* are regularly taught in courses spanning a wide range of academic disciplines, and comics studies is emerging as a recognized scholarly discipline, as indicated by the existence of scholarly monograph series like this one. In the wider cultural sphere, new graphic novels are regularly reviewed in the *New York Times Book Review* and the *New York Review of Books* and are a regular feature on year-end lists of best books. However, the importance of comics to discussions of materiality and the future of the book has not been sufficiently recognized.

Theorists of materiality such as Hayles, Drucker, and Kirschenbaum have largely ignored comics, with the exception of one essay by Drucker on Chris Ware, and critical accounts of the future of the book rarely if ever mention comics. This neglect has continued even as comics have acquired greater visibility among cultural critics and literary scholars. This, I suggest, is attributable to the way in which the field of comics studies has developed. In North America, the academic field of comics studies has coalesced around a very small canon of texts—essentially, *Maus, Persepolis,* and *Fun Home,* as mentioned above, plus works by a few other artists, such as Lynda Barry, Chester Brown, Chris Ware, and Joe Sacco. These are the comics that have attracted the most scholarly attention, including entire monographs or edited collections in the case of *Maus* and Barry's work. Based on my anecdotal experience, when nonspecialists choose to teach a comic in a course primarily focused on texts other than comics, it will almost always be a comic from the above list. Comics scholars do, of course, write about and teach many comics that don't fall into this canon, notably including superhero comics. But for scholars and teachers who are not comics experts, the common perception is that "comics" or "graphic novels," as an object of academic study, means Spiegelman, Bechdel, Barry, and so forth, and that superhero comics and comic strips, for example, are something different.[5]

While all the texts in the academic comics canon are clearly major works with significant value for scholarship and pedagogy, the fact that the comics canon has coalesced around these texts has created distorted views of

5. Moreover, work on superheroes is defined by its focus on a particular genre rather than a particular medium or form of materiality, and it often focuses on film instead of comics. See, for example, Dan Hassler-Forest, *Capitalist Superheroes.*

the field, causing scholars to identify comics as a whole with one particular genre of comics. Almost all the works in the academic canon are graphic memoirs or works of graphic journalism, and they tend to deal with issues of memory, trauma, history, and ethnic and queer identity. Since Marianne Hirsch's pioneering work on *Maus* and postmemory was published, such issues have been seen as central to comics studies. Hillary Chute has even made the explicit claim that autobiography and childhood memory are the privileged subject matter of comics:

> The form of comics has a peculiar relationship not only to memoir and autobiography in general, as I will note, but to narratives of development. Additionally, comics and the movement, or act, of memory share formal similarities that suggest memory, especially the excavation of childhood memory, as an urgent topic in this form. . . . Through its hybrid and spatial form, comics lends itself to expressing stories, especially narratives of development, that present and underscore hybrid subjectivities. (2010, 4–5)

Chute goes on to suggest that "historical graphic novels are the strongest emerging genre in the field" (9) and that "the autobiographical genre of comics . . . has become the dominant mode of contemporary work" (17). The influence of scholars like Hirsch, Chute, and Julia Watson has reinforced this belief that autobiography, history, and journalism are the dominant genre of comics. This view of comics has been reinforced by the fact that most North American comics scholars come from a background of literary scholarship. Texts like *Maus, Persepolis,* and *Fun Home* are easy for literary scholars to appreciate, and the issues they address are already central topics in literary studies.

This focus on a narrow canon of autobiographical, historical, and journalistic comics has limited the scope of comics studies in two ways. First, one particular genre of comics has become the privileged object of study at the expense of all others. Second, more attention has been devoted to themes such as autobiography, trauma, and history than to questions of materiality and mediacy, with the result that comics scholars have sometimes offered insufficiently theorized accounts of the latter topics.

Materiality has emerged as a significant topic in comics studies thanks to the work of scholars like Ernesto Priego and Ian Hague. Moreover, other scholars like Charles Hatfield, Hillary Chute, Jared Gardner, and Jean-Paul Gabilliet have provided useful insights into the materiality of comics, though sometimes without specifically using that term. Comics scholars have increasingly recognized that our interpretative and affective experience of a comic is fundamentally conditioned by the particular form in which we encounter that comic. However, existing comics theory often provides an incomplete account of materiality that is frequently biased by a focus on nonfiction genres. For example, Hillary Chute's work on Alison Bechdel and Lynda Barry is based on a naive assumption that printed comics are literal replications of the author's handwriting, as we will see in my own discussions of these authors. Chute's privileging of handwriting in comics is tied to her assumption that autobiography, a genre intimately linked to the self-representation of the author, is the dominant genre of comics.

The neglect of questions of mediacy in comics studies is starting to reverse itself. Critics such as Priego, Hague, Hatfield, and Gardner have drawn more attention to the complex material interactions that exist in comics. Therefore, this book does not break completely new ground in advocating for the importance of materiality in comics. However, even when comics scholars have written about materiality, they have not paid sufficient attention to what comics can tell us about shifts from print to digital forms of materiality. For instance, Gardner's book *Projections* intentionally declines to address digital comics for reasons of scope. A recent major work on the materiality of comics is Ian Hague's *Comics and the Senses,* but while Hague's work significantly advances our understanding of the various sensory modalities at work in comics reading, it is concerned primarily with expanding our understanding of comics reading and not with relating comics to larger problems in the field of materiality. We are therefore currently without an account of materiality in comics that takes full account of the evolution of comics in the digital era. This is an error that needs to be rectified because comics can significantly add to our understanding of questions of materiality.

WHAT COMICS CAN TELL US ABOUT MATERIALITY

Comics help us understand questions of the materiality of the book because they prevent us from being distracted by the crystal goblet illusion. Of course, in comics, distinctions such as substantive/accidental, medium/message, sensible/intelligible, and form/matter don't make sense. In comics, it is impossible to dissociate the semiotic content of the text from its physical form, or even to imagine the two as separate. Even more generally, I would argue, in comics, attention to materiality is the *default* position. Comics call the reader's attention to their visual and physical structure almost automatically. In reading comics, it is often more difficult to *ignore* visual features such as page layout and draftspersonship than to consciously notice them. This is certainly not true in all cases, and it tends to be less true for comics that adopt familiar or stereotyped artistic styles. One can easily read a volume of manga or a Marvel superhero comic without paying attention to its materiality, especially if one is already an experienced reader of these genres of comics.[6] Frederik L. Schodt wrote in 1983 that readers took an average of 20 minutes to finish a 320-page manga magazine, or 3.75 seconds per page (18). Nonetheless, at a basic level, every comic *looks* visually distinct from every other comic, whereas one prose novel or academic monograph looks much like any other prose novel or academic monograph, and this means that materiality tends to be far more noticeable in comics than in prose.

Another way to put this is to observe that the comics text is always instantiated in a specific visual and typographic form, and this form cannot be changed without radically altering the text itself. As Chute writes:

> Writing about avant-garde poetry . . . Drucker observes "the use of visual information as a material in its own right. These are works that cannot be translated—either linguistically or typographically—without losing some essential value performed by the original work." This sense of the poetic page as the space of performance opened my eyes to how comics functions narratively and graphically. Comics is a site-specific medium; it can't be re-flowed, re-jiggered on the page; hence, it is spatially located on the page the way that poetry often must be. (2013 n.p.)[7]

Noah Berlatsky clarifies: "This is in contrast to prose, where the position of the words on the page isn't important and can change from edition to edition" (n.p.). In comics, any alteration of the visual form of the text—or the publication format, as I will argue in the next chapter—has significant *and visible* effects on meaning. This has to be emphasized: in prose as well as in comics, changes in the spatial arrangement of the text affect the reading experience, but the difference between comics and prose is that in comics, the *ways* in which this happens are more immediately obvious.

---

6. I thank Corey Creekmur for raising this objection. Of course, some manga do employ highly ornate and elaborate page layouts that require more active attention from the reader. For example, the Year 24 Group of female shoujo manga artists were noted for their radical departures from standard page layout techniques (Gravett 79).

7. I will critique this argument in chapter 3, but my objections to it can be ignored for the moment.

Of course, materiality is not always an active element in the reading of comics. It is certainly true that comics *can* be designed in a crystal goblet fashion and that they are often read in a transparent fashion, without awareness of materiality. Again, manga, in particular, seem explicitly designed to evoke this sort of reading practice. Moreover, some aspects of comics tend to be more transparent than others; for example, a common piece of conventional wisdom is that when comics lettering is done effectively, the reader doesn't notice it. Finally, if comics are typically read in a nontransparent fashion, it is the result of both formal and cultural factors. On the one hand, comics are typically designed in a manner that forces the reader to pay attention to parameters such as page layout, draftsmanship, and often even publication design and typography. In other words, golden goblet design (the mentality that Warde opposes to crystal goblet design) is much more common in comics than in literary prose, and is almost ubiquitous in comics with artistic intent. At the same time, especially in North America, comics tend to be an "unfamiliar" medium. Most readers of comics have less experience with comics than with other media and are therefore not socialized into ignoring the material properties of comics as they would do when reading prose. Therefore, comics may be read in a nontransparent fashion regardless of whether they are designed to evoke such a reading practice.

I do suggest, however, that golden goblet design and nontransparent reading are much *more* standard in comics than in literary texts. When reading a comic, as opposed to when reading a prose literary text, the reader finds it much more difficult to fall into the illusion that he or she is having a purely cognitive and disembodied experience. In particular, in the avant-garde or noncommercial segment of the comics industry, golden goblet design is ubiquitous; it would be difficult to think of a single major avant-garde comic that solicits a transparent mode of reading. Even in comics that employ deliberately understated visual strategies, like the work of Seth (the pen name of Gregory Gallant) or Chester Brown, the reader is always aware that the artist's work *looks* different from that of other artists. Seth's transparency is not the same as Chester Brown's transparency. In contrast, even though golden goblet design has become steadily more important in English-language fiction, the vast majority of literary novels and short stories are still designed and typeset in a crystal goblet style, and that style is similar from one book to another.

Because comics take advantage of their own materiality as a signifying resource, and because they deliberately cultivate awareness of materiality, they are useful for understanding the current debate between print and digital literature. When we consider materiality from the perspective of comics rather than that of print, we avoid being distracted by the crystal goblet phenomenon, because we can literally *see* how alterations in materiality lead to alterations in content and affective response. Comics lay everything out flat on the page and make the act of reading visible, and it is for this reason, I argue, that comics need to take center stage in debates over materiality and the future of the book.

OUTLINE OF CHAPTERS

In chapter 1, I argue for the importance of an analytical practice that pays attention to the effect of mediacy and materiality on the rhetorical experience of comics—that is, I argue for the application to comics of what Katherine Hayles calls media-specific analysis. I model this analytical practice with a discussion of Alison Bechdel's *Fun Home.* Furthermore, I suggest that by studying comics from a media-specific perspective, we can develop insights that are generalizable to books in general. Because comics make visible the difference between alternative print editions of a book or between print and digital editions, they help us literally see what happens when books move from print to digital form or vice versa.

With this analytical foundation established, I spend the rest of the book examining what comics can tell us about the effect of digitization on the future of the book. In chapter 2, I begin by examining how authors of print comics have responded to digitization. I argue that digitization represents a "crisitunity" for print comics, in that it not only creates a sense of impending crisis but also provides creators with a previously absent incentive to explore the unique creative affordances of print.

Chapter 3 proceeds from the opposite angle, examining how, contrary to Scott McCloud's predictions in 2000, print remains central to the way in which the contemporary digital comics industry has been constituted. In the first place, webcomics are not completely ethereal and weightless artifacts—some webcomics are just as tactile as print comics, or even more so, since they exploit tactile functionalities that are not available in print. In the second place, because sales of print editions are a vitally important source of revenue for webcomics creators, there is an economic incentive for webcomics to be produced in a form that is adaptable to print.

These chapters suggest that an antagonistic relationship exists between print comics and digital comics, but in chapter 4, I suggest that the opposite is the case. While many contemporary comics are "fixed" to either the print or the digital medium, many other comics are "flexible" in that they are designed to be publishable in either print or digital form without significantly degrading the reading experience. Chapter 4 argues that the contemporary comics distribution system has evolved in a way that allows it to facilitate remediation between print and digital in both directions at once. ComiXology, the leading digital comics website, publishes both digitized versions of print comics and digital comics that are intended to subsequently appear in print. I discuss examples of comics that have passed through the filter of ComiXology in both directions.

But if comics can be designed to move smoothly from digital to print form and back, then we can take one step beyond that. What if a comic existed in both print and digital versions, but each version was formatted differently in order to take advantage of the unique affordances of its medium, so that reading the two versions concurrently would become an interesting exercise in comparative media studies? Chapter 5 begins by examining two comics, Chris Ware's *Building Stories* and Jason Shiga's *Meanwhile,* that have been published in both print and digital forms. However, unlike in some of the cases discussed earlier, the print and digital forms of each comic are significantly different; each comic was originally published in one form but had to be reformatted substantially to preserve this functionality in the other form. These examples suggest one final possibility: a comic that exists interstitially *between* the print and digital media and is intended to be read in both media at once. Currently the best example of this approach is not a comic but an artist's book, Amaranth Borsuk and Brad Bouse's *Between Page and Screen,* but comics have the ability to extrapolate from the lessons offered by Borsuk and Bouse's book and to produce new and exciting work in its vein.

In the conclusion, I discuss possible pedagogical and scholarly applications of the perspective on comics outlined in this book. I suggest that whether we're specifically studying or teaching comics or not, we can draw inspiration from comics as texts which, at their best, display careful attention to materiality and design. I outline various assignments I've used that took inspiration from the approach to materiality demonstrated in comics. While this conclusion is written from my perspective as a comics scholar and a composition instructor who makes extensive use of comics, I hope its insights will be useful to teachers and scholars from other disciplinary backgrounds.

WHAT THIS BOOK IS NOT

This book is not a comprehensive study of the impact of digitization on the comics industry. The specific goal of this book is to examine how digital technologies have impacted the material rhetoric of comics—that is, the ways in which comics communicate through their audiences' interactions with them. Therefore, this book concentrates on the distribution and reception rather than the production of comics. Scott McCloud draws a distinction between *digital production* and *digital delivery* of comics, meaning respectively "the creation of comics with digital tools" and "the distribution of comics in digital form" (2000, 22). This book touches on the question of digital production of comics but is principally about digital delivery. The past two decades have seen many radical innovations in comics production technology, such as the widespread adoption of Wacom and Cintiq tablets as drawing tools, but a full examination of the effect of digital technology on comics production methods will have to wait for another book.

Furthermore, this book is admittedly biased toward the print side rather than the digital side of comics. I emphasize print in this way for reasons of scope and expertise, as well as personal preference. I grew up reading print comics and have never gotten used to reading comics on a screen or on the Kindle. Even when I lived in a town with no comic book store, I chose to use a mail-order comic book subscription service rather than downloading new comics from ComiXology. This is purely a personal inclination on my part, and I mention it merely to make my biases clear, not to argue that print is objectively superior to digital. The other reason for my emphasis on print is that print is currently perceived as the more embattled of the two media. The future survival of the print book seems much more in doubt than that of the digital book. Therefore, it seems necessary to use the example of comics to demonstrate that print books can not only survive the challenge of digitization but can even productively draw inspiration from digital books. At the same time, I do hope to also use comics as an example of how digital texts can adopt some of the cherished properties of print.

Finally, my goal is neither to predict nor to prescribe what the future of the book should look like. I am trying neither to make definitive forecasts as to what the book of the future will be nor to offer advice to artists or to industry professionals on how to create or market books. All of this is beyond my expertise.

In particular, I am not qualified to comment on the economics of the comics or book industries. For example, while I end by suggesting that books which blend print and digital functionality are an exciting way forward, I do not propose an economic model for how such books might work. My argument is that such books are artistically and rhetorically necessary, independently of their economic justification. When, at some points in this book, I do discuss economics, I seek to avoid exceeding the limits of my expertise by framing such discussions in terms of rhetoric and aesthetics. For example, in chapter 3, I explain why people are willing to purchase print editions of webcomics that they can already read for free. While this discussion uses readers' economic preferences as evidence, it does so in order to prove claims about authors' and publishers' rhetorical and aesthetic choices.

My goal, then, is not to propose economic models but simply to suggest that comics are an effective way of thinking about and imagining the future of the book. My basic theoretical claim, as I will explain in the conclusion, is that *every* book is a comic insofar as it makes thoughtful use of images in relation to text. Comics offers a model and a vocabulary for thinking about book design as an expressive process. If we think about books in this way, then the question of the future of the book stops being exclusively a question of which medium offers the most efficient ways of delivering information. It also becomes a question of which medium can provide the most visually and materially rich experiences, or how the phenomenological, material, and visual experiences of the two media differ from and also resemble each other.

To this extent, my argument is addressed primarily to comics scholars, and secondarily to scholars in other related fields such as rhetoric and composition, media studies, games studies, and book history. As I suggest below with a different emphasis, I want to suggest that we can leverage our intuitive understanding of materiality and mediacy in order to comment on and perhaps transform the debate over the future of the book. A possible tertiary audience for this book includes comics artists, publishers, and book designers. I hope that for professionals in the comics and book industries, this book may offer intriguing insights or possible ways forward. But I don't intend to offer practical artistic or publishing advice, nor am I qualified to do so; I only present a theoretical framework that can be put into artistic or publishing practice in a variety of ways.

WHO SHOULD READ THIS BOOK, AND WHO WROTE IT

This book is intended to speak to many academic and nonacademic audiences. My argument is addressed primarily to comics scholars, as this is the scholarly community with which I identify most closely. My primary rhetorical aims in this book are to encourage comics scholars to think differently about mediacy and materiality and to reorient the field of comics studies toward such questions. As previously suggested, I also hope that this book will be useful to scholars in rhetoric and composition, games studies, book history, and so on. I hope that such scholars will be patient if I make theoretical claims that seem excessively obvious to them, because these claims are not yet common in comics studies. Finally, I hope that this book will also have a broader appeal and even that it will be interesting to comics fans outside the academy. One of the pleasures of comics scholarship is the close relationship that exists between creators, scholars, and fans.

I'm an example of that close relationship because I was a fan before I was a scholar, and my motivations for writing this book are deeply influenced by my fandom. I write as what Henry Jenkins calls an "aca-fan," a scholar who also self-identifies as a fan of his or her object of study. I have been reading comics since I was seven years old, I have been attending comic book conventions and participating in online comics fandom since I was in junior high school, and I have spent several years as a moderator at *comicbookresources.com*, one of the World Wide Web's most heavily trafficked comic book forums. I even worked in the comics fan press for two years as an editorial intern for Jon B. Cooke's magazine *Comic Book Artist*. Thus, like many other comics scholars, I came to comics scholarship from comics fandom. My arguments in this book are informed not only by scholarly research but also by firsthand knowledge acquired through many years of involvement in comics fandom. Furthermore, as seems to be the case with many comics scholars, the motivation behind my research is my desire to increase the academic respectability of a medium that I deeply love. As a comics fan, I want other academics to sympathize with my fandom: I want my colleagues to see comics as the ninth art, an artistic medium as respectable as literature or film. I want comics studies to develop as an academic discipline: I want there to be more departments or programs in comics studies, I want to see more peer-reviewed journals and major national conferences devoted into comics, and I want more comics scholars to get tenure-track jobs. In that sense, I am a comics evangelist.

However, I believe that many scholars are currently engaging in comics evangelism in an excessively narrow way that is doomed to have only limited success. As I discussed above, comics scholars often try to promote comics by showing that particular examples of the medium are relevant to discussions of established topics of the humanities. For example, each chapter of Rocco Versaci's *This Book Contains Graphic Language* focuses on different preexisting literary genres (e.g., memoir and journalism) and describes examples of comics relevant to the genre. This approach succeeds only in demonstrating that *particular* comics are relevant to discussions of particular literary genres or problematic; it fails to suggest why comics *as a medium* are worth discussing in the context of literature. I believe that if we want comics studies to develop as a discipline, we need to show why comics are relevant in a more general sense. We need to prove that comics are as relevant to the mission of the humanities academy (however that may be defined) as cinema or video games, other media that also emerged from mass culture but that now enjoy a degree of academic legitimacy that comics still lack. The present book attempts, rather overambitiously, to contribute to that goal by showing how comics help us develop a better understanding of a pressing question in academic and popular debate over the humanities: the question of the nature of the book of the future.

CHAPTER 1

MY MOTHER WAS A TYPEWRITER

Fun Home and the Relevance of Materiality to Comics Studies

THIS CHAPTER sets the stage for the chapter 2 discussion by demonstrating the ways in which materiality affects the reading experience of comics.[1] Thanks to the work of textual critics like Jerome McGann and D. F. McKenzie, as well as material rhetoricians like Jack Selzer and Sharon Crowley, it has long been known that the physical and technological form of a text affects the way in which the reader comprehends its meaning. However, my contentions in this chapter are that comics scholars have not been sufficiently sensitive to questions of materiality and material rhetoric, and that comics scholars need to pay more attention to such questions because comics are an important test case for broader discussions of textual materiality, insofar as the rhetorical effects of materiality are frequently more visible in comics than in prose texts. I demonstrate this through an analysis of one graphic novel, Alison Bechdel's *Fun Home,* which offers particularly important insights about textual materiality.

1. This chapter is a somewhat revised version of Kashtan 2013. Material from that article is reproduced by kind permission of Taylor & Francis. See http://www.tandfonline.com/doi/full/10.1080/21504857.2012.718290 for the original article. I'm indebted to Rachel Dean-Ruzicka, Roger Whitson, and Meg Worley for their assistance with the earliest version of this material.

Fun Home is perhaps the most widely discussed graphic novel since Art Spiegelman's *Maus*. However, the critical literature on this text is primarily concerned with questions of theme rather than medium, as is also true of comics scholarship and pedagogy more generally. In this chapter I use *Fun Home* to model a practice of what Katherine Hayles (2000) calls "media-specific analysis" of comics: a mode of analysis that pays attention both to the physical and material parameters of a text and to the ways in which these parameters are involved in the creation of meaning. Instead of treating "comics" as an a priori, Platonic concept which exists prior to the way it gets instantiated in particular media and technologies, media-specific analysis pays more attention to how the technological parameters of comics help to shape what comics are. Because of its explicit engagement with questions of materiality, particularly questions of handwriting and the physical form of the book, and also because of its prominence within academic comics studies, *Fun Home* is an appropriate text to use as a test case of this type of analysis. In subsequent chapters, I use the mode of media-specific analysis demonstrated in this chapter to explore more specific questions involving the transition of comics from print to digital form and back.

My claim that comics scholars have been inattentive to questions of media seem counterintuitive given the frequency with which comics scholars employ the term *medium*. However, comics scholars typically use the term *medium* in an excessively abstract way. In comics studies, the term *the comics medium* often means comics as a generalized, Platonic form, which is independent of the technologies used to display comics. For example, Henry John Pratt writes: "My aim is to investigate the most prominent narrative functions of the comics medium (both in its newspaper and its book form, though I will explain some differences between these where warranted) and to show how these are similar to and different from related media" (108). In this sense, newspaper comic strips, comic books, graphic novels, webcomics, and comics viewed on an e-book reader are all instances of "the comics medium," though they may differ in some details, and questions of "medium" have to do with the difference between comics and other artistic "media" such as prose, poetry, or film. Specifically, under this view of "medium," any individual comic—Alan Moore and Dave Gibbons's *Watchmen*, for example—is the same comic regardless of the particular form in which it exists. Whether *Watchmen* is read as a graphic novel, a hardcover, a series of twelve pamphlet-sized comic books, or a digital file, it remains an example of the comics medium.[2]

2. As a counterexample, Randy Duncan and Matthew Smith write that "there is no distinct medium known as comics" (3) and that under some perspectives, comic books and comic strips constitute different media (5).

I suggest, however, that it's more productive to understand the term *medium* in Bolter and Grusin's sense: as something that remediates (65). For the purposes of the present analysis, I will define a medium as a historically and culturally situated assemblage of technologies and physical parameters, which is employed for the delivery of some sort of content. In Bolter and Grusin's sense, or in the sense of Katherine Hayles's "media-specific analysis" (2002, 29), comic strips, graphic novels, webcomics, and so on, are all different "media," and they are not neutral relative to content. A media-specific analysis of a text asks how it engages with its material and technological conditions of production and distribution—meaning both how its content is shaped by its material parameters and how it uses those same material parameters as a signifying resource. The term *media* in this sense therefore overlaps with *materiality,* a term that also appears in the published literature on comics, albeit with much less frequency (see my definition of this term in the introduction). What I hope to demonstrate in this chapter is that materiality, in this sense, plays a crucial if easily under-appreciated role in our understanding of comics and that as comics scholars we need to take materiality into account.

I would contend, for example, that *Watchmen* is not the "same" text when read as twelve individual comic books, or as a perfect-bound trade paperback, or as a digital file on Amazon's Kindle Fire—and that these are all different media through which the art form of comics can be delivered. Comics creators, retailers, and fans know this intuitively, as illustrated by recent controversies in creative and fan circles over practices like "waiting for the trade" or the digital distribution and downloading of comics.[3] Fans like me intuitively know that comics don't "read" the same when read in trade paperback, or in single-issue, or in digital format. Moreover, the controversial nature of these practices indicates that the physical form of a comic is not culturally neutral. When comics are repackaged in different print or digital formats, this repackaging affects the cultural and economic status of these texts. For example, when a story originally published in serialized comic books and sold in specialty stores is repackaged as a trade paperback and sold in chain bookstores, this changes who has access to the comic and also alters the cultural connotations of the comic. I will discuss below how *Fun Home* both comments on the importance of the materiality of texts and serves as an example of the importance of materiality because

3. Indeed, *Watchmen* itself has been the subject of such controversies. In September 2011, *Watchmen* was one of 100 DC graphic novels that were announced as exclusives for the Kindle Fire. Barnes and Noble reacted to this announcement by discontinuing sales of those graphic novels in its brick-and-mortar stores (R. Johnston, "Barnes & Noble Pulls Watchmen," 2011).

of both the physical and the cultural differences between its various incarnations as hardcover, paperback, and e-book.

Comics scholars have treated mediacy and materiality as mere accidental features of comics or incidental devices for the transmission of meaning, and they have therefore been inattentive to the ways in which materiality also shapes meaning. A full attention to this question is essential given that comics texts are inseparable from their material and medial conditions of production in a way in which literary texts are not. As discussed in the introduction, when a literary text is reprinted on new paper or with a different typeface, this change is not typically seen as an alteration of the essential nature of the text. Literary works that cannot be reprinted in this way because their visual, typographic, and tactile properties are essential to their meaning—for example, George Herbert's pattern poetry or Mark Z. Danielewski's novels—are typically seen as exceptions rather than the rule.[4] The identity of the text appears to reside in the text itself, that is, the ordered string of signifiers it comprises, and not in the way in which this text is instantiated. For purposes of text encoding, it often makes sense to view the text as an "Ordered Hierarchy of Content Objects" (OHCO) (Renear 224–25), in which all that matters are the pieces of linguistic content and the hierarchical relationships between them, not the specific material forms in which these pieces of content are embodied.[5] In comics, this distinction between the text and its physical and graphic instantiation hardly seems to exist. When a comic is reprinted with different coloring or lettering, such as when old comic books are recolored via computer, the effects are dramatically obvious.[6] The materiality of comics is hard to ignore.

Even in the case of text-based literature, scholars have long since recognized that a literary text is not a transhistorical, Platonic essence. Critics like W. J. T. Mitchell and Jerome McGann have shown how the experience of reading a literary text is affected by the particular material form in which that text is instantiated. McGann, for example, observes:

---

4. For more on this type of literature, see the introduction and the section on "Kindle-proofing" in chapter 2.

5. This term will be discussed further in chapter 4.

6. For examples, see Whitbrook. In extreme cases, such recoloring can change the storyline. Phil Sandifer told me about the following example: In the original version of *Sandman* #4, when Morpheus speaks to his ex-lover, the African queen Nala, in hell, he has his usual chalk-white skin. In the *Absolute Sandman* version, he has brown skin the same shade as Nala's, implying that she perceives him as having the same physical form he had when he was her lover. This implication does not exist in the original comic book.

> When texts are interpreted, the readings frequently . . . avoid reflecting on the material conditions of the works being "read" and the readings being executed. Those material and institutional conditions, however, are impossible to set aside if one is editing a text. . . . Consequently, one comes to see that texts always stand within an editorial horizon (the horizon of their production and reproduction). (21)

Comics scholars, however, still tend to treat material conditions of production as a mere adjunct to the reception of a text that is not altered by changes in those conditions. For example, Charles Hatfield argues: "Like traditional books, but perhaps more obviously, long-form comics can exploit both design and material qualities to communicate or underscore the meaning(s) available in the text" (58). This formulation implies that meaning exists before "design and material qualities" and that the latter serve only as a vehicle for emphasizing the former. Hatfield probably does not literally believe this, given that elsewhere in the same book, he shows very persuasively how the generic features of alternative comics were shaped by the form of the pamphlet-size comic book and by the institution of the comic book specialty store (25–29). Hatfield acknowledges that alternative comics evolved as they did because they were being produced in a specific format (the comic book) and distributed through a specific distribution system (the direct market). Yet he seems to treat these physical and material parameters of comics as mere historical accidents that are separable from the essential meaning of comics. However, my contention, which will be demonstrated in my analysis of *Fun Home,* is that comics don't have a preexisting meaning that is prior to material parameters like lettering, publication design, or methods of distribution. Rather, the meaning of comics is *created* by these material parameters.

Furthermore, this claim does not apply only to comics published as paper books. I have argued elsewhere (Kashtan 2011, 84) that the alternative comics community has fetishized comics published as paper artifacts. As Emma Tinker argues in an article provocatively titled "Manuscript in Print: The Materiality of Alternative Comics," the archetypal alternative comic is produced by means of hand drawing and hand lettering and is distributed as a printed book, often with high-quality paper and elaborate publication design. This perception is strong enough to create the impression that comics produced or distributed by other means are somehow *devoid* of materiality, or materially impoverished. According to this perception, other types of comics—for example, comics assembled in Photoshop or drawn on a graphics tablet, or comics distributed via the Internet—are not material artifacts, but mere digital facsimiles. I argue, however, that these latter types of comics are not devoid of materiality; rather, they have their own modes of materiality which need to be evaluated independently. Again, I will demonstrate this through an analysis of *Fun Home* itself.

HANDWRITING AND TYPEWRITING

The first way in which issues of materiality manifest themselves in the text of *Fun Home* is through the juxtaposition of two writing technologies: handwriting and typewriting. On one reading, *Fun Home* appears to reproduce a standard opposition between handwriting, viewed as a subjective, personal, and material medium, and typewriting, viewed as a machinic, impersonal, and immaterial medium. However, a closer reading reveals how *Fun Home* actually presents a more nuanced view of materiality, indicating that typewriting, despite its lesser degree of embodiment, is a no less material process than handwriting. This insight can then be extended to the digital processes that Bechdel used to produce the text of *Fun Home* itself. *Fun Home* needs to be analyzed as what Hayles calls a technotext—a text that "interrogates the inscription technology that produces it," setting up "reflexive loops" between its content and its material substrate (2002, 25).

Handwriting is often viewed within modern Western culture as a privileged channel for the expression of selfhood, subjectivity, and personality. Because of its origin in the unique, irreproducible movements of the body, handwriting seems to express the self of the writer far more effectively than more mechanical writing technologies such as typewriting and word processing. Susan Stewart summarizes this conventional wisdom:

> Because writing by hand assumes the speed of the body, it is linked to the personal. It is not quite polite to type condolence notes and heartfelt letters to friends or lovers. To sign your name, your mark, is to leave a track like any other track of the body; handwriting is to space what the voice is to time. (14)

This understanding of handwriting is frequently reflected in alternative comics and in the criticism thereof. Hilary Chute explains why the use of handwriting seems essential to the alternative comics project:

> Handwriting underscores the subjective positionality of the author. . . . What feels so intimate about comics is that *it looks like what it is*; hand-

> writing is an irreducible part of its instantiation. The subjective mark of the body is rendered directly onto the page and constitutes how we view the page. This subjective presence of the maker is not retranslated through type, but, rather, the bodily mark of handwriting both provides a visual quality and texture and is also extrasemantic, a performative aspect of comics that guarantees that comics works cannot be "reflowed": they are both intimate and *site specific*. (2010, 11)

This argument logically implies that other types of literary works are not "intimate and site-specific" in the same way as comics. For example, a printed copy of a novel does not bear the imprint of the author's hand, even if the copy-text for the novel was a handwritten manuscript, because the text has been filtered through multiple levels of mediation. Comics reproduce the mark of the artist's hand in a way that other media don't. Therefore, if a comic were to be produced through means other than handwriting—a Wacom tablet or Photoshop, for example—it would be a less genuine comic. This perception indeed exists in some segments of the comics fan community. Relative to handwriting, such technologies seem more removed from the artist's body, inasmuch as they impose an extra layer of technological mediation between the artist's hand and the drawn line.

This binary opposition between handwriting and typewriting seems to be reflected in *Fun Home* itself. We see this most strikingly when Alison comes out to her parents. (I refer to the author as Bechdel and the protagonist as Alison.) Despite the intensely personal nature of this declaration, Alison "d[oes] it via letter—a remote medium, but as I have explained, we were that sort of family" (2007, 77/1). What makes this announcement even more "remote" is that the letter is composed on a typewriter, which, as the above quotation from Stewart indicates, is a notoriously impersonal medium. A typewriter reproduces letters perfectly every time, and the appearance of those letters is the same between one writer and another, regardless of differences in the physical movements each writer uses to operate the keys; this makes it impossible to tell who wrote a typescript.[7] The font of Alison's letter is impersonal and mechanical, with fixed-width characters devoid of any variations in stroke widths that would indicate a handwritten origin. (As reproduced by Bechdel, however, these letters are visibly handwritten.) Alison's mother, Helen, responds to this letter with another typewritten letter (see figure 1.1) disapproving of Alison's "choice" (77/5).

7. On typewriting generally, see Wershler-Henry.

On receiving the letter, Alison tries to comfort herself by buying a pocket knife. "Opening it back in my room, I accidentally cut my finger. I smeared my blood into my journal, pleased by the opportunity to transmit my anguish to the page so literally" (78/4–5). She then goes on to write in her journal[8] with a fountain pen, an act that not only expresses her subjective emotions but does so through the means of the trace of her unique physical movements (see figure 1.2).

Alison then goes on to write another typewritten letter to her mother (see figure 1.3). It appears as though Alison's diary entry represents her authentic, innermost self, while her letters to her mother represent an inauthentic facade, a veneer of coldness and professionalism that she hides behind because she is uncomfortable relating to her mother in a more authentic manner. Alison's typewriting represents her public self, while her handwriting represents her private, authentic self. One reading of this sequence would be that Alison has an authentic, irreducible core of selfhood which can be either revealed or concealed, depending on the writing medium she uses in order to share her selfhood with the world: handwriting expresses that core of selfhood, while typewriting conceals it. An alternative reading would emphasize embodiment rather than selfhood. Alison's handwritten trace, and even more so the track of her blood, is a mark of the (former) presence of her subjective body. With the typewriter, the imprint of Alison's body is invisible. Even though her typewritten letters were generated by an act of direct bodily engagement between her fingers and the typewriter keys, there is no evidence that it was *her* fingers that pressed the keys; the words "I am a lesbian" could have been written by anyone.

I'll deal with the former reading first, since it's more naive and therefore easier to critique. The understanding of handwriting as a pure reflection of selfhood seems commonsensical, but it was given perhaps its most definitive formulation by early twentieth-century practitioners of the pseudoscience of graphology. Graphologists claimed that a person's character traits could be inferred from the graphic properties of his or her handwriting—for example, slant (left or right), pressure (soft or hard), and direction (up or down)—because handwriting depends on unconscious impulses. For practitioners of this science, "a man's words offered unreliable evidence of character, for speech is a willed and therefore potentially duplicitous act, but a man's unconscious gestures, especially the act of writing, were a dif-

8. The cover of this composition book is not shown, but it looks like the same kind of composition book I discuss in the next chapter, in the section on Lynda Barry's *Syllabus*.

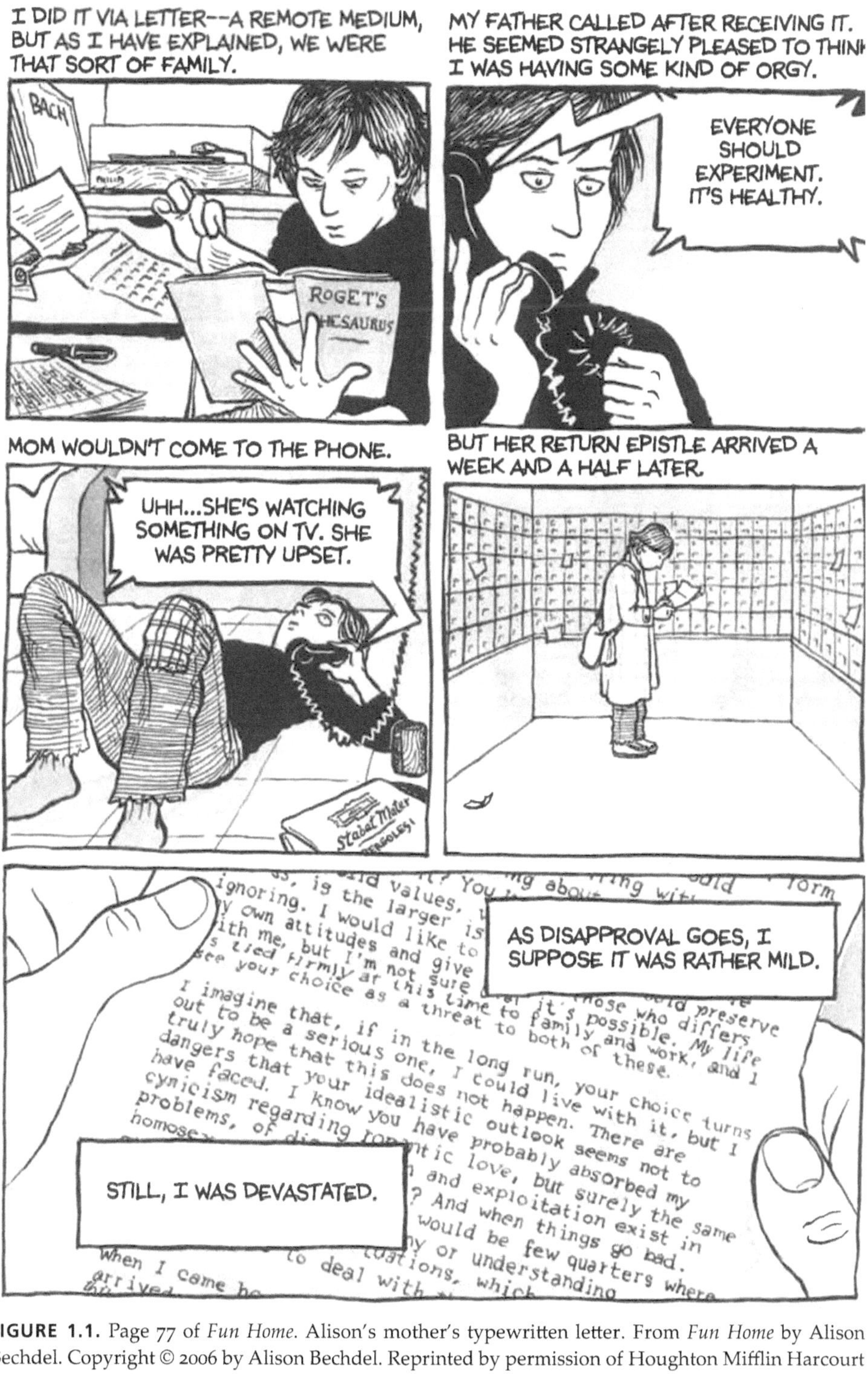

FIGURE 1.1. Page 77 of *Fun Home.* Alison's mother's typewritten letter. From *Fun Home* by Alison Bechdel. Copyright © 2006 by Alison Bechdel. Reprinted by permission of Houghton Mifflin Harcourt Publishing Company. All rights reserved.

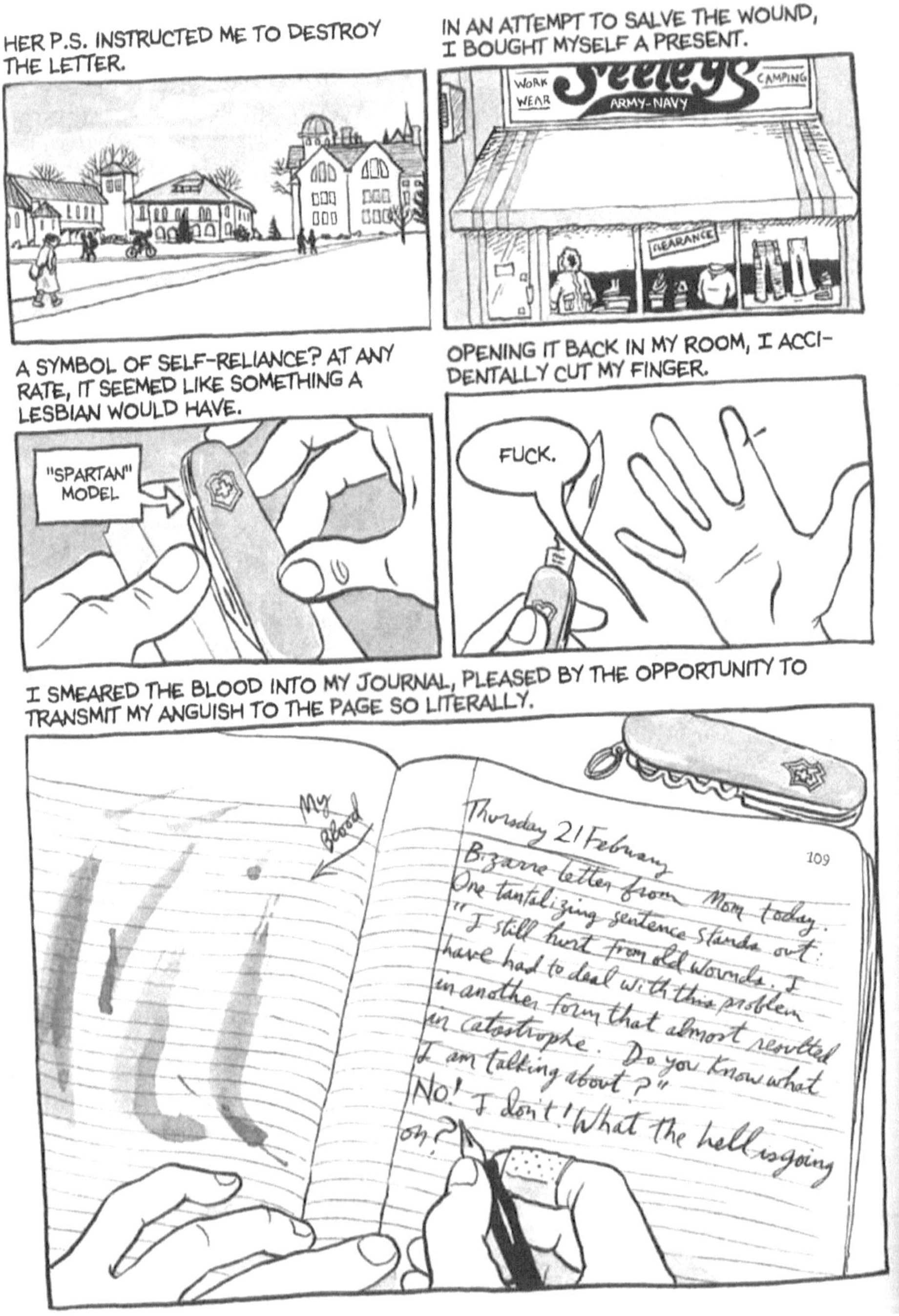

FIGURE 1.2. Page 78 of *Fun Home.* Alison's handwritten journal entry, accompanied by her blood. From *Fun Home* by Alison Bechdel. Copyright © 2006 by Alison Bechdel. Reprinted by permission of Houghton Mifflin Harcourt Publishing Company. All rights reserved.

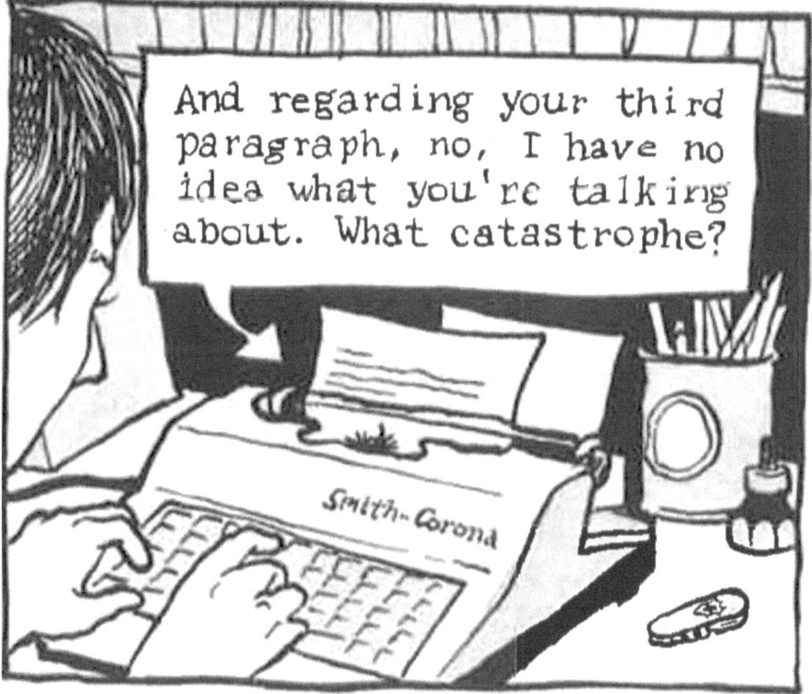

FIGURE 1.3. First panel of page 79 of *Fun Home*. Note the realistically drawn Smith Corona typewriter. From *Fun Home* by Alison Bechdel. Copyright © 2006 by Alison Bechdel. Reprinted by permission of Houghton Mifflin Harcourt Publishing Company. All rights reserved.

ferent story altogether. . . . Handwriting, because it is an unconscious act, reveals the self for what it is" (Thornton 94). Graphology's premise was that since handwriting is involuntary, it represents a privileged means of access to subjective truth, to the authentic meaning of the self.

This premise presupposed that there *was* a self that could be revealed for what it was, a self independent of the act of writing. Indeed, this was one of the primary selling points of graphology. At a historical moment when identity was increasingly being understood as a series of masks or facades adopted successively in different social situations, graphology offered people the comforting illusion that they could know who they "really" were behind all the masks:

> Character, a fixed nucleus of identity, had best served the interests of a society in which production was the imperative, but the shift to a consumer

> society demanded a new form of the self. That new self, personality, consisted of a series of carefully managed presentations, each designed to please a different audience. But as the ever-changing mask of personality displaced the solid core of character, some experienced the eerie sensation that their self had ceased to exist altogether. . . . What graphologists responded to was the fear that there was no face behind the mask. (Thornton 131–32)

The trouble with this graphological understanding of handwriting, however, is that it assumes that the relation between selfhood and writing technology is a one-way street: writing merely expresses the self but does not change the self. In simpler terms, the assumption is that the mode of expression is independent of what is being expressed. And this was not a bug but a feature. The ostensible purpose of graphology was to give its subject an insight into his or her innermost self, but its deeper effect was to reassure the subject that he or she *had* a singular, stable core of selfhood, which was always the same however much it might seem to change from one communicative context to another.

In reading *Fun Home,* then, a graphologist might assume (1) that Bruce and Alison have stable and immutable selves, (2) that their selves are capable of being revealed or made manifest, and (3) that the privileged way in which this revelation or manifestation occurs is through their handwriting. However, *Fun Home* implicitly argues against at least assumptions (2) and (3). (And if these two are false, then assumption [1] becomes uninteresting even if true: What is the use of knowing that Bruce or Alison "has" a unique, immutable self if that self is not knowable?) To begin with assumption (3), throughout *Fun Home,* handwriting serves as a vehicle for *concealing* rather than revealing uncomfortable truths about the self. Bruce Bechdel's letters are written to assure his future wife—and probably also himself—of his heterosexuality. In Alison's diary she dances around or avoids topics like her habit of masturbation and her father's arrest.

A graphologist might argue that the *content* of these handwritten texts is irrelevant, because even if Bruce and Alison don't tell the truth about themselves, that truth can still be inferred from the graphic properties of their handwriting. However, there are two problems here. First, Bechdel vehemently resists the notion (which constitutes assumption [1]) that there *is* a single truth about her father or about herself. *Fun Home* is emphatically *not* about uncovering the "secret" of either Bruce Bechdel's life or his death. It is not a detective story that seeks to strip away his various masks and arrive at the truth. "*Fun Home* is not a book about 'what happened' to Bechdel's father. Rather, it is a book of ideas about what happened to Bruce Bechdel" (Chute 2010, 180). Bechdel never arrives at a definitive explanation of why Bruce had sex with teenage boys or an answer to whether he committed suicide or not. The truth about these matters, as Chute goes on to indicate, is like the Lacanian Real, that which cannot be symbolized (191). Even if we accept assumption (1), then, it does not imply assumption (2); that is, if there is a single "truth" about Bruce or Alison's character, that truth may not be susceptible to being divined, even by a trained graphologist. Indeed, one present day graphologist emphasizes that graphology can't detect a writer's homosexuality unless the writer is aware of it:

> It is very difficult for a graphologist to say definitely whether an individual is a homosexual. What he can detect is that the person thinks of himself as sexually unusual. Distortions in the lower zone or strangely shaped letters show a sex life that is of an uncommon sort, but not necessarily homosexuality. Remember that this is what the writer himself feels. The homosexual who does not consider homosexuality strange will not reflect this in his writings. (Engel n.p.)

If we think about handwriting in *Fun Home* as a means of revealing subjective truth, we quickly encounter the difficulty that Bruce and Alison don't or won't understand the truth about themselves. For example, if the teenage Alison had been told that her handwriting proved her to be a latent homosexual, she would have violently denied this (though of course *Fun Home* is written by the adult Bechdel, who now knows this truth about herself).

But the second problem with a graphological reading of *Fun Home* is that it assumes that the "truth" of Bruce or Alison's self is independent of the medium in which this truth is expressed. Again, graphology assumes that the role of handwriting is simply to act as a conduit or channel for the self, which implies that the self is not altered by being filtered through particular material processes of writing. Indeed, graphology holds that the self *cannot* be altered in this way, because it's inherently unchangeable. However, this premise is questionable. As I have already observed, the college-age Alison is much more willing to discuss and explain herself in her handwritten diary than in her typewritten letter to her mother. Doesn't this imply that the "self" who writes the diary is not the same as the "self" who writes the letter? Precisely *because* handwriting has connotations of personality and intimacy which typewriting lacks, Alison is willing to be more personal and intimate when she writes in her diary than when she writes on her typewriter. Differences between these two technologies of self-expression result in real or perceived differences between the qualities of the selves that Alison uses them to express.

A possible objection to this argument would be to frame the difference between the pen and the typewriter in terms of embodiment rather than selfhood. For Chute, *Fun Home* is fundamentally concerned with "comics as a *procedure of what I [Chute] am calling embodiment,* and the instantiation of handwriting as a gripping index of a material, subjective, situated body" (2010, 193). From this perspective, the difference between pen and typewriter comes down to subjective *embodiment*: the pen reveals the unique properties of Alison's body in a way that the typewriter doesn't. What this reading misses is that the typewriter is still a material, embodied medium. No less than the pen, the typewriter represents a means of producing discourse by means of physical interaction with the world. As such, the typewriter has its own materiality which is encoded into texts produced with it.

"The" typewriter is incorrect, here, however, because Alison does not use "the" typewriter in an abstract sense, she uses *a* typewriter. Bechdel is careful to identify which typewriters Alison is using. The typewriter Alison uses at age seven is a Remington (129/2). At college, Alison uses a Smith Corona (58/1 and 79.1). Her mother, Helen, uses a third typewriter to write her MA thesis (177/2); this one is a Selectric typewriter, although it's not identified as such (Bechdel, personal communication). Each of these typewriters is visually distinct from the other two; in drawing each of them, Bechdel clearly intended to depict a specific model of typewriter, rather than just any generic typewriter. All of these typewriters are individual, unique artifacts. Each of them has a unique history, including a unique pattern of deterioration. All the typewriter *fonts* in the book look alike, but if an expert were to compare an actual copy of one of Alison's typewritten letters to, say, the police report on Bruce's arrest (161/2; see figure 1.4), he would be able to tell that these documents were produced on different machines, just as reliably as an expert in forensic document identification could distinguish between the handwriting of two different people.

Accordingly, in an 1891 Sherlock Holmes story, Arthur Conan Doyle had Sherlock Holmes observe that "a typewriter has really quite as much individuality as a man's handwriting, Unless they are quite new, no two of them write exactly alike" (qtd. in Gitelman 214–15). The typewriters in *Fun Home,* then, are in no way devoid of materiality; they are specific artifacts, each with an individual history. Moreover, these artifacts are specifically associated with Alison and her mother. Throughout chapter 6 we watch

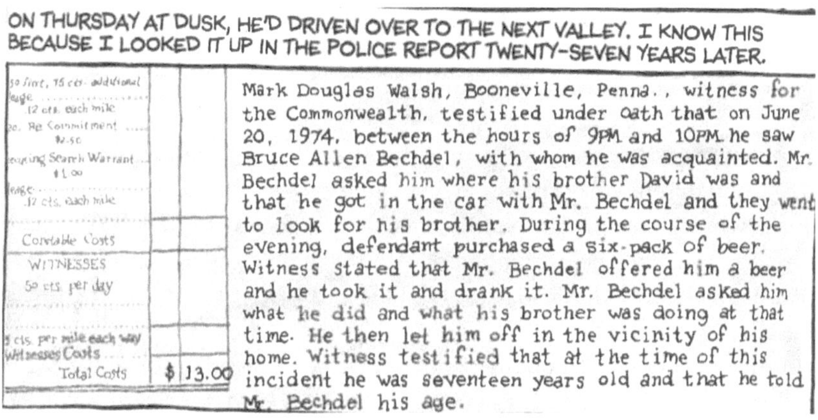

FIGURE 1.4. The second panel of page 161 of *Fun Home*. Note Alison Bechdel's painstaking handwritten reproduction of Bruce Bechdel's typewritten arrest report. From *Fun Home* by Alison Bechdel. Copyright © 2006 by Alison Bechdel. Reprinted by permission of Houghton Mifflin Harcourt Publishing Company. All rights reserved.

Helen typing her thesis (Bechdel 2007, 158/3), rewriting it when her advisor demands revisions, and finally retyping the whole thing after the original typescript is destroyed by rain (179/2). This sequence is one of the few instances in the book in which Alison's mother, as opposed to Alison herself or her father, is shown writing.

It's also relevant that Alison and her mother both use this particular writing technology, because the typewriter has specifically female associations. Friedrich Kittler observes that stenography, the predecessor of typewriting, was a professionalized occupation requiring extensive training and was thus exclusively male. This fact led to an association of the handwritten word with the male gender: "Prior to the invention of the typewriter, all poets, secretaries, and typesetters were of the same sex" (184). The masculine associations of the pen are also present in alternative and underground comics, largely for obvious symbolic reasons; the famous splash page to Justin Green's *Binky Brown and the Holy Virgin Mary*, in which the pen metaphorically represents the penis, is a notable example. In contrast, because typewriting required much less specialized skill, it opened up the written word and the labor force in general to women:

> The fact that "the female clerk could all-too-easily degrade into a mere typewriter" made her an asset. From the working class, the middle class, and the bourgeoisie, out of ambition, economic hardship, or the pure desire for emancipation emerged millions of secretaries. It was precisely

> their marginal position in the power system of script that forced women to develop their manual dexterity, which surpassed the prideful handwriting aesthetics of male secretaries. (Kittler 194)

Typewriting may therefore be considered a writing technology with specifically feminine associations, as indicated by the ambiguity of the word itself, which "meant both typing machine and female typist" (183). (Such was also initially true of computers, and this ambiguity is exploited in the title of Hayles's book *My Mother Was a Computer,* which inspired the title of the current chapter.)

Alison's use of a typewriter connects her to her mother specifically and to a more general notion of the female writer. It is therefore significant that the typewriter figures prominently in chapter 6, which heavily emphasizes Alison and Helen's relationship, depicting Alison helping her mother memorize lines, swimming with her mother, and (very reluctantly) talking to her mother about puberty. Paradoxically, when Alison comes out to her mother by means of a typewritten letter, she not only distances herself from her mother but also demonstrates their closeness. Her use of a stereotypically female inscription technology testifies to the body of female experiences she and her mother share. More specifically, it connects them both to a tradition that includes the exploitation as well as the empowerment of women. The introduction of the typewriter allowed women to enter the workplace in unprecedented numbers, but only because their labor could be acquired more cheaply than that of men. Moreover, if the typewriter gave women the ability to write, it did so by reducing the status of writing. "Male" writing (stenography) was an expert craft that involved a full command of the written word and was practiced by professional craftsmen. "Female" writing (typewriting) was a mechanical, assembly-line process that was practiced by interchangeable and temporary laborers. Alison's and her mother's use of the typewriter thus connects them to a more general pattern in which women's writing and women's labor are seen as minor and lacking in inherent importance. This pattern is reproduced in the Bechdel household, where Bruce is the primary breadwinner and Helen's work on her thesis appears to be subordinated to her domestic duties.[9] In a

---

9. The larger question of Helen's role in *Fun Home* is beyond the scope of this essay. Adrielle Mitchell argues intriguingly that while Helen seems to be "a nearly absent figure, receiving far less coverage than Alison's father," she is in fact constantly present at the margins of the image: 'The reader, however, does not fail to register Helen's steady physical presence in the panels, and thereby some of her eclipsed story" (paragraph 18). For reasons of scope, I do not discuss Bechdel's book *Are You*

more abstract sense, Alison herself struggles with the social devaluation of women's writing inasmuch as she defines her work in relation to a literary canon composed largely of works written by men.

Finally, while the typewriter may have seemed an immaterial and disembodied technology when compared to handwriting, it has now been nostalgically reimagined as a symbol of a condition of materiality that is allegedly vanishing with the advent of digital technology. The typewriter is often characterized as a more material, mechanical, physical writing technology than the computer, which seems to generate text out of nothing. Accordingly, Sven Birkerts aligns the typewriter and the pen against the computer, arguing that the typewriter entails a "commitment to truth" that the computer lacks. With both the pen and the typewriter, the difficulty of correcting errors obliges the writer to think about his/her words before setting them down (157). Of course this is why comics are typically drawn in pencil first, but even though pencil lead is erasable, doing so requires nontrivial effort and leaves a physical reminder, just like hitting the delete key on the typewriter. On the computer, words "can be transferred with a stroke or deleted altogether. And when they are deleted it is as if they had never been" (157). Even if typewritten text is in many ways far less "personal" than handwriting—a graphologist couldn't determine anything about Alison or Helen from reading their typescripts—it now seems far *more* personal than what has replaced it. Furthermore, this perception is partly independent of the physical properties of the typewriters; it also exists simply because the typewriter is now obsolete and has therefore become an object of nostalgia. The typewriter now serves as a living relic of an earlier, precomputer age; the appearance of typewriters situates *Fun Home* in a bygone era (and for a reader like me, it creates nostalgia for that era—I have distant childhood memories of the sound of my mother's typewriter). Moreover, all the typewritten documents appearing in *Fun Home* were laboriously hand copied by Bechdel; the fact that she put so much effort into recreating these documents indicates that she views them not as anonymous mechanical texts but as cherished testaments to the past.

In *Fun Home* the apparently simple opposition between handwriting and typewriting turns out to be more complex than it appears. Neither is purely personal or purely impersonal; both have their material and their immaterial aspects. It is fitting, therefore, that the lettering of *Fun Home* itself is a hybrid of handwriting and typography. The captions and word

---

My Mother, which was released after I completed the first draft of this essay and which is primarily about her relationship with Helen.

balloons in *Fun Home* are set in a digital typeface (i.e., a font produced and distributed digitally rather than as metal type), but one based on Bechdel's own handwriting.[10] As I discussed in a previously published essay (Kashtan 2011), alternative and autobiographical comics are almost always hand-lettered, to the point that Chute, as seen above, assumes that hand lettering is an *inherent* aspect of comics. Besides its previously discussed graphological implications, the use of hand lettering indicates a devotion to materiality, a preference for manual over mechanical labor. Therefore, alternative cartoonists who use digital fonts, such as Jeff Smith, are sometimes criticized for doing so.[11] Bechdel, however, was not willing to make the sacrifice of efficiency that the use of hand lettering would have required:

> I did not handletter my book, I cheated and used a digital font. . . . I was experimenting with what it would look like to do the lettering myself, but it would have taken forever and I don't think it would have been legible enough for the kind of material I was writing. The digital font is made up from my own letters. (*Fun Home* 2007, n.p.)

Given that Bechdel was willing to invest massive amounts of time and effort in other aspects of the book—she posed for reference photographs for every panel (Chute 2010, 200) and redrew numerous archival documents and photographs by hand—it seems paradoxical that she would be unwilling to do the lettering by hand as well. Indeed, Bechdel seems to regret this decision, as the word *cheated* indicates, and she wanted to use hand lettering for her next book but was apparently again unable to do so.[12] Perhaps the extremely laborious nature of other aspects of the book made Bechdel unwilling to go to the additional trouble of hand lettering. Nonetheless, it seems fitting that this book is not hand lettered. As I have just argued, *Fun Home* demonstrates that typewriting is not purely immaterial or impersonal, any more than handwriting is purely material or personal. Like

10. A distinct font also based on Bechdel's handwriting is used for the author's name on the front cover of the paperback edition. Various other digital fonts, notably what appears to be Times New Roman, are used for other text on the covers and the front matter. All the documents depicted in the book, whether handwritten or typewritten, are reproduced by hand.

11. In an interview, Smith was somewhat apologetic about his decision to use a digital font, admitting that "I believe that a person who draws a strip should letter it, because graphically that makes it whole. They should be organic to each other" (qtd. in DuPont 2003).

12. In a 2011 blog comment, she wrote: "I have talked in the past about how much I wanted to hand-letter this book, instead of using a digital font like I did for *Fun Home*. But in fact, I'll be using a digital font for this book too" (Bechdel 2011).

handwriting, but in its own distinctive way, typewriting both reveals the self and alters the nature of the self that is revealed. And the same is true of the handwritten font that Bechdel uses. By employing a font based on her own handwriting, Bechdel combines the self-revelation (stereotypically) associated with handwriting and the self-concealment associated with typing. If the reader notices that the font is a digital font rather than actual hand lettering, then this indicates that the self that is revealed in Alison's words is a self that is personal and distinctive, but also reserved and reticent. It exposes itself to the world, but only to a limited degree. By using this font, Bechdel partly embraces and partially rejects the graphological myth. If the reader is fooled by the digital font and mistakes it for hand lettering, then this is also appropriate; it means that Alison's depiction of her self is to some extent a façade, an artifice designed to appear to be something it's not, much like Bruce Bechdel's carefully constructed persona.

But in the end, neither the naive reading of handwriting as an authentic depiction of Bechdel's self, nor the sophisticated reading of handwriting as a facade, captures the full truth. To balance these two views, we need to remember that what matters in comics is the *appearance* of handwritten-ness or hand-drawn-ness, not the reality. As I suggest elsewhere in this book (page 165), no commercially published comic is truly hand lettered or hand drawn. The comic that the reader encounters is a printed version of the artist's original artwork. Even before being printed, any modern comic passes through multiple other layers of mediation, including scanning, retouching, digital coloring, digital lettering, and so forth. Thus, the reader who imagines that she is coming into direct contact with the stamp of the artist's hand (as I suggest on page 165) is engaging in a fantasy. What ultimately matters in comics is not the *reality* of touch or trace but the *appearance* thereof. For example, as I suggest in an essay on comics lettering, comics letterers seek to make their work look hand lettered even—or especially—when it's not. "One of the things readers desire out of comics is the *appearance* of handmadeness, even if this appearance does not reflect an actual reality, and hand lettering fonts satisfy this desire" (Kashtan 2017). Instead of actual contact between writer and artists, comics offer an experience of haptic visuality, a "close-up and tactile way of looking" (Marks 4) in which "the eyes themselves function like organs of touch" (2). The comics reader uses his eyes to figuratively feel the surface of the page and the trace of the artist's hand.

While Marks develops her concept of haptic visuality with reference to cinema, haptic visuality also operates to both a greater and a lesser degree in comics. On one hand, comics have a greater capacity to evoke haptic visuality because they are less tied to the contrasting notion of optic visuality, in which the viewer beholds the screen from a disembodied, external perspective (5). In comics, the image almost always betrays its nature as a flat plane covered with inscriptions, rather than a transparent window into a three-dimensional perspectival space. The reader is almost always aware of the physical surface of the comics page. This awareness may be even stronger in comics than in cinema because in cinema, the viewer typically looks at the screen but does not touch it, but in comics the reader can and must touch the page in order to continue reading. At the same time, actual touch and haptic visuality may interfere with each other, because the page's actual texture may not match its apparent texture. This occurs with Lynda Barry's collage pages, discussed in chapter 2, or when comics originally drawn on one type of paper are reprinted on a different type of paper, as mentioned in my discussion of *MIND MGMT* in chapter 4.

Indeed, this complex interplay between actual and apparent touch, or more broadly between what Matthew Kirschenbaum calls formal and forensic materiality, is one of the stranger material properties of comics. This complex interplay is visible in *Fun Home,* where a constant oscillation occurs between handwriting, typing, hand-drawn reproductions of typing, typing that looks like handwriting, and digital reproductions of all of the above. What matters in comics is not only the reality of handmadeness or tactility, but also the appearance thereof, and the play between reality and appearance is an important source of comics' poignancy.

PRINTED BOOKS AND E-BOOKS

The above discussion focuses on the way in which *Fun Home* represents the materiality of writing and drawing, but *Fun Home* is also about the materiality of reading, which is the central topic of the present book. The second way in which issues of materiality appear in *Fun Home* is through its depiction of the physical form of the book. The alternative comics community has fetishized the book as a physical and handmade object. Tinker observes that "throughout this period in which the conventions of comics publication have been shifting, the authors and artists of alternative comics have paid increasingly close attention to the formal qualities of their books" (1173). Specifically, "with many small press comics, the handmade quality is part of the appeal. Many have hand-coloured covers, have fabric or other materials glued to them, are tied together with string, are made of different coloured paper or have varying page sizes" (1172). Similarly,

Bart Beaty introduces his comparison between alternative and commercial comics by comparing a handcrafted, limited edition comic book by Nadia Raviscioni to a mass-produced album by Zep [2007, 3–5], although Beaty is discussing European rather than American comics. Thus, within the alternative comics community, the physical codex book is typically viewed as the privileged, authentic form of the comics text. This is further indicated by the existence of artifacts like *Kramer's Ergot* 7 (2008), a 16-inch-by-21-inch volume that cost $125 and "ha[d] to be bound by hand, since no binder at that size exists" (Spurgeon n.p.). Conversely, the alternative comics community often exhibits a dismissive attitude toward less durable and more commercial modes of comics production. The terms *floppies* and *pamphlets,* frequently used within the alternative comics community to describe monthly comic books, have negative connotations, implying that these artifacts are insubstantial and disposable. Alternative comics publishers like Fantagraphics and Drawn & Quarterly, unlike commercial publishers like Marvel and DC, have mostly abandoned the disposable form of the comic book in exchange for the more durable form of the codex book.[13]

In *Fun Home,* Bechdel initially seems to exhibit a similar attitude: Bruce and Alison are both fetishistically devoted to the physical form of the codex book. Chute observes the omnipresence of books in Alison's milieu:

> It is hard to overstate the fascination with books that the Bechdel family exhibits; reading in their household is valued above all else. . . . Her father is depicted reading *Anna Karenina* on *Fun Home*'s very first page, and he goes on, within the space of the text, to be shown reading or discussing an additional twenty-one different books (Alison, for her part, is shown reading or discussing over fifty separate titles). (2010, 184–85)

However, these books are important not just as containers for literary texts but as physical objects. In *Fun Home* the physicality of books is a recurring trope; books are presented as insistently material objects. Bruce's books are expensive "calf-bound" hardcovers (Bechdel 2007, 5) and he enshrines them in a purpose-built room with expensive furnishings, including a "mahogany and brass second-Empire desk" (60/1) and a "massive walnut bookcase" (61/3) with glass doors (see figure 1.5).

The physicality of books is further underscored by their function as objects of exchange, including exchange of a sexual nature. Alison and her lover Joan use books as sexual props (80–81). Less innocently, Bruce alleg-

13. On this topic, see the stories on the inside back covers of Adrian Tomine's *Optic Nerve* #12 and #13.

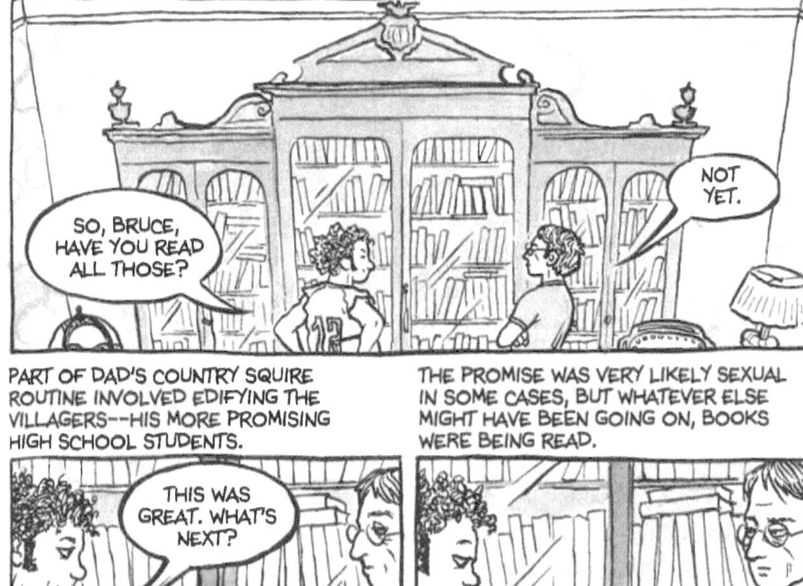

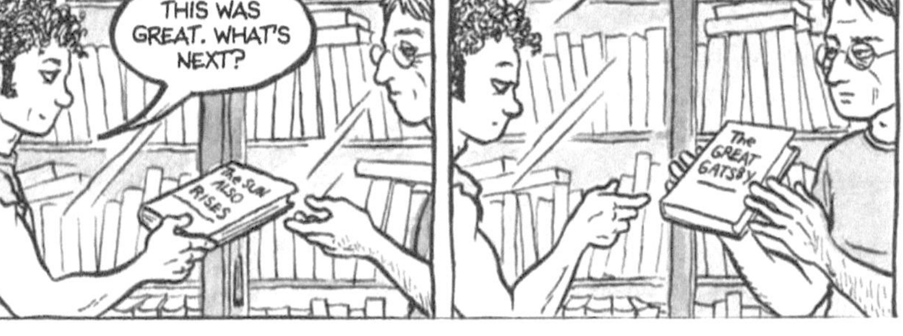

FIGURE 1.5. Detail from page 61 of *Fun Home,* showing Bruce Bechdel's "massive walnut bookcase." From *Fun Home* by Alison Bechdel. Copyright © 2006 by Alison Bechdel. Reprinted by permission of Houghton Mifflin Harcourt Publishing Company. All rights reserved.

edly lends books to his students as part of his efforts to seduce them (61). Karim Chabani argues that this "establishes a clear connection between the transmission of books and a more physical expression of mutual affection" (9), but I'd suggest that "more physical" is the wrong choice of words. The point is that the exchange of books *is* a physical exchange. As Whitman writes: "Camerado! This is no book / Who touches this, touches a man; / (Is it night? Are we here alone?) / It is I you hold, and who holds you; / I spring from the pages into your arms" (382). The physicality of the book is what matters here, not just its function as a container for knowledge. A book given as a gift is a memento of its former owner, and, specifically, the physicality of the book is a reminder of its owner's unique body.

Thus, when Helen gives Joan a book, Joan commemorates the occasion by writing a poem which highlights the materiality of the book: "She tells me to choose a book. // Cloth-bound, grey and turquoise / heavy in my hand as a turtle shell filled with mud" (Bechdel 2007, 82/2). Chabani observes that books function in this way because they serve as a material metaphor for relationships:

> Communication can only be effective in *Fun Home* if it is somehow mediated. The failed attempts at immediate physical and verbal communication end in painful disasters. . . . A remarkably fruitful exchange between Alison and her father is mediated by an exchange of books. On pages 204–205, one can see that books literally become replacements for paternal love. (9–10)

However, books can fulfill this function of mediating relationships only because they are physical objects, which can be traded or given as gifts, and not mere containers for knowledge. Finally, for the Bechdels the physical attractiveness of a book seems to be an index of its literary value. Helen tells Joan: "Don't just pick a cheap paperback. Take something good" (Bechdel 2007, 82), implying that cheapness and paper covers are incompatible with "goodness"; the durability and attractiveness of a book are physical signs of the quality of the book's contents.

Because of its careful attention to the physicality and materiality of books, *Fun Home* calls attention to its own physical and material features, presenting itself as "something good" rather than a "cheap paperback" (see figure 1.6). As Julia Watson comments:

> The hardback's front cover, an elegant color scheme of teal and silver on black, frames themes of the memoir: a close-up drawing of a tabletop with an embossed silver tray for calling cards at a funeral home (with cut-outs on the tray's edges revealing the contrasting orange book binding) holds the book's title like a card. . . . On the back are other early review endorsements of the memoir, topped by a drawn photo. . . . The book's end papers, featuring green-shaded white chrysanthemums on a silvery teal background, imitate the wallpaper in the funeral home. By contrast, the book's binding, in a vivid light orange, is a blowup of the panel depicting each family member inside a black-edged bubble in different parts of the house. (130–31)[14]

14. By *front cover* Watson means the dust jacket, and by *binding* she means the actual front cover. Notably, Bechdel did not design either this cover or that of the

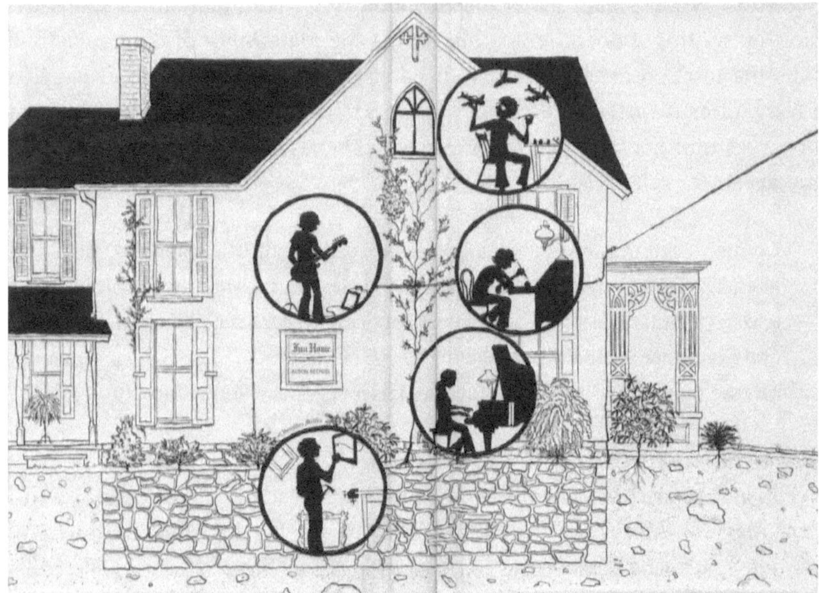

FIGURE 1.6. Cover of the hardcover edition of *Fun Home.* From *Fun Home* by Alison Bechdel. Copyright © 2006 by Alison Bechdel. Reprinted by permission of Houghton Mifflin Harcourt Publishing Company. All rights reserved.

All of this leads Watson to conclude that "*Fun Home*'s elegant presentation as an artifact invites readers inside its decorous exterior for an encounter with its graphic—in both senses—disclosures about life between the covers" (131). In its earliest published form, therefore, *Fun Home* uses its own paratextual materials as signifying resources. Though Bechdel is less obsessively attentive to publication design than an artist like Chris Ware or Seth, *Fun Home*'s publication design emphasizes the physicality and materiality of the book in the same way as its content does. It's also significant that *Fun Home* was conceived and published *as* a book. Until the late 1990s, the privileged publication format for alternative comics was the serialized comic book, and the collected single-volume edition was more of an afterthought (Hatfield 25–29).[15] *Fun Home,* however, was always meant to be stored on bookcases rather than in longboxes.

---

paperback edition, discussed below; Michaela Sullivan designed the former, and Christopher Moisan the latter.

15. As a sign of how times have changed, in *Optic Nerve* #12 (Drawn & Quarterly, September 2011), Adrian Tomine depicts himself agonizing over his continued allegiance to the single-issue format after all his peers have abandoned it.

Yet if we argue that *Fun Home* is a "good" book, an artifact whose attractive material form reflects and enhances the literary quality of its content, then we run into the difficulty that there is *also* a "cheap paperback" edition of *Fun Home*. Watson's claims apply specifically to the hardcover edition and are no longer true of the paperback edition, which I am using to write this essay and which I have ordered for my students when I have taught the book. All the specific paratextual features Watson mentions are absent from the paperback version. The cover of the paperback depicts three photographs and a calling card depicting the work's title, but the silver tray is absent. There is no photo on the back cover, and the endpapers are absent. Since there's no dust jacket, the vivid orange cover is also gone, although the paperback edition does try to emulate it: the first page of the paperback edition is printed on glossy paper and depicts Alison and Bruce's silhouettes against a vivid orange background (see figure 1.7).

We might assume that the paperback edition of *Fun Home* is an inferior substitute intended for less materiality-conscious readers—that the paperback is aimed at a reader who wants or needs to read the book once, while the hardcover is aimed at a reader who wants to make it a part of his or her permanent library and is willing to pay more for this privilege. On this reading, the hardcover is the "real" *Fun Home*, the privileged version of the text, while the paperback is a mere knockoff.

This reading, however, is unsustainable because it reproduces a fetishistic attitude to the printed book, and it turns out that *Fun Home* actually criticizes this attitude. Bechdel hints that there is something fetishistic and fantastic about her father's attachment to books:

> For anyone but the landed gentry to refer to a room in their house as "the library" might seem affected, but there really was no other word for it. And if my father liked to imagine himself as a nineteenth-century aristocrat overseeing his estate from behind the leather-topped mahogany and brass Second Empire desk, did that require such a leap of the imagination? (2007, 60)

Bruce's expensive books and library furnishings are important tools he uses to create his constructed persona. In building and using this library, Bruce is presenting himself as the sort of person who owns expensive books and spends most of his time at home surrounded by them. This explains Alison's reference to the library as "a fantasy," albeit "a fully operational one" (61). She goes on to claim that "Gatsby's pristine books and my father's worn ones signify the same thing—the preference of a fiction to reality"

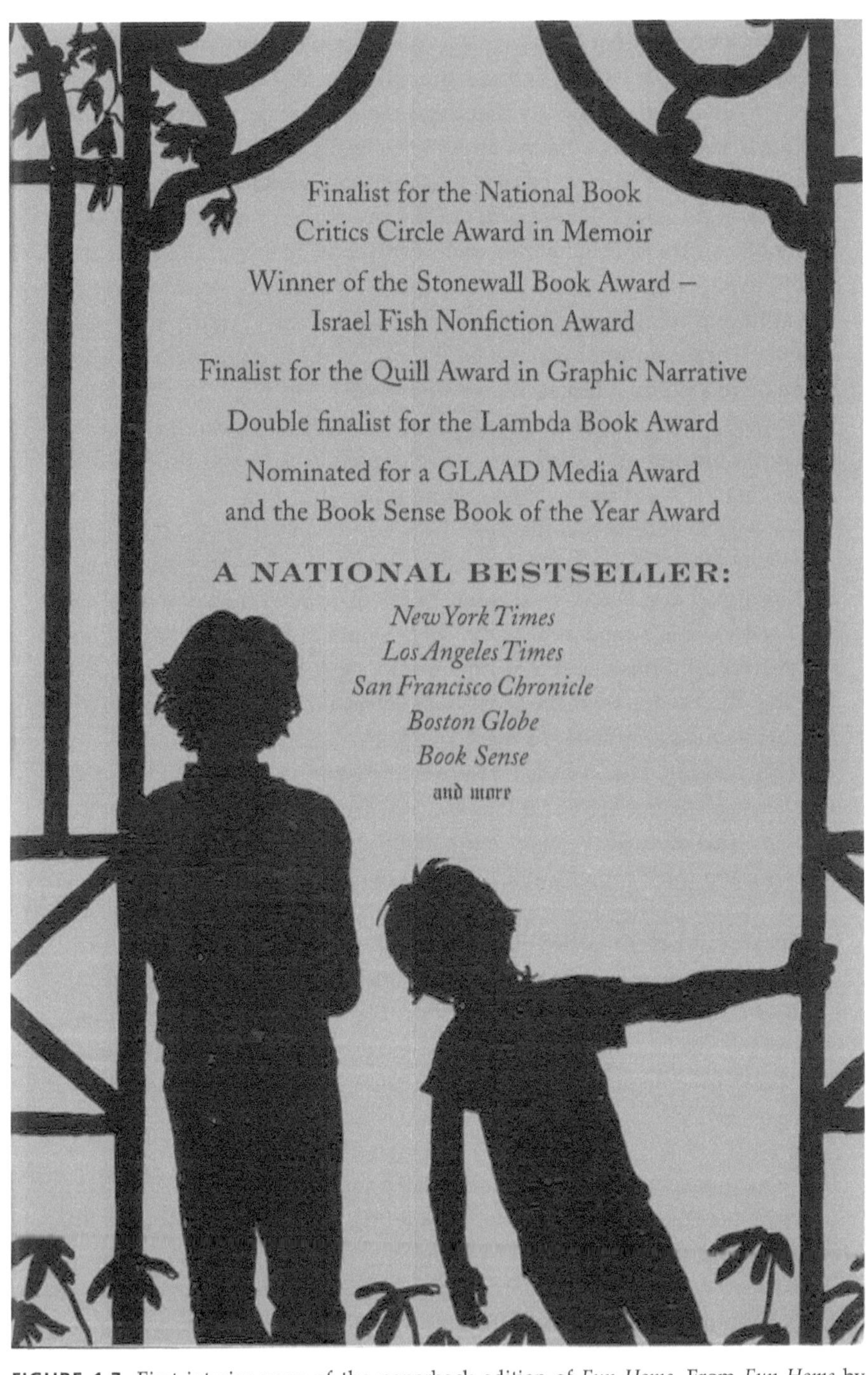

FIGURE 1.7. First interior page of the paperback edition of *Fun Home*. From *Fun Home* by Alison Bechdel. Copyright © 2006 by Alison Bechdel. Reprinted by permission of Houghton Mifflin Harcourt Publishing Company. All rights reserved.

(85). Just as Gatsby exhibits his wealth by displaying real books (albeit with uncut pages) rather than cardboard mock-ups, Bruce reveals his erudition and culture by displaying expensive books that show visible signs of having been read. Bruce's attachment to books is one of the ways in which he constructs a false persona. Bruce's bibliophilia is fetishistic both in the ordinary sense and in the Freudian sense whereby the fetish hides an underlying reality that the subject is not willing to face.[16]

By critiquing Bruce's book fetishism, *Fun Home* asks us to reevaluate our attitude toward its own materiality. One way we might do so is by questioning the implicit value hierarchy of the hardcover and paperback editions. Instead of seeing the paperback as a mere inferior substitute for the hardcover, we could evaluate it as a different but equally valid incarnation of the same text. From this perspective, there is no single, authoritative edition of *Fun Home*; rather, *Fun Home* is a text that exists in multiple independent material instantiations. Thus, the paperback does not simply lack features that are present in the hardcover; it also has its own unique material features that are potentially productive of different emphases and different layers of meaning. This is illustrated by the fact that even though the cover of the hardcover and the first page of the paperback use the same shade of orange, the images are different. For the hardcover, the image is panel 3 of page 134, which shows the five Bechdels ensconced in separate circles; for the hardcover, the image is panel 3 of page 150, which shows Alison and Bruce watching a sunset together (see figures 1.6 and 1.7). Although these images come from the same chapter of the book, they have opposite connotations. The former emphasizes the mutual isolation of Alison and her parents and siblings, while the latter emphasizes Alison's closeness to her father. (The previous panel on page 134 shows Alison dictating a diary entry to her mother: "Dad and I watched the sunset. It was beautiful.") Similarly, the cover of the paperback features the same business card that appears on the dust jacket of the hardcover, but on the paperback, the business card lies atop a photograph of Alison and her father, rather than on a silver tray. The two pieces of art generate different first impressions as to what this book will be about: the hardcover dust-jacket art is an immaculate still life with no people in it, while the paperback cover art emphasizes Alison and her father.

16. I have also felt for a long time that there is something fetishistic or fantasized about Alison's and Bruce's attachment to classic literature. Bechdel seems to emphasize the similarities between her story and various canonical literary texts as a way of protesting (too much) that her book is a literary text and not a mere comic book. However, I am not able to develop this argument here.

It's true that compared to the hardcover, the paperback looks less like a handcrafted work of art and more like a commercial product. Reviewers' blurbs feature prominently on the front and back covers and occupy the first four interior pages. Besides the handwritten title, all of the text on the covers and spine is typeset rather than handwritten. However, this does not imply that the paperback is merely a subordinate, commercial version of the hardcover. I argued above that typewriting is not simply a less material process than handwriting. It doesn't make sense to say that handwriting has more materiality and typewriting has less. Both of these processes are equally material; what differs is the specific nature of their materiality, including both the material processes they involve and the cultural and historical connotations attached to those processes. The same can be said about the difference between the hardcover and the paperback book, at least in the case of *Fun Home.* Both of these books are material artifacts. The latter is not simply a "less material" version of the former. Each deserves to be considered and appreciated for itself rather than by reference to the other.

It is crucial to keep this argument in mind when we consider the third material form in which *Fun Home* has been instantiated, because this form is so radically different from either the paperback or the hardcover that it may seem like an entirely different object. Many readers, including many of my students, now encounter *Fun Home* not as a physical book but as an e-book. *Fun Home* is available for the Amazon Kindle device or as a Google eBook. Amazon.com does not offer a preview of the Kindle edition, but the Google eBook edition appears to feature the same artwork as the paperback edition. The electronic *Fun Home* is clearly not the same artifact as the physical *Fun Home,* but these two artifacts need to be interpreted as equally valid alternative versions of a single underlying text. The electronic *Fun Home* needs to be interpreted on its own, not simply dismissed as an immaterial substitute for the real thing.

For reasons of scope, I limit myself to one example of how the differences between these two artifacts result in differing reading experiences. In the printed *Fun Home,* pages 100 and 101 form a two-page spread that depicts Alison holding Bruce's photograph of his lover Roy; the spread is located at the exact center of this book. This latter fact is central to Watson's interpretation of these pages:

> Bechdel and her father could meet only at a phantom middle, a "slender demilitarized zone," in the appreciation of the pubescent male body as an epitome of androgynous beauty (*Fun Home* 99). At this evanescent point the family legacy of desire materializes across generations and genders. A

> double-page literal centerfold at the middle of the chapter, and the book, stages this insight. (Watson 136)

By virtue of being the literal centerfold of the book, pages 100 and 101 can also be read as a "centerfold" in the *Playboy* sense and as a meeting point between Alison and Bruce. This reading, however, makes sense only if the reader is experiencing *Fun Home* as a printed book rather than an electronic book. The e-book version obscures the crucial fact that this image is the centerpiece of the book. Upon reaching pages 100 and 101 in the printed book, the reader sees that he or she is at the center of the book and feels that the number of pages on the left is equal to the number of pages on the right. E-readers do have on-screen indicators of the reader's position within the book, such as the Kindle's progress bar, but such indicators provide a much weaker understanding of where each page is located relative to the rest of the book. Recent research in neuroscience suggests that the e-book may have detrimental effects on memory because it lacks these spatial cues, as Maia Szalavitz summarizes in a *Time* magazine article:

> The more associations a particular memory can trigger, the more easily it tends to be recalled. Consequently, seemingly irrelevant factors like remembering whether you read something at the top or the bottom of page—or whether it was on the right or left hand side of a two-page spread or near a graphic—can help cement material in mind. . . . E-books, however, provide fewer spatial landmarks than print, especially pared-down versions like the early Kindles, which simply scroll through text and don't even show page numbers, just the percentage already read. In a sense, the page is infinite and limitless, which can be dizzying. Printed books[,] on the other hand, give us a physical reference point, and part of our recall includes how far along in the book we are, something that's more challenging to assess on an e-book. (n.p.)

The lack of spatial cues in e-books, therefore, has significant effects on the reading experience. The question Szalavitz doesn't consider, however, is whether the less spatial nature of the e-book may also have positive effects. If the page in the e-book is "infinite and limitless," then this might be liberating instead of "dizzying." Early hypertext critics and practitioners like George Landow and Michael Joyce embraced electronic texts precisely because of their freedom from the unidirectional spatiality of print. We therefore have to ask whether the less spatial nature of the e-book version of *Fun Home* might be productive of new readings as well as destructive of old ones. *Fun Home* is a notoriously nonlinear text; rather than following simple chronological order, its narrative jumps forward and backward and traverses the same territory multiple times. Perhaps it's appropriate that this story is now available in a format where any page is equidistant from any other and where no single page enjoys absolute priority as the beginning or the center of the narrative. We could also consider whether *Fun Home*'s critique of book fetishism is strengthened or weakened when we read *Fun Home* in a format that is not subject to such fetishism. When we read *Fun Home* digitally, are we sympathizing with Allison's claim that book fetishism is harmful? Or does reading *Fun Home* in this format instead create nostalgia, making us wish we were reading it in the expensive hardcover edition? I will provide further examples of this type of analysis in my discussion of Carla Speed McNeil's *Talisman* in chapter 2.

What all of this suggests is that the e-book version of *Fun Home,* like the paperback version, is an interesting artifact in its own right. *Fun Home* exists simultaneously as three or more different artifacts—the hardcover, the paperback, and the various e-books—and each artifact presents a similar but subtly different reading experience. In interpreting *Fun Home,* it's necessary to take these differences into account, rather than reproducing the fetishism of the printed book that *Fun Home* itself criticizes. In its depiction of books, just as much as in its depiction of handwriting, *Fun Home* has more to say about the productive differences between modes of materiality than about the superiority of any specific material artifact or process.

CONCLUSION

I contend that as comics scholars, we need to be more attentive to the kinds of questions about materiality that *Fun Home* raises. If we treat comics as idealized, insubstantial forms that are independent of their physical, material instantiation, then we miss some of the most crucial questions we can ask about comics. Literary critics from W. J. T. Mitchell to Katherine Hayles have become increasingly interested in the question of how the visual and material features of texts shape their meaning and their cultural importance. This question has become increasingly central to the discipline of literary studies at a time when the materiality of the printed book is changing rapidly. Comics should be among the central case studies in this debate because they represent unusually powerful examples of how visuality and materiality affect the reading experience. I therefore contend that materiality and mediacy should be topics of central importance for the study of comics. Now more than ever, comics studies and media studies need to inform each other.

But on an even broader level, my discussion of *Fun Home* suggests why comics can be an important test case in the debate over the effect of technological change on the embodied experience of reading. The two printed editions and the digital edition of *Fun Home* each differ from the others in ways that dramatically impact the reading experience. I would contend that the differences between these texts are greater than the differences between the hardcover, paperback, and Kindle editions of any typical prose novel—or, at least, that the reader of *Fun Home* is more aware of these differences than the reader of such a prose novel would be. Therefore, comics enable us to literally *see* what happens to the reading experience when texts move from print to digital form or vice versa. The remainder of this book will explore numerous examples of comics that change significantly when remediated from print to digital form or in the opposite direction, as well as comics that can't be remediated in this way because they're too tightly bound to one medium or the other. It's my hope that these examples will allow us to extrapolate from comics to books in general.

With this foundation established, I begin my exploration of the effects of digital technology on the materiality of comics in chapter 2. In that chapter, I examine how print comics have responded to the (perceived) threat posed by digital comics.

CHAPTER 2

TALISMANS

How Print Comics Have Responded to the Crisitunity of Digital Media

THE PREVIOUS chapter established the parameters for this book by explaining the importance of considerations of materiality and material rhetoric to comics studies and by analyzing the kinds of changes that occur when comics are remediated from print to digital. My basic argument was that comics are bound to their physical and material form in ways which are much less noticeable in the case of prose fiction, and that therefore comics offer an effective test case for how digitization affects the material rhetoric of texts. In this chapter and in the rest of the book, I examine specific categories of cases where digitization affects material rhetoric.

I begin by examining what digitization does to print comics. Within both popular and literary circles, the most common account of the effect of digitization on the print book is that the latter is inevitably doomed to obsolescence. Digital proponents like Scott McCloud (discussed in the next chapter) celebrate the impending liberation of the book from the physical constraints of print, while digital skeptics fetishize the print book and engage in anticipatory mourning for its inevitable death. This latter reaction is what Ben Ehrenreich calls biblionecrophilia, or "the retreat of the print-faithful into a sort of autistic fetishization of the book-as-object" (n.p.).

Because of the centrality of print to the comics medium, biblionecrophilia has expressed itself perhaps even more strongly in the comics community than elsewhere. Some of the strongest proponents of biblionecrophilia (though they obviously wouldn't self-identify as such) are cartoonists like Carla Speed McNeil and Lynda Barry.

However, a close reading of the work of these cartoonists demonstrates the blind spots of the biblionecrophilic position and suggests ways that digital technology can inadvertently serve as an inspiration for authors of print texts. McNeil's and Barry's work elegantly demonstrates the continuing appeal of the print book, but it also shows that merely advocating for the survival of print is not enough to guarantee its continued existence. Instead, when we look at Barry's work and that of Matt Kindt, we realize that the best way to defend the print comic book is to create work that takes advantage of the unique affordances of print and that could not be reproduced digitally. Competition from digital technologies can be viewed as a creative challenge to print cartoonists, encouraging them to use the print medium in more exciting ways—much like how, according to the standard narrative, competition from photography forced painting to identify and accentuate its unique properties. To this extent, comics demonstrate how the advent of digital media need not be purely a crisis for print. It can instead be a *crisitunity,* a Chinese word that (according to the noted scholar Homer J. Simpson) means both "crisis" and "opportunity."

TALISMAN: COMICS AND BIBLIONECROPHILIA[1]

The rise of the digital book has led to a discourse of biblionecrophilia, which celebrates the alleged superiority of the printed book and laments its alleged supplantation by the digital book. Biblionecrophiles argue that the intangible, ethereal nature of the digital book makes it inferior to the printed book, with its physical weight and resistance. One of many commonly cited examples of this inferiority is that in the e-book, progress is represented by a sliding bar, rather than by the number of pages in the reader's left and right hands. This allegedly makes the reading of a print book a physically meaningful experience, whereas the reading of an e-book is an ephemeral process that leaves no physical traces.

1. This section incorporates some material that was previously used in Kashtan 2015. The material is reprinted from *Class, Please Open Your Comics: Essays on Teaching with Graphic Narratives,* © 2015, edited by Matthew L. Miller. Used by permission of McFarland & Company, Inc., Box 611, Jefferson, NC 28640. www.mcfarlandpub.com.

The biblionecrophilic position has been advocated not only in nonfiction works like Sven Birkerts's *The Gutenberg Elegies* and Andrew Piper's *Book Was There,* but even in prose novels such as Robin Sloan's *Mr. Penumbra's 24-Hour Bookstore.* Carla Speed McNeil's graphic novel *Talisman* (in the *Finder* series; see below) advocates for the importance of print at least as powerfully as any of these works do. However, it must be evaluated differently from other texts that participate in the discourse of biblionecrophilia because, as a comic book, it has the ability to exploit the visual and tactile resources of the printed page in ways that are not available to print literature. Through multimodality and material rhetoric, McNeil has the ability not only to describe but also to demonstrate the material richness of the printed book as compared to the ephemerality of the e-book.

However, *Talisman* fails to make maximally effective use of the capacity of the comic to demonstrate the material-rhetorical superiority of print to digital, and this failure is all the more notable because it's a comic book. *Talisman* doesn't exploit the unique affordances of print—it doesn't do anything that couldn't have been done digitally—and because of this, it could be and has been translated into digital form. When read in digital form, *Talisman* contradicts its own argument for the superiority of print, and thus it ultimately suggests the blind spots of the biblionecrophilic position and serves as a negative example of how print comics can advocate for the superiority of the print medium.

To clarify this argument about the future of the book, some background information is necessary. *Talisman* originally appeared as issues 19 through 21 of McNeil's self-published comic book series *Finder,* which ran from 1996 to 2005. *Finder*'s current publisher, Dark Horse, describes it as follows:

> *Finder* is aboriginal science fiction, set at street-level in a far-future world of domed cities and clans and high technology.
>
> Finder is fantasy: magic and myth, and the hunger of memory, and the power of story. Its protagonist, Jaeger, the titular Finder, is a tribal detective and a Sin Eater, a ritual scapegoat; like *Finder* itself, Jaeger straddles the worlds of science and myth with astonishing grace. (Edidin n.p.)

The first *Finder* story arc, *Sin-Eater,* is set in the city of Anvard and revolves around Jaeger's encounter with an occasional lover named Emma Lockhart; her abusive husband Brigham Grosvenor; and their three daughters, Rachel, Lynne (a transgender character), and Marcie. By the end of the story, Brigham is insane and paralyzed. Emma is caring for him permanently, while Jaeger has left Anvard because of his chronic wanderlust. *Talisman,* the third *Finder* story arc, begins as Jaeger returns to Anvard, but

Jaeger appears only in the first of its three chapters; the protagonist of this story is Marcie, Emma's youngest daughter.

Talisman's theme is Marcie's relationship with books over the course of her childhood, adolescence, and young adulthood. Its title refers to the way in which physical objects, including books, can serve as quasi-magical facilitators of creative activity and as embodied metaphors for creative agency. Its story covers three different periods in Marcie's life during which books function for her in this capacity. In chapter 1, originally published as *Finder* #19, Marcie is seven years old but cannot read because chronic illnesses have kept her out of school. Jaeger buys her a book as a present (untitled, but let's call it The Book) which happens to have her name in it, and he reads to her from it. Marcie's encounter with The Book becomes the central event of her childhood. For Marcie, The Book is "the greatest gift I was ever given." It seems to contain an infinite plenitude of stories: some of the sentences from The Book that McNeil quotes are actually the work of Lewis Carroll, Stephen King, and J. M. Barrie, while others are her own inventions, suggesting that the book contains all the stories in the world and more besides (McNeil 624–25).[2] Yet "strangest of all . . . it all seemed somehow to be about me . . . my home" (522). In short, this is the ultimate book, the greatest book there ever was or could be, as suggested by Marcie's intoxicated expression after Jaeger reads to her (see figure 2.1).

Yet Marcie values The Book not only for the stories it contains but also for its physicality. Marcie's reading sessions with Jaeger become safe spaces in her life, allowing her to escape from her home life with her paralyzed and verbally abusive father. At one point, Marcie literally clings to the book against a background of her father's screams (see figure 2.2).

To that extent, *Talisman* emphasizes the affective experience of reading, the ways in which reading is more than just semantic processing of content. For Marcie, the book itself, as an object, has an emotional value independent of the information it contains—it functions as her security blanket.

However, Jaeger, a compulsive wanderer, leaves before finishing The Book, and Marcie's older siblings either refuse to read it to her or are unable to read it in the same way Jaeger did. Rachel even physically places the book out of Marcie's reach when she discovers something inappropriate in it, without explaining why. Therefore, Marcie resolves to learn to read. Although it proves difficult because she belongs to a subculture that values beauty and etiquette over intellectual achievement, she ultimately succeeds in learning to read her own name. Yet on the very day she does so,

---

2. All page references to *Talisman* refer to the version included in *Finder Library Volume 1*. The differences between the various versions of *Talisman* will be discussed below.

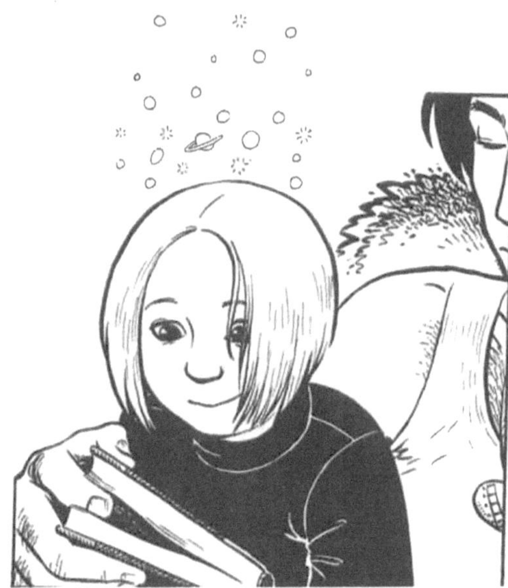

FIGURE 2.1. *Talisman,* detail from page 522. Note the upper left panel showing Marcie in a state of bibliophilic intoxication.

Marcie discovers that her mother has thrown The Book away, for reasons explicitly related to its physicality: "Those old-fashioned paper-pulp books are perishable. It would only have gone to rot; it was already turning yellow." As we learn in the next chapter, Emma created a 3D digital model of The Book before throwing it away, but ironically the digital version of The Book proves less durable than its physical counterpart, because the digital file proves to be corrupt and unreadable. Chapter 1 ends here, with the line "The greatest gift I ever had taken away from me was a book" (539).

In chapter 2, which is set several years later, a now teenaged and fully literate Marcie tries to compensate for the loss of The Book by reading voraciously. Books become so crucial to Marcie that they orient her experience of the physical world around her: "I knew my home city as a huge empty space with constellations of bookstores and libraries" (550). Marcie also tries to become an author herself, but her friends find her literary efforts less interesting than "the movies," which, in this science-fictional world, involve multisensory as well as visual and audio input (554). Marcie therefore becomes convinced that she needs to find The Book again in order to activate her literary talent.

Miraculously, she does find The Book—in the window of a store that's gone out of business—and her desire for it is so strong that she breaks

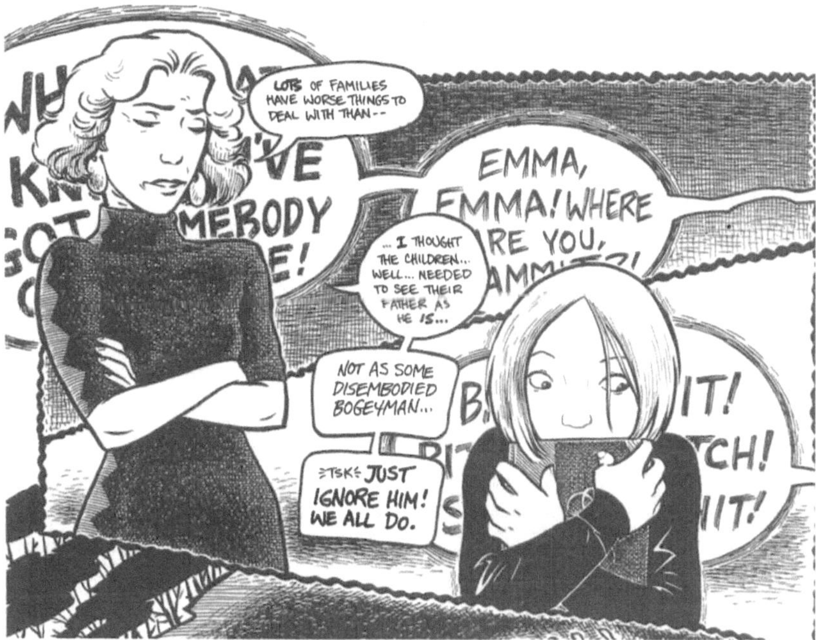

FIGURE 2.2. *Talisman,* page 524, showing Marcie literally using her book as a shield against her father.

the window and steals it. Yet on rereading it, she finds it to be completely banal and nonsensical, lacking any of the stories Jaeger read out of it. At this point, Marcie's sister Lynne reveals Jaeger's secret: The Book was never what it appeared to be. It was actually just a personalized children's book created as part of a marketing scam: "You'd fill out your kid's name, age, friends' names, favorite foods, pets' names . . . the company sends you a storybook with all that information inserted. It was just a scam, a way to start dossiers on future consumers at a really young age" (562). When Jaeger pretended to read to her from The Book, he was only making the stories up. Marcie realizes that if she ever wants to recreate the experience of reading The Book, she will have to write it herself.

In chapter 3, which takes place soon after chapter 2, Marcie finds that her attempts to write The Book are still unsuccessful because she is missing the proper talisman (hence the title of the story), the "perfect blank book" (582) that will act as a material incarnation of her creativity. However, blank books are difficult to find:

> Most shops carry tons of movies and data plugs, but comparatively few real, bound books. Environmentalists hate paper books. They say it'd be

> better if *all* books were digital files. But people *like* books [. . .] I don't want a fancy digital day planner. Nor do I want a cheap cardboard jacket to make a *plain* digital day planner look fancy. I want a *book*. (583, emphasis in original)

This claim again reinforces the superior material richness of the physical book compared to the digital book: for Marcie, writing in a blank book with a pen represents a physically meaningful act that is not compatible with the act of creating digital files. What happens next reinforces this argument. Unable to find the perfect printed book, Marcie buys one that has the ideal shape and size, but a blank cover. She plans to buy another one with the perfect cover image—a sphinx, the guardian of knowledge—so that she can cut out the cover image and glue it onto the cover of the first book. However, in a repeat of Marcie's two earlier disappointments (when her mother threw The Book away and when she discovered that it wasn't what she thought), the sphinx book is sold out when Marcie goes to buy it. Therefore, she is again forced to resort to drastic measures. She buys a $200 e-book device that has a sphinx on its cover, then cuts out the sphinx, glues it onto the cover of her blank book, and throws the actual device in the trash—an act that seems like the ultimate rejection of digital technology. The book ends by showing Marcie happily writing with a pen in a different blank book, with the talismanic blank book resting, unused, on a shelf above her desk (589; see figure 2.3). Although she's not ready to use it yet, its mere physical presence has the magical effect of activating her creativity. In some but not all versions of *Talisman*, this page is followed by a splash page showing a hand holding a pen over a blank page.

Talisman argues that books are valuable not only as vehicles for words, but also by virtue of their physical form. Reading a book or writing in a blank book is a physical, affective experience, and the value of the words written in a book is connected to the value of the book itself. Indeed, sometimes the best book can be a blank one. This is demonstrated both in chapters 1 and 2, where The Book's emotional significance turns out to be vastly greater than the intrinsic value of its content, and in chapter 3, where Marcie's book ends up being valuable purely as a talisman, whose blank pages are too valuable to tarnish with any actual writing.

In short, *Talisman* is a deeply biblionecrophilic work, in both a positive and a negative sense. It's a text committed to the value of the printed book as an affectively significant object and not just as a container for text. The fact that *Talisman* is a comic book rather than a work of prose science fiction gives added strength to its rhetoric of biblionecrophilia, because as I argue

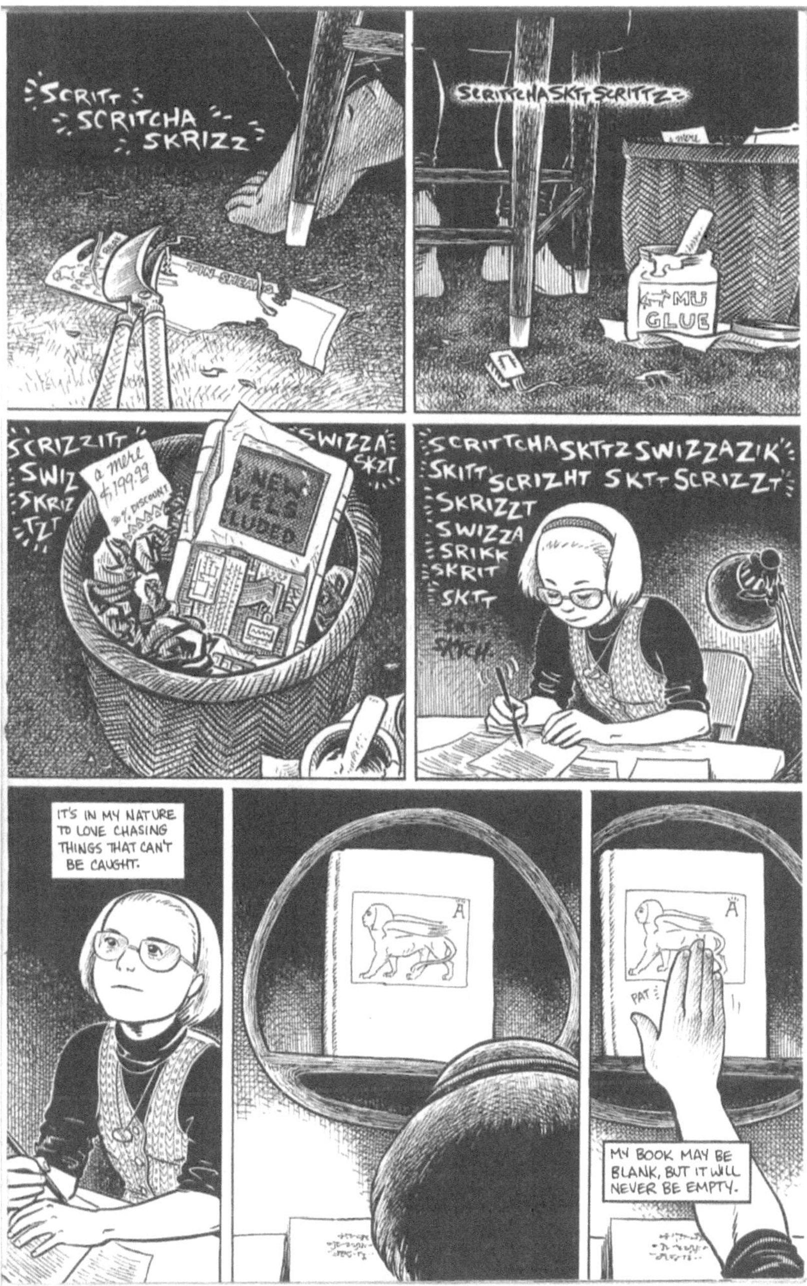

FIGURE 2.3. *Talisman,* page 589, showing Marcie's blank book serving as a talisman. Note the e-reader device in the trash.

throughout this book, the reader of a comic is more insistently aware of its physical and material properties than the reader of a prose book. In reading a comic, one can't easily forget that one is having a technologically mediated experience rather than an actual one. As a comic, *Talisman* can become a talisman itself, with less difficulty than if it was a printed book.

But what kind of talisman is *Talisman*? It turns out that the answer depends on the specific form in which the reader encounters the text. *Talisman* currently exists in at least five different physical forms, not to mention digital forms, and each version of the book offers a subtly but significantly different reading experience. The fact that *Talisman* is not fixed to a particular physical form means that the book doesn't prove its own arguments about the impact of materiality on the reading experience—it doesn't practice what it preaches, and therefore its biblionecrophilic arguments ultimately deconstruct themselves. In the vocabulary I will introduce in chapter 3, *Talisman* is a flexible text when it should be fixed to the print medium. As a result, *Talisman* suggests that if cartoonists want to use comics as a tool for demonstrating the continued relevance of the print medium, they need not only to praise print but also to exploit its material affordances, and this is what Lynda Barry and Matt Kindt have done.

Talisman originally appeared as issues 19 through 21 of McNeil's self-published comic book *Finder*. Subsequently, it was collected in a trade paperback, which was the edition that most of my students used when I taught it, and then included in an omnibus volume that also contains *Finder* #1–18 and #22, which is the edition that I cite in this chapter. Finally, in late 2012 two additional versions appeared: an oversized hardcover and a signed, limited-edition hardcover. Each of these versions has unique features missing from the others and has unique physical properties that affect the reader's experience. Thus, some of them are more effective as talismans than others.

In its original form as issues 19 through 21 of *Finder, Talisman*'s biblionecrophilic message takes on added resonance through its physical instantiation as a comic book. The comic book was designed as a disposable medium, cheaply printed and not intended for long-term storage: hence high-grade copies of comics from the 1950s and earlier are extremely scarce. But by the time *Talisman* appeared, the comic book had become a collector's medium, marketed to fans who lovingly maintained and curated their collections. I obtained my copies of *Finder* #19–21 when Carla Speed McNeil gave them to me for free at Comic-Con, an event that was originally designed largely as a meeting place for such collectors, although that is no longer its primary function. And though the comic book may seem like an even more doomed medium than the book, people like me continue to buy them as obsessively as ever. I would suggest that one reason for the resilience of the comic book is its combination of visual and tactile richness. As Ian Hague explains in *Comics and the Senses,* touch plays a significant role in the reader's experience of a comic. The comic book offers tactile pleasures that the trade paperback doesn't: it's flexible and soft to the touch and can be easily slotted into a box containing hundreds of other comic books. Finally, the object the reader touches bears the physical stamp of the artist's hand. As will be discussed in chapter 5, when I read a comic book, I have to touch the pages to turn them, and in doing so, I put my hand on a piece of artwork that bears an indexical relationship with the artist's originary act of drawing.

This indexical relationship also exists when comic books are reprinted in trade paperback form, but the trade paperback has other differences from the comic book. In *Talisman*'s case, the trade paperback of *Talisman* lacks the original cover art, inside cover illustrations, letter columns, and advertisements for original art that appeared in the original issues. It seems like a secondary, knock-off artifact, lacking the aura of the original comic (though obviously a comic book is not an auratic text in the strict sense). At the same time, the *Talisman* trade paperback is a more permanent, durable artifact and offers a more complete and sustained reading experience, which are among the reasons why "waiting for the trade" has become a common fan practice. Compared to the trade paperback, the comic books seem flimsy and insubstantial: hence some fans derisively refer to comic book as "floppies." Furthermore, the trade paperback has an added feature: several pages of endnotes written by McNeil. These endnotes provide important information not given in *Talisman* itself, as well as fleshing out the book's world-building. The reader of the trade paperback needs to check the endnotes constantly, which is another reminder of the book's physical materiality and its random-access nature.[3]

The giant omnibus edition of *Finder* #1–22 is still more cumbersome, and more likely to show the physical effects of reading. My copy has a prominent crease on the spine, offering physical proof that it was read to completion. Most dramatically, the limited-edition, signed hardcover is designed to look like The Book itself (see figure 2.4). This edition is apparently supposed to be the ultimate version of *Talisman*: a beautiful, durable book that presents McNeil's story in the way it was meant to be read. More-

3. I thank a reviewer for this suggestion. *Talisman*'s use of endnotes is not unique. The most famous example of a graphic novel that uses endnotes in a similar way is Alan Moore and Eddie Campbell's *From Hell.* Another example is Chester Brown's *Louis Riel.*

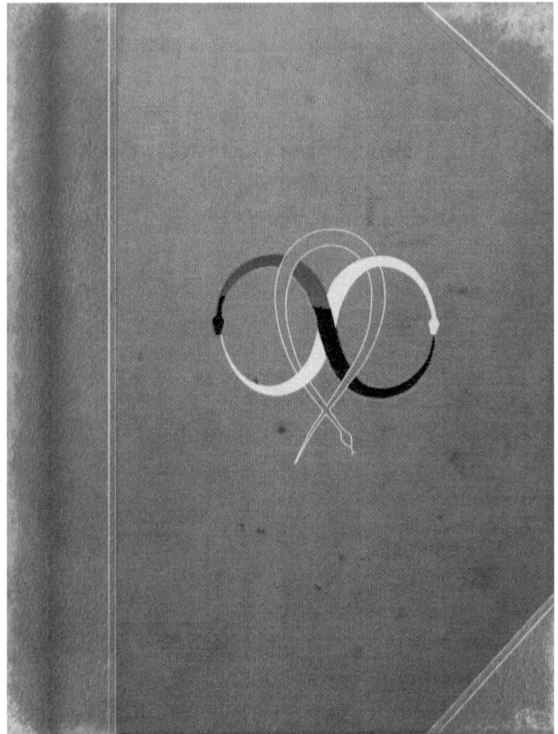

FIGURE 2.4. Cover of the limited-edition, signed hardcover version of *Talisman.*

over, its resemblance to The Book seems to imply that like The Book, it has the potential to activate the reader's creativity. Yet there is another possible reading here, which may well have been intended: if the limited-edition hardcover is like The Book, then perhaps it, too, is a cynical marketing scam whose actual content is completely banal.

Again, as with *Fun Home,* the point here is not that any of the five print versions of *Talisman* is any better or worse than any of the others. The point is that *Talisman* is unlike either The Book or Marcie's blank book because it's not strongly bound to any one particular physical instantiation: it's capable of remediation into a variety of forms. This was most strikingly demonstrated when *Talisman* was made available in digital form. *Talisman* can now be read digitally via Dark Horse Comics's digital app and also via ComiXology, which is discussed in chapter 4. Many of my students read it in this form; some of them probably even read it on real-life versions of the e-book device that Marcie throws in the trash. Indeed, as I was writing this chapter, I myself used the digital version of *Talisman* to check the quotation about constellations of bookstores and libraries. When read in this form, *Talisman* seems to deconstruct itself—it critiques digital reading devices in the strongest terms, yet it can now itself be read with a digital device. This may be taken as evidence that the biblionecrophilic project is inevitably doomed because digital reading devices are inescapable.

However, I don't want to engage in a hostile critique; I think that *Talisman* is a beautiful and honest work and that its celebration of printed books is deeply resonant. The problem with *Talisman,* if anything, is that it doesn't go far *enough*: it doesn't use its physical form as support for its argument about the value of printed books, and therefore it is not resistant to translation into digital form. In this sense, *Talisman* is not taking full advantage of the "crisitunity" offered by the threatened status of print. In order to see how comics can be used to both argue for and physically demonstrate the continuing value of the printed book, we need to look at other works that not only make explicit arguments in favor of print but also serve as physical examples of what print can do that computers can't.

SYLLABUS: USING THE MATERIAL PROPERTIES OF COMICS TO CREATE MEANING

Compared to McNeil, Lynda Barry is more interested in using the physical design of her works to support her arguments about materiality. While Barry's work contains an element of extreme hostility toward digital technology which is at odds with my own project (and which, as I show later, is potentially separable from the more productive elements of her work), she ultimately goes further than McNeil in suggesting ways of using comics to reimagine the future of the print book as a physical artifact and an expressive medium.

Lynda Barry's work has recently been the subject of significant critical interest, including a monograph by Susan Kirtley. This section here focuses specifically on the attitudes toward the materiality of the book that are revealed in her recent autobiographical/instructional trilogy: *What It Is* (2008); *Picture This: The Near-Sighted Monkey Book* (2010); and *Syllabus: Notes from an Accidental Professor* (2014). Like McNeil, Barry sees the printed book as an almost magical artifact that has the power to transport the reader and to activate creativity. But unlike McNeil, Barry's work demonstrates how this commitment to materiality can be translated into actual bookmaking practice, resulting in the creation of books that are tightly bound to their specific physical instantiations and that exploit their own physical properties in a way that *Talisman* does not.

Barry's perspective on the printed book is rooted in her view of handwriting. A full treatment of Barry's treatment of handwriting and drawing is outside the scope of the present chapter, and I hope to explore this topic elsewhere, but in short, Barry views handwriting and drawing as having an almost magical power to inspire creativity. For Barry, "handwriting *is an image* left by a living being in motion *it cannot be duplicated* in time or space" (*What It Is* 108).[4] Throughout the instructional section of *What It Is,* Barry repeatedly emphasizes that handwriting and hand drawing are physical processes that trigger mental activity. By writing and drawing, the reader activates a circuit between the body and the unconscious memory, bypassing the conscious mind. These ideas appear to have some basis in neuroscience, given the number of neuroscientists that Barry cites in *Syllabus,* but Barry never explains the scientific basis for her theory of handwriting. Therefore, the mechanism by which handwriting activates creativity is unclear; this mechanism appears to operate by magical means, like Marcie's talismanic book. Because of this extreme allegiance to manual writing technologies, Barry explicitly rejects digital writing technologies. In *Picture This,* Barry states that the use of a laptop made her writing process slow and frustrating, and she describes how her creativity was reactivated when she started to use a paintbrush instead (198–200). Barry therefore used a paintbrush to write her illustrated prose novel *Cruddy,* even though it was published in typeset form (*Picture This* 200–202). In her instructional writings, Barry insists that her students similarly disavow the use of digital technologies: "If you have a cell phone you must turn it off" (*What It Is* 175). (More examples of how Barry's pedagogy is explicitly antidigital will be mentioned below.)

Barry's views of writing technologies are reflected in her views of reading technologies. Like McNeil, Barry emphasizes the printed book's talismanic quality, its ability to magically inspire creativity.[5] In addition to emphasizing the magical power of writing, *What It Is* also emphasizes the magical power of the book. As a child, Barry had no books in her house; her

---

4. In *What It Is* and *Picture This,* Barry writes in a combination of upper-case block letters and lower-case cursive. Rather than reproducing Barry's style of capitalization, I use Roman lettering to represent the former style of text, and italics to represent the latter. Barry also sometimes uses line breaks rather than punctuation to suggest interruptions in the flow of thought. I use slashes to represent such line breaks.

5. Barry's almost magical view of the printed book is related to her even more mystical views of handwriting and drawing, but this topic is outside the scope of the present chapter and deserves a separate treatment elsewhere.

parents were "not reading people" (26).[6] For the same reason, Barry had limited access to paper:

> I got screamed at a lot for using up paper. The only blank paper in the house was hers, and if she found out I touched it she'd go crazy. I sometimes stole paper from school and even that made her mad. I think it's why I hoard paper to this day. I have so much blank paper everywhere, in every drawer, on every shelf, and still when I need a sheet I look in the garbage first. I agonize over using a "good" sheet of paper for anything. I have good drawing paper I've been dragging around for twenty years because I'm not good enough to use it yet. Yes, I know this is insane. (qtd. in Schappell 53–54)

When "*thanks* to a summer supermarket give-away, four *books* made it *into our* household" (*What It Is* 27), they seem to have acted to spark Barry's creativity. On pages 27 and 28 of *What It Is,* Barry shows herself reading Hans Christian Andersen and the Brothers Grimm, and on the left side of page 28 she reproduces a quotation from William Blake, another visual-verbal artist who was deeply interested in the physical form of the book (see figure 2.5).

She continues: "But paper and ink have conjuring abilities of *their own.* Arrangements of *lines* and shapes, *of* letters *and* words *on* a series of pages *make a world we* can *dwell* and travel in" (38). This is accompanied by an image of the child Lynda reading an unidentifiable book, as shown in figure 2.5. The notion Barry describes here—that books transport the reader into another world—is not unique. It's familiar from Emily Dickinson's statement: "There is no Frigate like a Book / To take us Lands away" (553), or the opening animation of *Reading Rainbow,* where spacesuits and dragons explode out of children's books.[7] But given Barry's preoccupation with materiality, it's significant that she specifically references paper and ink and that she describes literature in visual terms, as "arrangements of lines and shapes, of letters and words on a series of pages." In conventional versions of the book-as-frigate fantasy, the book serves merely as a vehicle for the transformative experience it provides. By comparing books to ships, horses, and chariots, Dickinson emphasizes their relative frailty. Her poem concludes: "How frugal is the Chariot / That bears the Human soul" (553), emphasizing the flimsiness of books rather than their solidity. In the *Reading Rainbow* opening sequence, the children discard their books after the

6. Barry's family's lack of intellectualism is a common theme in her work.

7. Coincidentally, Barry quotes Dickinson repeatedly in *Syllabus,* though not this poem.

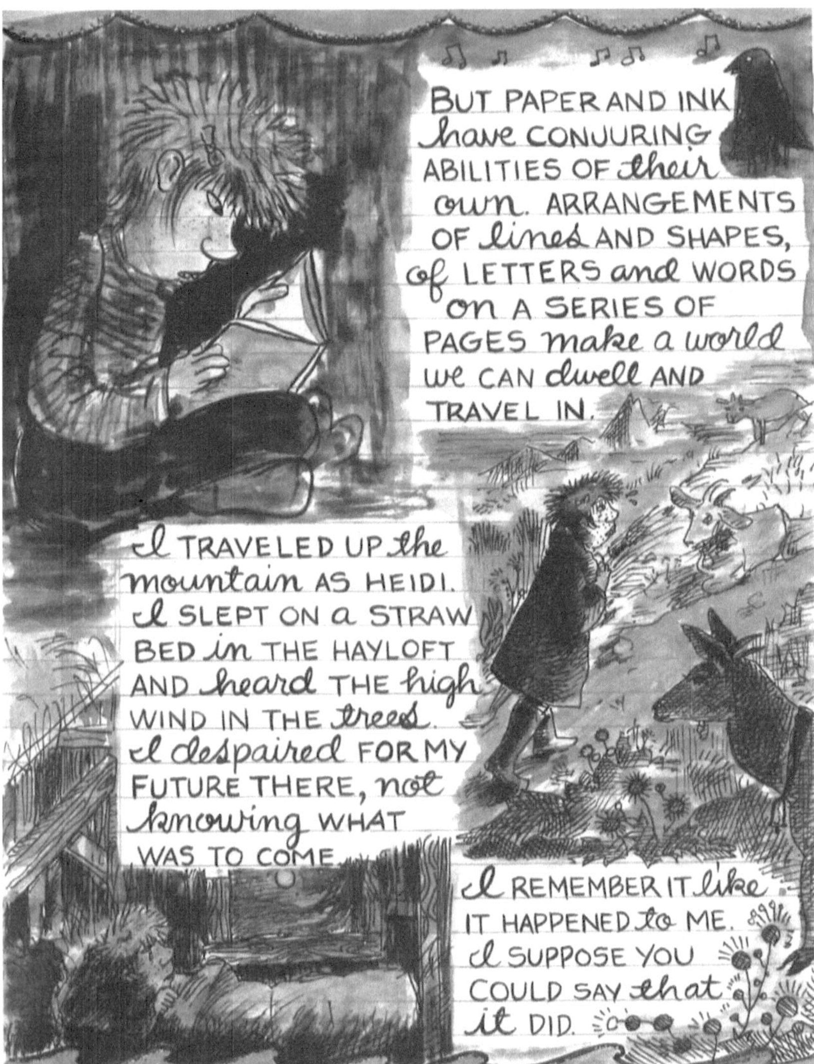

FIGURE 2.5. Page 38 of *What It Is.* Note the image of Lynda reading an unidentifiable book.

books transform them into kings, pirates, and so on, again suggesting that the book as an object is less valuable than its content. In contrast, Barry conceives of books as visual and tactile objects, and for her, the inhabitable world contained in the book is inextricably linked to the book's physical form and never achieves an existence separate there from.

Barry's investment in the physical form of books, as well as the imaginative experiences they provide, helps explain why she takes a more active role than McNeil in designing her own books. In *Picture This,* Barry writes: "*I remembered making my own books when I was a kid* / IT / STILL / WORKS" (202). It is important to note that Barry does not literally make her own books, unlike such artists as Nadia Raviscioni or Jason Shiga, who have produced hand-bound limited editions of their work (see Beaty 3–5 and the last chapter of this book). Her works are not handwritten, handmade artifacts—they are printed books, mediated through the print process. When Chute writes that "Barry underlines the link between this scene of creation and the actual materiality of the book by the fact that she incorporates pieces of pajamas into her collages" (2011, 307), she neglects the difference between what Matthew Kirschenbaum calls *formal* and *forensic materiality*—essentially, what a text appears to be made of versus what it actually is made of (11). Barry's original collages do include pieces of pajamas, but her published books only *look* like they include pieces of pajamas (see figure 2.6). What they actually include is *photographs* of pieces of pajamas, and presumably these photographs were taken digitally, given that nearly all professionally published books are produced using digital methods. Indeed, digital printing methods were probably required in order to accurately reproduce the quality of Barry's colors.

Nonetheless, Barry's books create the *suggestion* of physicality. Both books attempt to activate the reader's tactile memory, reminding the reader of the texture of the artifacts depicted on the collage pages. Barry's books invoke a haptic or tactile mode of visuality in which the reader is invited to imagine what the original collages must have felt like. (Of course, the tactile visual aesthetic of Barry's pages is contradicted by the fact that the viewer *can* and *must* touch the pages in order to read the book, and she or he is therefore necessarily aware that the pages feel smooth and flat, unlike the collages they represent. By contrast, in what Laura Marks calls *haptic cinema,* the viewer does not have to touch the screen in order to view the image.) Moreover, *Picture This* and *What It Is* are heavy, inconvenient artifacts, as I learned when I walked a mile from my house to my office while carrying two of them. As with European bande dessinée albums, the sheer size of these books is essential to their visual appeal. They could not be remediated into another format without mangling the reading experience, and neither book is currently available on Kindle.

The key example of Barry's deployment of the materiality of the book is *Syllabus,* the third volume in her instructional trilogy. In *Syllabus,* one particular type of book—the composition notebook—emerges as a crucial symbol of the creative process, and the publication design of *Syllabus* reflects the centrality of the composition notebook to its argument.

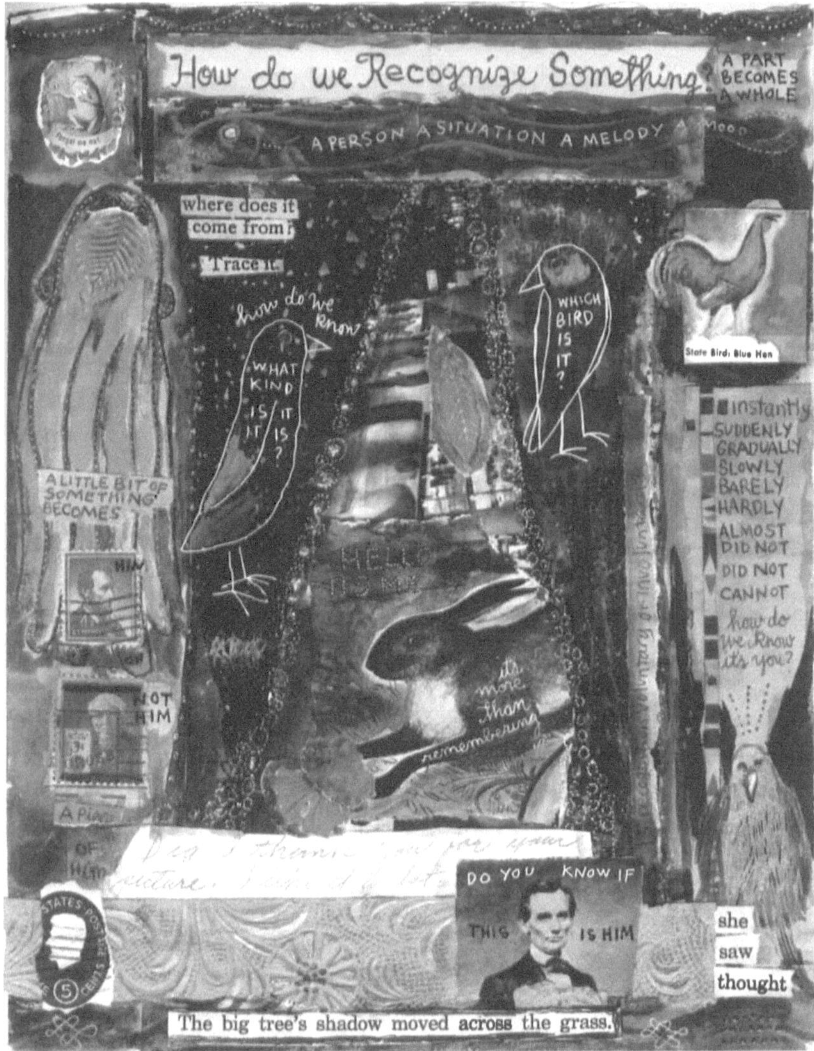

FIGURE 2.6. Page 32 of *What It Is,* showing Barry's collage technique.

Syllabus is a collection of exercises and assignments from Barry's courses at the University of Wisconsin. In each of these courses, students are required to take notes in a "standard composition notebook / B&W marbled cover, 200 pages" (48) and to submit these composition notebooks to Barry at regular intervals. The notebook is of central importance to the class, as Barry explains:

> Keeping an active comp book is at the heart of this class. . . . Keep the comp book with you at all times—or as often as you can—and use it for everything. Along with diary pages, writing and drawing assignments, I'd like you to use it for work in other classes you may have, lecture notes, ideas, rants, plans, insults, first drafts of any sort on any subject, reviews. And I'd like you to include some of the ephemera from your daily life: ticket stubs, candy wrappers. . . . Decorate the covers any way you wish. Think of your composition notebook as a catch-all that collects samples from all of the elements of your day-to-day life. . . . I think of the comp book as a place for the back of the mind to come forward. (62)

For Barry, the composition book is the equivalent of a medieval commonplace book, which was "filled with items of every kind: medical recipes, quotes, letters, poems, tables of weights and measures, proverbs, prayers, legal formulas. Commonplaces were used by readers, writers, students, and scholars as an aid for remembering useful concepts or facts they had learned. Each commonplace book was unique to its creator's particular interests" ("Commonplace Book"). Like commonplace books, Barry's students' composition books serve as externalized records of their minds. Each student's composition notebook—or notebooks, plural, since Barry expects students to compile three or four each semester (55)—is supposed to be a record of all the important things the student did, felt, or thought during the semester.

Crucially, however, the composition book is supposed to be physical rather than digital. Barry suggests that as a basic diary exercise, the student should "relax and draw a spiral for about a minute while remembering the day as it comes to you," then spend short periods of time writing down things she did, saw, and heard, and then draw a picture. Drawing a spiral is intended as "an exercise in both relaxation and concentration—your task is to get the lines as close together as possible without letting them touch. If they touch, you get electrocuted" (76). The motivation for this exercise is that Barry believes drawing is a means of activating creativity, as she explains at much greater length in *What It Is*. The very act of writing or drawing, even just drawing a spiral, is valuable because it creates a circuit between the hand and the brain. More generally, Barry sees the physicality of writing as a means of creating "muscle memory":

> We know that athletes, musicians and actors all have to practice, rehearse, repeat things until it gets into the body, the "muscle memory," but for

> some reason, writers and visual artists think they have to be INSPIRED before they make something. Not suspecting the PHYSICAL act of writing or drawing is what brings that inspiration about. (163)

For Barry, writing and drawing are physical as well as mental activities, and they require practice just as other physical disciplines do.

Barry's belief in the galvanizing powers of handwriting and hand drawing also explains her hostility toward digital communication technologies, hostility that is displayed on several occasions in *Syllabus*. Barry explicitly states: "No activated electronic devices are allowed in our classroom between 12:00 pm–4:00 pm. Please do not check your devices during our break" (73). Barry doesn't explain the reason for this policy, but we can infer that she does not believe typing or using a smartphone is a physically meaningful act in the same way as drawing is. Barry's dim view of digital devices is also reflected in her description of the hand as "the original digital device" (8), which implies that hands are less primal or originary than so-called digital devices (though this phrase could also be read against the grain as implying that the human body is always already technological).[8] For Barry, writing on a screen does not generate the same sort of physical-mental engagement that handwriting creates.

More broadly, Barry's pedagogy involves an approach to time that is at odds with the dominant temporality of digital culture. She expresses frustration that "sometimes right before class I'll see students rushing to finish the homework I gave them," because "they'll get nothing from the work without the state of mind that comes with it" and "we can use writing and drawing to get to that state, but not by rushing" (128). To get the full benefits of Barry's approach, one must be willing to spend as much time writing and drawing as necessary. This sort of approach to the utilization of time is more characteristic of print culture or even manuscript culture than digital culture, in which both students and employees are required to work according to a relentless schedule and to be constantly on call.[9] Barry's only concession to digital culture is that she maintains a class Tumblr page which students are required to check regularly.

---

8. Clay Shirky, who is much less a digital skeptic than Barry, has adopted a similar no-laptops policy in class because "multi-tasking is bad for the quality of cognitive work, and is especially punishing of the kind of cognitive work we ask of college students" (n.p., hyperlinks removed). This is the same rationale that leads Nicholas Carr to prefer print culture to digital culture.

9. See Jonathan Crary's *24/7: Late Capitalism and the Ends of Sleep*. *The Onion* satirized the temporality of digital culture with a November 4, 2014, article titled "Laid-Back Company Allows Employees To Work From Home After 6 P.M."

Up to this point, Barry's argument about the superiority of books and handwriting to computers and typing is similar to McNeil's argument in *Talisman*. The reason *Syllabus* represents an advance over McNeil's work is that Barry uses the physical properties of her book as a means of augmenting its meaning. *Syllabus*, the book, is not just a container for content but a carefully designed artifact, whose publication design intersects with its content in such a way as to create meanings that wouldn't exist otherwise.

Let me explain this by describing my own encounter with *Syllabus*. On December 3, 2014, I received my copy of Barry's *Syllabus*. Retrieving the Amazon.com package from my mailbox, I was surprised at its light weight and floppiness—I had expected a large, bulky hardcover volume, similar to *What It Is* and *Picture This*. Opening the package, I understood why, and I experienced a pleasurable shock of recognition. *Syllabus* is designed to look like a composition book with a duct-taped spine and a faux-marble cover—the same kind of composition book that Barry's students are required to purchase (see figure 2.7).

I immediately recognized what *Syllabus* was supposed to resemble, because as a child, I received the exact same type of composition notebook as a present from my favorite babysitter, and I proceeded to fill it with all sorts of drawings and lists. I wouldn't be surprised if that notebook was still in my parents' house somewhere, though efforts to find it have been fruitless. I am not alone in having very specific memories of notebooks like this one. When I posted a message to WPA-L asking if anyone knew the history of this type of notebook, several people responded and mentioned having used them in the 1970s or 1980s. They date back much further than that—according to the Fountain Pen Network forum, the exact origin of this style of composition book is unclear, but examples have been found that date back to the 1870s, and they continue to be widely available today. Composition books have also been remediated digitally. As Karen Evans pointed out: "One of the theme templates in Blackboard is based on the marbled cover of those composition books" (quoted with permission).

As the above discussion suggests, black marbled composition books tend to be associated with specific memories of childhood—at least among certain persons—and *Syllabus*'s resemblance to such a composition book is designed to activate such memories (see figure 2.8). For Barry, according to the theories she outlines in *What It Is*, creativity is effectively a matter of activating buried memories—creative writing is about resurrecting images from your past that you didn't know you still had. *Syllabus*'s physical form is designed to achieve this effect. *Syllabus* argues that

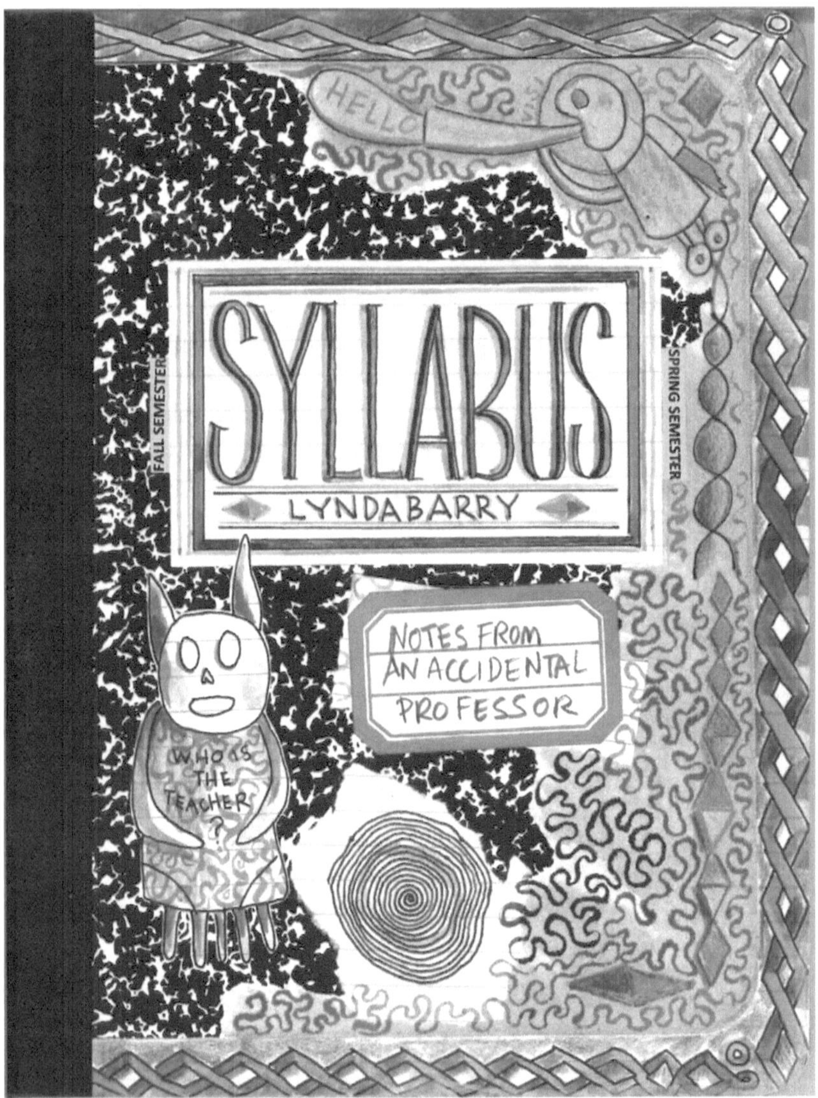

FIGURE 2.7. Lynda Barry's *Syllabus*.

if a book can be a "frigate . . . to take us lands away" (Dickinson), this is not just because of the information in the book, but also because of the ways in which its physical substance serves to activate the reader's memory. Yet the book demonstrates this point through its physical design as well as through its content. The physical design of *Syllabus* is intended to encourage the reader to practice the sort of creative behavior that the book describes.

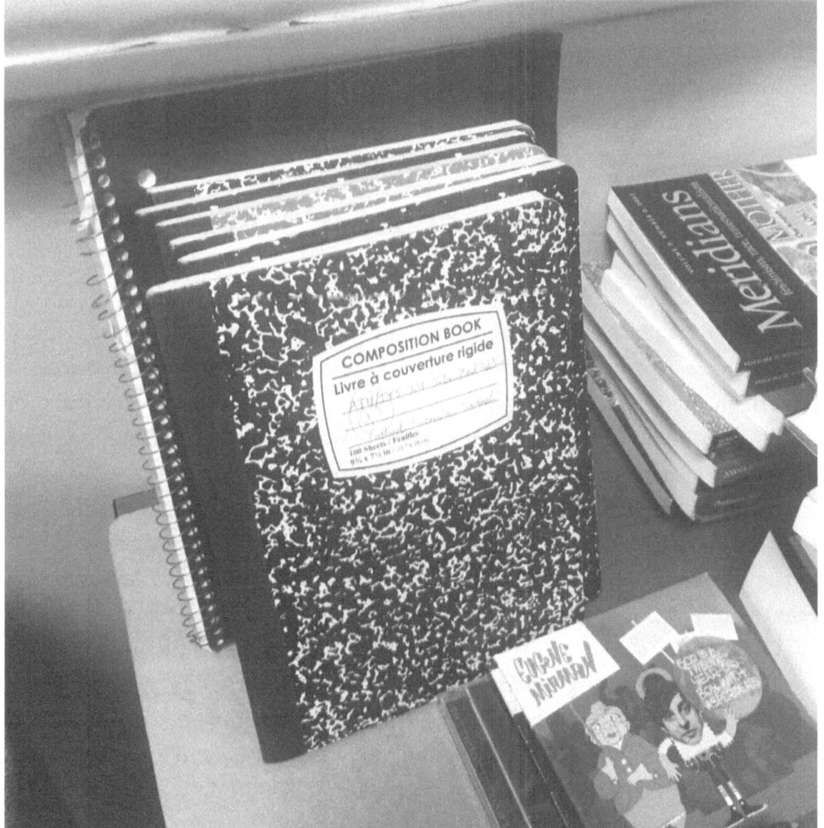

FIGURE 2.8. Composition books in the wild. Photo by the author.

At one level, Barry's decision to format her book in this way is motivated by her lifelong interest in the materiality of writing and reading processes. Yet the design of *Syllabus* can also be read as a deliberate act of resistance to digital technology. As discussed above, Barry is a committed digital skeptic and is deeply resistant to the replacement of the printed book by digital alternatives.[10] Barry's publication design practice can therefore be seen as a political strategy, motivated by the desire to defend the printed book against the threat of digitization. By publishing books like *Syl-*

10. Barry has not completely eschewed the use of digital technology. *One! Hundred! Demons!* was initially published as a webcomic, and in *Syllabus*, Barry describes her use of a course Tumblr page. However, the webcomic version of *One! Hundred! Demons!* is no longer available and has been supplanted by the print version. And Barry's course Tumblr page seems more like an adjunct to her class than a central component to her pedagogy, given how little space she devotes to it in *Syllabus*.

labus, Barry seeks to resist the creeping onslaught of digital technology. Her publication design practice is motivated by her view of digitization as a crisis for the printed book. In this sense, Barry participates in the contemporary literary trend that Garth Risk Hallberg describes as "Kindle-proofing."

"KINDLE-PROOF YOUR COMIC IN SEVEN EASY STEPS!"

As I briefly mentioned in the introduction, unusual typographic, photographic, and other techniques have started to take on a central role in American literature. Leading representatives of the contemporary trend of multimodal fiction include Mark Z. Danielewski, Jonathan Safran Foer, and Salvador Plascencia. The trend of literary exploitation of multimodality was given official institutional recognition when Jennifer Egan won the 2011 Pulitzer Prize for *A Visit from the Goon Squad,* whose final chapter is formatted as a PowerPoint presentation.[11] Nor is this trend limited to American literature; one of its outstanding representatives was the late German author W. G. Sebald (1944–2001), whose novels include photographs interspersed with the text. Kindle-proofing has become an increasingly popular strategy for contemporary authors of prose literature, yet comics can implement this strategy even more effectively than prose texts can, and another way to understand Kindle-proofing is as a process by which the prose novel accentuates its resemblance to a comic book.[12]

Of course, literary works that exploit their own visual and tactile properties are hardly a new phenomenon. The notion of a book as a transparent container for meaning, an invisible vehicle for the literary experience, is an artifact of the Gutenberg era. In the manuscript age, all literary experiences would have been strongly visual—as well as auditory, since silent reading is itself a modern practice.[13] Even after the invention of print, the use of images and innovative typography continued to be an important tradition, as with Renaissance emblem books and George Herbert's pattern poetry. As Johanna Drucker documents in *The Visible Word,* the exploitation of the

11. Barry has assigned this book in her classes and has required her students to create a hand-drawn version of the PowerPoint chapter (*Syllabus* 185).

12. One of the ultimate examples of a Kindle-proof comic is Marc-Antoine Mathieu's *Julius Corentin Acquefacques,* which I do not discuss here because the scope of this book is limited to English-language comics. This series has unfortunately not been translated into English.

13. See Hayles and Pressman's *Comparative Textual Media* as well as Alberto Manguel's *A History of Reading.*

material properties of typography was an important trend in twentieth-century avant-garde literature, appearing in the work of Modernists like Marinetti, Apollinaire, and Khlebnikov as well as in mid-century concrete poetry. The use of nonstandard book designs and nonlinear orders of reading is a distinct but related phenomenon with an equally long history. Distinguished modern examples that preceded the current digital age include Raymond Queneau's *Cent mille milliards de poèmes* and Julio Cortázar's *Hopscotch*. Finally, the artist's book emerged as a significant form of visual art in the twentieth century; notable commercially published examples include Theresa Hak Kyung Cha's *Dictée* and Tom Phillips's *A Humument*. We might refer to all these phenomena with the umbrella label of *multimodal literature*.

However, at earlier periods in the history of print, multimodal literature was typically a marginal and avant-garde phenomenon. "It was not until the late 1960s and early 1970s that visual poetry began to be recognized as a literary movement of any consequence. . . . Pattern poetry . . . generally existed in the margins of poetic discourse, especially in English-speaking cultures" (Thomas 86). For example, George Herbert's pattern poetry was traditionally seen as an aberration and a departure from the dominant poetic tradition. In the twentieth century, phenomena like pattern poetry and nonlinear narrative tended to develop out of an avant-garde context. Authors like Marinetti and Queneau, though in very different cultural contexts, were seeking to push the boundaries of what was acceptable as literature, so their work was extremely atypical relative to the literature of their time.

By contrast, in contemporary America, multimodal literature has become much more central to the literary scene. Works by authors like Danielewski, Foer, and Egan routinely appear on bestseller lists. Why is multimodal literature starting to move from the margins to the center? Partly this is due to the same phenomenon that led to the rise of the graphic novel, namely, the visual turn in American culture. The use of images in all cultural spheres is becoming more ubiquitous and more acceptable than it was for most of the twentieth century. But more specifically, with recent works of multimodal literature, the stakes are significantly higher than in the past because the printed book is now haunted by the specter of digital media, particularly e-reading platforms such as the Kindle and iPad.

Thus, recent works of multimodal literature may be read either as attempts to demonstrate the continuing importance of the printed book at a time when other, more efficient reading devices seem poised to replace it, or as nostalgic monuments. In his essay "Kindle-Proof Your Book in Seven

Easy Steps!" from which I borrow the term *Kindle-proofing,* Garth Risk Hallberg begins by quoting Balzac's lament for the wooden printing press in *Lost Illusions*: "[Now] the rapid spread of machine presses has swept away all this obsolete gear to which, for all its imperfections, we owe the beautiful books printed by Elzevir, Plantin, Aldus[,] Didot, and the rest" (n.p.). Subsequently, "in honor of the future that never was, the durable pigments of the almost obsolete," Hallberg provides a list of multimodal techniques for making books impossible to remediate on the Kindle.

Some of these techniques—like "Use Color," "Illustrate, Illustrate, Illustrate," and "Play with Text, Typeface and White Space"—are predicated on the fact that the Kindle and the iPad are designed primarily for rendering text and have limited capacities for rendering images and effective typography. As Joe Clark suggested in a comment to Hallberg's blog post, books that use these techniques are Kindle-proof only because of the present impoverished state of the Kindle's visual rendering technology. Future versions of the Kindle will probably be able to more effectively replicate the visual experience of a book like Foer's *Extremely Loud and Incredibly Close* or Plascencia's *People of Paper.* However, even if these techniques don't inherently make a book Kindle-proof, they still represent a break from "the unmarked text, the even gray page of prose and poetic convention" (Drucker 1997, 46). They help books emulate the visual appeal of other media. Comics, of course, use most of these techniques almost universally.

Other items on Hallberg's list involve exploitation of the physical and tactile properties of print books, and the use of these techniques makes a book inherently Kindle-proof. These items include "Run with Scissors" and "Put It in a Box." Examples of books that use these techniques include Foer's *Tree of Codes,* Anne Carson's *Nox,* and Queneau's *Cent mille milliards de poèmes.* Such books are inherently Kindle-proof in a way in which a normal print novel or Carla Speed McNeil's *Talisman* is not: they couldn't be remediated into any other format without removing essential elements of the reading experience. *Syllabus* is also a Kindle-proof book in this sense, as are other books I will describe later, such as Chris Ware's *Building Stories* or Jason Shiga's *Meanwhile*—which *has* been remediated into a digital format, but as we will see in chapter 5, this was done in a sensitive and thoughtful way and resulted in a new book that complements the original book rather than replacing it.

Here is where comics can help us understand what Kindle-proofing means and why it matters. As described by Hallberg, Kindle-proofing is motivated by nostalgia for a dying age of print. As used by Barry, Kindle-proofing is motivated by the related phenomenon of hostility to digital technology. The reason why one would want to Kindle-proof one's book is to frustrate any attempt to transform it into a digital text.

However, this prompts the question of whether the strategy of Kindle-proofing can be separated from its associated politics of opposition to digital technology. Is it possible to produce comics that are Kindle-proof but are also compatible with digital technology? Can comics help us imagine a way to rethink the printed book in terms of compatibility with the digital book, rather than in terms of opposition to it? Many current comics suggest a positive answer to this question. For these and other authors, digitization represents not a crisis, but a crisitunity.

Ian Hague suggests that the rise of digital technology means that books published in print form now need to have a *reason* to be published in that form (133–34). Print publishing is no longer the unquestioned default. Therefore, a book published in print must do something to justify its use of the print medium. Hague's claim is somewhat excessive, at least if we take it to imply that all print books must do creative and experimental things with the print medium, since we have already seen that the vast majority of print books do not do this. A more moderate version of Hague's claim might be that in the digital era, there is often a need to justify why a book must be published in print rather than digital form. Some categories of books have indeed disappeared for this reason: because of their inability to compete with digital alternatives. For example, the *Encyclopedia Britannica* and the *Oxford English Dictionary* are no longer published in print, and the gamebook genre, as I discuss in chapter 5, went extinct due to competition from video games.

For Barry, as well as for traditionalist critics like Andrew Piper or John Updike, the fact that print is no longer the unquestioned default mode of publishing is a negative development; it represents a crisis for the printed book. However, it is also possible to see this development as a crisitunity, in that it forces authors to think critically and sensitively about the expressive possibilities of the printed book. When Kindle-proofing is understood in this way, it doesn't need to be mutually exclusive with the thoughtful exploitation of digital technology; instead, it can be a technique for rethinking the ecological relationship between print and digital books. As evidence of this, I turn to the work of a cartoonist who does not necessarily share Barry's polemical opposition to digital technology, but who also makes extensive and effective use of the medium of the printed book: Matt Kindt.

MATT KINDT: HOW THE THREAT OF DIGITAL CAN HELP REVITALIZE THE PRINT MEDIUM

Among all the artists working in the higher-end segment of the commercial comics industry, Matt Kindt is perhaps the one who has devoted the most effort to reimagining the print medium. In works such as *Pistolwhip* and *Superspy,* Kindt uses the physical materiality of the comics medium as a tool for creating meaning. For example, *Superspy,* like Cortázar's *Hopscotch,* can be read either from start to finish or in an alternative, nonlinear order described at the start of the book. Here, however, I specifically want to focus on Kindt's most recent completed work: his comic book series *MIND MGMT,* which was published by Dark Horse from 2012 to 2015. *MIND MGMT* is a key example of what I mean when I describe the rise of digital technology as a crisitunity for print comics, because it creatively rethinks the almost obsolete format of the pamphlet-size comic book in ways that would not have been necessary at a time when this format was the dominant delivery vehicle for comics.

Famously invented by M. C. Gaines in 1933, the pamphlet-sized, four-color comic book was one of America's most popular print media for much of the prewar and immediate postwar periods. Following the 1950s anti-comics campaign, the comic book went into a slow decline from which it has never recovered.[14] Even after it began to decline in commercial importance, the comic book remained the standard delivery mechanism for both commercially and artistically oriented comics until well into the 1990s. As Charles Hatfield explains in *Alternative Comics,* comic books served as the medium of choice for major creators like Chris Ware, Chester Brown, and the Hernandez brothers, who later moved into graphic novels, and the comic book store was the emotional heart of the comic book community. However, in recent decades the monthly comic book has been eclipsed in importance by the original graphic novel, the trade paperback and, more recently, the digital edition. (In this context, the difference is that a graphic novel consists of original material not previously published, while a trade paperback collects stories previously published in another form.) Perhaps as a result of the extraordinary success of the trade paperback ("TPB" or "trade") collections of Neil Gaiman's *Sandman* (1989–96), almost all monthly comics are now collected into TPBs after their initial serial publication. "Waiting for the trade"—that is, waiting to read a comic book storyline

14. See Gabilliet for a definitive historical account of the evolution of the comic book format in America.

until it's been collected in trade rather than buying the individual serialized issues—is now a common practice among fans.[15] Many comics sell better in trade form than as single issues,[16] and some publishers use single issues as a loss leader, intended to fund the publication of the trade paperback and not to make a profit. Trades are typically considered more attractive and easier to store and transport, and they sometimes contain special features absent from serialized comic books. Meanwhile, most monthly comic books now use a "decompressed" style of storytelling, in which each individual issue only tells a minor part of a larger story rather than being complete on its own, and the bonus features formerly included in comic books, such as letter columns, have been increasingly phased out. Monthly comic books are now frequently referred to as *singles, pamphlets,* or *floppies,* terms that emphasize their insubstantiality relative to the comic book. The two most recent issues of Adrian Tomine's comic book *Optic Nerve* both include Tomine's rueful meditations on the death of the comic book form, which his publisher, Drawn & Quarterly, has almost abandoned. As Tomine's reflections indicate, the comic book, even more so than other print media, is now considered a moribund format. Of course, both the trade paperback and the comic book now face competition from the digital edition, as will be discussed in the next chapter.

This context helps us understand the innovative nature of Matt Kindt's comic book series *MIND MGMT,* which was published by Dark Horse starting in 2012 and is scheduled to conclude in 2015.[17] *MIND MGMT* is the story of Meru, a true crime writer who discovers the existence of the eponymous MIND MGMT, a massive network of espionage agents with psychic abilities. As the series progresses, Meru discovers that she herself was raised by MIND MGMT, and she engages in a struggle for control of the organization with another agent known as the Eraser. In a one-issue epi-

15. "Waiting for the trade" was already common enough by 1998 that Bart Beaty coined the term "the Cerebus effect" to describe it, referring to Dave Sim's long-running series of that name (Hoffman and Grace xiii). As early as 1999, comic book writer Steven Grant predicted: "The future of the comic book as we know it is to be a loss leader for the trade paperback" (n.p.).

16. I thank Kevin A. Boyd for confirming this. See also Kieron Gillen's blog post at http://kierongillen.tumblr.com/post/121756273497/market-maven-is-the-wicked-the-divine-in.

17. My discussion of *MIND MGMT* is heavily indebted to Drew Bradley's "Minding MIND MGMT" column at Multiversity Comics, which includes extensive annotations for each issue. Throughout this section, "*MIND MGMT*" in italics refers to the comic book, and "MIND MGMT" in non-italic text refers to the fictional spy organization that the comic book is named for.

logue, *NEW MGMT,* Meru becomes the new leader of MIND MGMT and recreates it in a new and more socially beneficial form.

While it explores the same themes of espionage and secrecy that inform Kindt's earlier work, *MIND MGMT* uses materiality in ways that were new to him at the time. Coming to *MIND MGMT,* Kindt only had experience working in the graphic novel form, although he had grown up reading comics in the single-issue format. Therefore, when Dark Horse approved his proposal for a monthly series, "I [Kindt] thought 'This is great!' but at the same time I thought, 'I don't enjoy the format as a reader anymore. Why did I do this?'" (Phegley n.p.) Kindt's creative challenge was to make the individual issues interesting in their own right, thereby rewarding readers who purchased the series in that format rather than waiting for the trade.

Therefore, *MIND MGMT* includes a letter column, a feature that was borrowed from science fiction magazines and was standard in all comic books until the early 2000s. The letter column's title, "T**h**e Official L**e**tter Co**l**umn and Corres**p**ondence Re: **M**ind Manag**e**ment", even contains bold letters that spell a hidden message (like the title of this section). But it also goes beyond that. The inside front covers of each *MIND MGMT* issue are devoted to one-page strips that detail the history of the title organization, often introducing characters who later appear in the main story. These strips, collectively titled "The Second Floor," are exclusive to the single issues and are not reprinted in the trade paperbacks. The back cover of each issue features a fake advertisement for an imaginary product that has something to do with the storyline. For example, the back cover of issue 8 is an ad for a romance novel written by the Perrier sisters, who are characters in the series. These fake ads even contain hidden content; for instance, the fake ad on the back cover of issue 8 includes the message "Start a real riot!" and the one on the back cover of issue 10 includes letters printed in a subtly lighter color, which combine to spell out the message "The Eraser must be stopped." Again, the back covers appear only in the single issues and not in the collected or digital editions. As Kindt explains:

> I'm actually trying to reward the reader that reads it monthly because I think that's a hard way to read something. . . . For one, it's a $4 book. I don't want you to sit down, read it and go "Now I've got to wait 30 days for the next one?" . . . I want to make this whole thing an experience. The inside cover is the history of MIND MGMT, and that stuff won't be in the trade because the trade will be a different reading experience. So I reward the monthly reader with a story they won't get any other way. (qtd. in Phegley n.p.)

The bonus features are intended as a reward for the reader; the point is to make the single issues of *MIND MGMT* a materially rich experience. At the same time, the collected editions *also* have bonus features, ensuring that the collections are not simply inferior to the single issues. As editor Brendan Wright states in the letter column of issue 19: "We've tried to make the extras in the issues a key element of enjoying the monthly series, but we put different things into the collections, so they're really two different reading experiences, which we hope both work independently and as complements to each other" (Kindt 2014, 25). For example, issue 17 contains a four-page splash that could be viewed in its entirety only by placing two copies of the issue next to each other, but in the collected edition, this image is printed as a four-page foldout (see figure 2.9).[18]

All the bonus features in the single issues are also included in the digital editions, which are effectively just facsimiles of the print comics. But what the digital editions lack are the physical features that contribute to the affectively rich experience the comic provides. As Kiel Phegley writes: "The series singles come with an almost found object quality that permeates the worn print style, fake advertisements and handmade quality of his watercolor art" (n.p.).

MIND MGMT is printed on newsprint, which was formerly standard for all comic books but is now unusual; since the late 1990s, nearly all commercial comics have used glossy paper instead. *MIND MGMT*'s use of newsprint gives it a rough, coarse feel and accentuates the gestural, physical quality of Kindt's watercolor artwork. Part of the sensuous pleasure of reading *MIND MGMT* is the rough, coarse feel of the paper. Even when one reads the *MIND MGMT* hardcovers, which are printed on smooth paper, or when one reads *MIND MGMT* in digital form, the pleasure of actually touching the newsprint is no longer available, but the artwork still retains the *appearance* of having been printed on newsprint (see figure 2.10). Thus, the pleasure of actual touch is replaced by the pleasure of what Laura Marks calls haptic visuality. The hardcover and digital versions of *MIND MGMT* evoke the reader's memory of what newsprint feels like, inviting the reader to "feel" or "caress" the image with his or her eyes. (A similar effect can be seen in the comics of Dustin Nguyen and Sarah Glidden, which also look as if they're printed on newsprint even when they're not.) The importance of newsprint to *MIND MGMT*'s visual and tactile aesthetic

18. Jim Steranko previously used a four-page splash in *Strange Tales* #167 (Marvel 1968). Again, the entire image could not be viewed in its entirety, but when the issue was reprinted in a trade paperback in 2000, the four-page splash appeared as a foldout. Even bigger panels have been attempted: *Ultimates 2* #12 (Marvel 2007) and *ODY-C* #1 (Image 2014) each contain an *eight*-page splash.

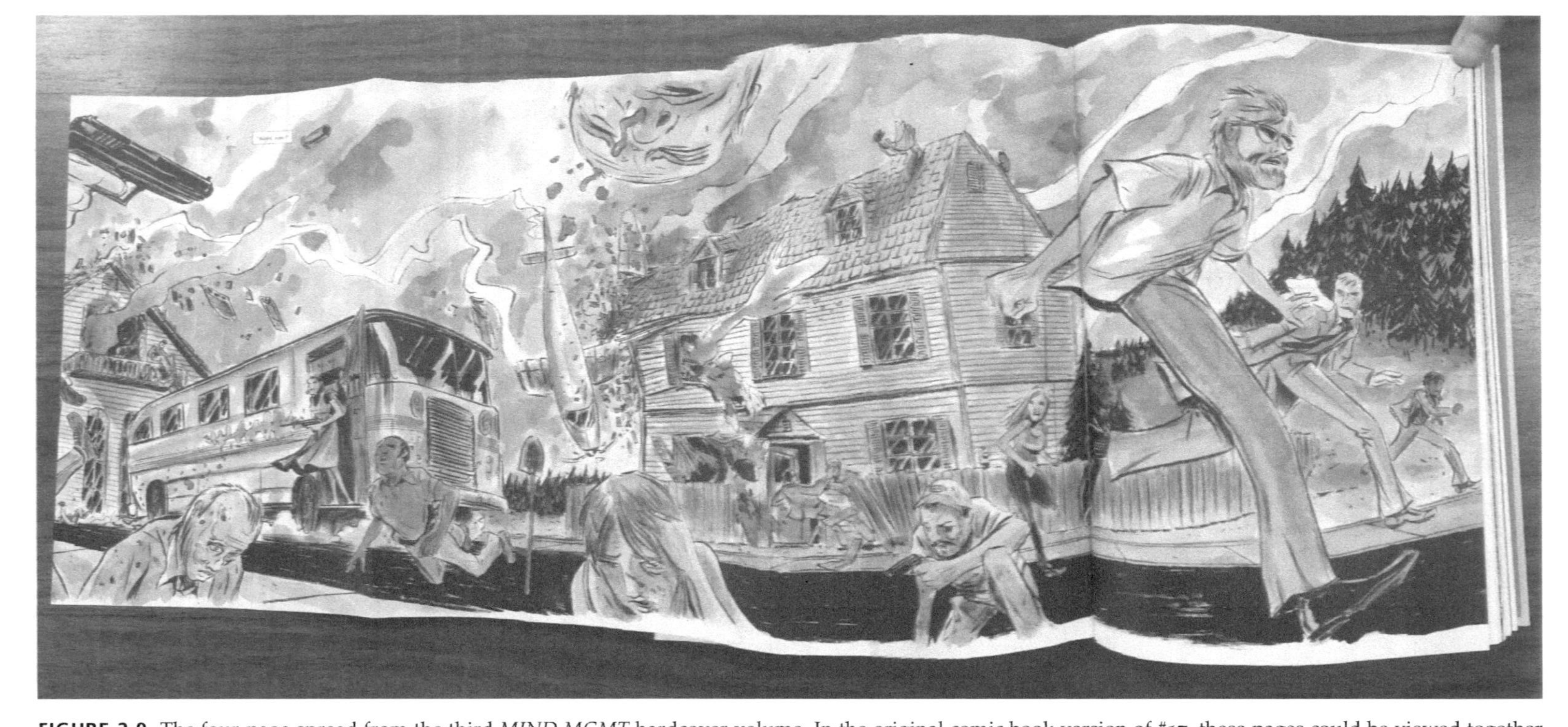

FIGURE 2.9. The four-page spread from the third *MIND MGMT* hardcover volume. In the original comic book version of #17, these pages could be viewed together only by placing two copies of the issue next to each other. Photo courtesy of Andrew Kunka.

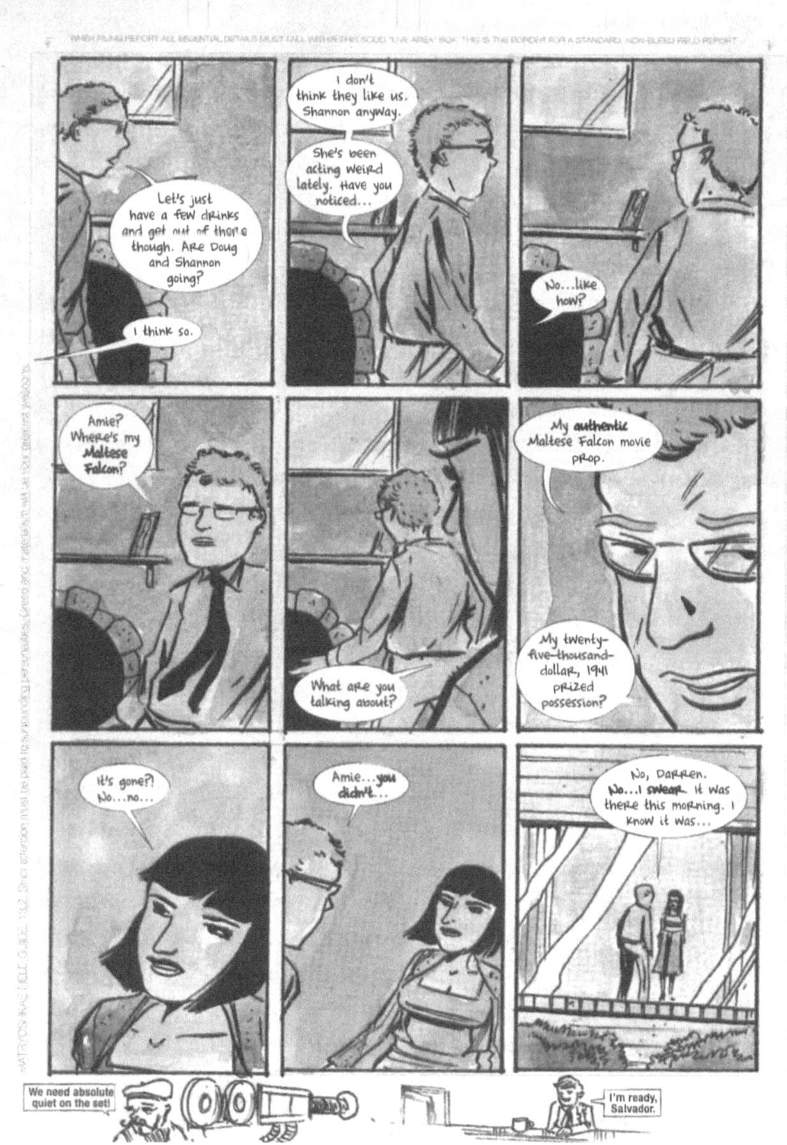

FIGURE 2.10. Page 2 of *MIND MGMT* #13. Note the paper texture, the coloring, the Field Guide excerpt (along the side), and the "live area" message (top). This particular page also includes images (bottom) that are located outside the "live area" and are therefore invisible to the MIND MGMT agents who would be reviewing this report.

was made clear when a *MIND MGMT* story appeared in the anthology series *Dark Horse Presents,* which is printed on glossy paper. Drew Bradley writes: "You'll immediately notice how different the art looks. It's still the same washed-out water colors, but somehow they have a different life on glossy paper. The newsprint-quality paper of the regular issues gives the impression of colors bleeding, but here the rough designs have very crisp edges." (Issue #1 n.p.)[19] *MIND MGMT* even acknowledges the sensuous appeal of paper. In issue 16, The Eraser mentions that one of her few memories from her college years is the paperbacks she read, because "I can still smell that musty paper. Paperbacks from the used bookstore down the street. I don't remember the street, but I remember the smell" (Kindt 2013, 3).

Besides the coloring and the paper, other features of *MIND MGMT* also work to actively draw the reader's attention to its materiality. Each page of the comic has a light blue border around the edge (again see figure 2.10). At the top of each page the following statement appears in the same light blue color: "When filing report all essential details must fall within this solid 'live area' box. This is the border for a standard, non-bleed field report." This implies that each page of the comic is an extract from a field report filed by an agent of the titular spy organization, and that these reports are filed in the form of original comic art pages. The terminology used here contributes to this impression. In a piece of original art, the live area is the area in which all artwork and lettering has to be contained in order to ensure that it will show up in the finished comic. A "bleed" is when the artist intentionally draws outside the live area in order to make the artwork extend to the very edge of the page. For knowledgeable readers, the blue borders and the terms *live area* and *bleed* act as reminders of the original artwork that served as a necessary precondition for the existence of the published *MIND MGMT* comic book. The impression is that the page we're reading is the same page that Matt Kindt originally drew. Moreover, *MIND MGMT* occasionally includes references to the three-dimensionality of the comic book form. In the April 2013 reprint of the first issue, the top of the back cover depicts the same three panels that appear on the last left-hand interior page. Below these panels is an advertisement for the series, and at the top of the advertisement is what looks like a rip or tear (see figure 2.11). The impression is that the advertisement is a ripped-off piece of newsprint that was placed on top of the last left-hand page. Drew Bradley writes: "The panels at the top are from the Mind Memo, and are actually situated such that, if you were to rip them off the back cover, the same pictures

19. For a further discussion of color in *MIND MGMT,* see Wilkins.

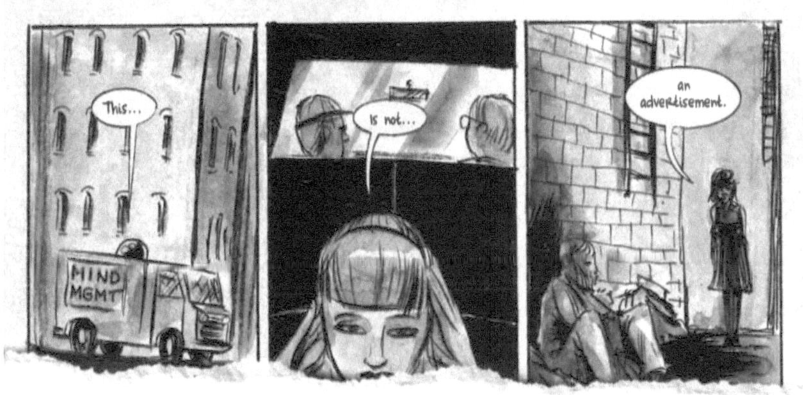

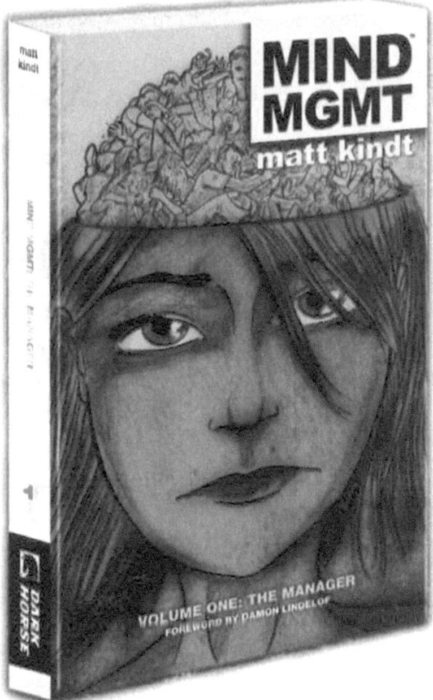

FIGURE 2.11. Back cover of the "#1 for $1" reprint of *MIND MGMT #1*. The three panels along the top are the same three panels that appear on the final left-hand page of the comic.

would still be there. If you have the opportunity to have this copy signed, don't be surprised if Matt really does tear it. He's funny that way" ("Minding *MIND MGMT*: Issue #1").

Finally, Kindt makes *MIND MGMT* a materially rich experience through his exploitation of the vertical dimension of the comics page. On the left-hand border of each page is an excerpt from the "MIND MGMT Field Guide" or, in some later issues, an excerpt from Meru's first book (again see figure 2.10). Because these excerpts are printed vertically from bottom to top, they force the reader to turn either her head or the comic book sideways. In my case, I usually move my head rather than the comic book, giving me a constant crick in my neck as I read. This acts as a constant reminder that the comic book is a physical artifact and that reading, even on a Kindle screen, is an embodied experience. Strangely, the more I read, the more it became second nature to turn my head sideways before reading each page, to the point that when I read issue 19, which doesn't include any vertical text, it seemed strange *not* to have to be constantly turning my head sideways.

But Kindt's use of materiality goes even further, because he incorporates the existence of the *MIND MGMT* comic book into the narrative universe of *MIND MGMT*. In other words, he creates the impression that the *MIND MGMT* comic book is an artifact that originated from within the same fictional universe it depicts. As noted, the Field Guide excerpts create the conceit that each *MIND MGMT* comic book is a report prepared by a MIND MGMT agent for submission to his or her superiors. Other bibliographic features of the comic reinforce this impression. For example, the back cover of issue 12 is designed to look like a torn-out page from a Mind Management Psychological Profile and Assessment Questionnaire. On this cover, the UPC code is incorporated into the narrative framework: below the UPC code it says: "When finished, please use the following code to catalog this entry." Here the UPC code is absorbed into the narrative framework of the comic, becoming a piece of the comic's fictional world rather than an intrusive reminder of the comic book's status as a commodity to be sold.

But even more radically, the comic's paratextual features penetrate its fictional narrative—or to reverse this formulation, the narrative of *MIND MGMT* bleeds out of the panels, word balloons, and caption boxes and contaminates the comic's paratexts. The rhetorical effects of media are an important theme of *MIND MGMT*, insofar as one of the title organization's standard means of mind control is through the production of mind-altering books, advertisements, films, and music. For instance, issue 7 introduces Brinks the Ad Man, a MIND MGMT agent who has the power to create texts that evoke specific reactions in the reader—"protection ads" that keep passers-by away from his building, graffiti that induces violence, even "assassination letters" that instantly kill the reader. When we read the ads on *MIND MGMT*'s back covers, we are invited to imagine them as the actual work of Brinks, and this produces a rather unsettling effect, despite our knowledge that Brinks's powers are purely fictional. Another example of how the paratexts become part of the narrative, or vice versa, is that some issues include additional short strips on the bottom of each page (again see figure 2.10). Including a short strip in the margin of a longer one is a time-honored tradition—*Krazy Kat,* for example, originated as such a strip. But in *MIND MGMT,* the bottom-of-the-page strips take on added significance because of the implication that they are visible only to the reader, and not to the hypothetical Mind Management agents who are reading the "field reports" that occupy the live area of the page.[20] When Meru encounters the First Immortal, Sir Francis, the *MIND MGMT* Field Guide starts to bleed into the space of the image. In issue 32, when Meru has reconstituted MIND MGMT in a new form as NEW MGMT, she is seen typing the new version of the Field Guide. On page 21, the first two panels carry the captions "This is all I have seen. / This is all I have learned" in the typewriter font that has been associated with Meru throughout the series. In the third panel, however, the caption "This is your field guide" appears on top of Meru's head in the same blue sans-serif font used for the Field Guide entries. The implication here is that Meru is now able to write the Field Guide as well as read it. She has gone from being one of MIND MGMT's manipulated and mind-controlled agents to being the architect of NEW MGMT, and this transition is indicated through the typographic cue of the appearance of Field Guide text on her forehead.

In scenes like this, *MIND MGMT* demonstrates that materiality in comics need not simply be used for cosmetic purposes, but that it can play a crucial role in the narrative. Throughout *MIND MGMT,* Kindt uses typography and publication design to enrich the narrative, to such a significant extent that a reader who consumes the series in trade paperback or digital format misses a large chunk of the story.

Such a materially rich comic book series *could* have appeared at any time in the history of the comic book medium, but the fact that it *didn't* appear until 2012 is evidence that digital technology is serving as "crisi-

20. This observation may not be original to me; I vaguely remember reading it in a review.

tunity" for the comic book. At the same time that digital reading platforms threaten to make printed comic books obsolete, they also give creators an incentive to create comic books that exploit the material resources of the medium in ways that might not have occurred to anyone before.

CONCLUSION

In this chapter I've suggested that the rise of digital reading technologies has created a crisis for print comics, but also a crisitunity. The perceived death of print has given cartoonists an incentive to use print in more active and creative ways. Cartoonists like Barry and Kindt have produced "Kindle-proof" comics that resist translation into digital form because their meanings are inextricably linked to their physical properties.

However, this chapter has given the perhaps false impression that print comics are inevitably doomed by the rise of digital comics. In the following two chapters, I suggest that the relationship between print and digital comics is less antagonistic than it initially appears. I begin by arguing that print remains essential to the current digital comics industry, both as a source of inspiration and as a channel for distribution.

CHAPTER 3

CLICK AND DRAG

The Continuing Relevance of Print to Digital Comics

IN *REINVENTING COMICS* (2000), which remains the foundational theoretical text on webcomics, Scott McCloud predicted a postprint future for comics. McCloud expected that improvements in webcomic technology would render print obsolete and that webcomics would prevail over print comics because of their ability to exploit creative possibilities not open to print. Webcomics offer access to interactivity, sound, moving images, and what McCloud calls the *infinite canvas,* or the ability to scroll indefinitely in any direction. As webcomics creators produced more and more work that could not be reproduced in print, print would gradually lose relevance as a delivery mechanism.

At the same time that McCloud praises digital comics, he argues against the continuing relevance of print. His specific claim is that print is no longer relevant because tactile contact with works of art is not required:

> Is there a fundamental need on our part to touch what we read in the form of books or magazines?[1] . . . Will comics lose their magic if we can

1. In McCloud's original text, the words *touch, books,* and *magazines* in this sentence are in boldface type, as well as other words in the rest of the quotation. I ignore

> no longer touch them? In the end, I don't think that comics readers need to hold or own comics to experience them fully. If physical contact were really so necessary to form an emotional bond with a work, how could we explain the lure of movies and music? (177)

McCloud further argues that the continuing relevance of print to comics readers is a historical accident:

> For comics readers everywhere, our primary emotional bond has been with the sensations of paper and ink. This is the only form of comics we've known throughout our lifetimes, so of course we're partial to it [. . .] but if it had been granite or sand or tin that cast that spell, would we feel any less of a debt?

He concludes: "After all, without the art and ideas [. . .] that have graced its surface for hundreds of years, print is nothing but flat, dead wood" (178–79).

More than fifteen years after *Reinventing Comics* appeared, McCloud's predictions have proven inaccurate. In the first place, print hasn't died. As explained in the previous chapter, print remains an important production and distribution technology for comics, and the crisitunity of digitization has inspired cartoonists to exploit the creative possibilities of print and explore the advantages of print over digital.

In the second place, digital comics haven't taken the path that McCloud outlines. Many digital comics do use the digital-specific features McCloud discusses, and therefore they could not be printed without destroying the reading experience. However, even these comics sometimes offer the kinds of tactile, physical pleasures that McCloud characterizes as exclusive to print. At the same time, many other webcomics have declined to exploit these features and are therefore fully compatible with print. Indeed, being printed is a mark of success for a webcomic, and webcomics creators often publish print editions of their work because their readers demand it. Many readers—even readers for whom print is no longer the "only form of comics [they've] known throughout [their] lifetimes"—still cherish the format of print. Readers still value the experiences that print can provide, whether those experiences are purely tactile, as McCloud suggests, or whether print also has other things to offer.

---

this. Citations of "McCloud" in this chapter refer to *Reinventing Comics* unless otherwise indicated.

In the current comics industry, readers value the unique properties of *both* print and digital, and this has resulted in an environment where print and digital modes of delivery have worked to support rather than replace each other. It has become increasingly common for comics to exist in both print and digital forms at once. Most commercially published print comics are now also published in digital form, with notable exceptions such as the output of Fantagraphics and Drawn & Quarterly, and many works that start out as webcomics are ultimately printed. This symbiotic relationship between print and digital comics is a challenge to Hillary Chute's claim that "comics is a *site-specific medium*; it can't be re-flowed, re-jiggered on the page; hence, it is spatially located on the page the way that poetry often must be" ("Secret Labor" n.p.). Comics *can be* reflowed, and a significant number of them *are*. A large percentage (if not necessarily a majority) of current comics are "re-flowed" or "re-jiggered" multiple times to fit multiple delivery channels.

Indeed, this was true even before the digital era. In an article in the *Atlantic*, Noah Berlatsky claimed that Chute's argument was disproved by counterexamples like Charles Schulz's *Peanuts*. This strip was originally published as a horizontally formatted, four-panel comic strip, as is typical of American daily newspaper comics. However, it was later reprinted by publishers such as Holt, Rinehart & Winston in paperback books which used vertical formats (with four separate tiers, each with one panel) or square formats (with two panels across and two down). For example, the *Peanuts* strip of September 20, 1960, consists of four equally sized square panels:[2]

- *Panel 1.* Charlie Brown walks toward Snoopy with a full bowl of food, saying: "Here you are, Snoopy. . . ."
- *Panel 2.* Charlie Brown continues to hold the food, saying: "An extra big supper to celebrate this being 'National Dog Week!'" Snoopy thinks "Well!"
- *Panel 3.* Charlie Brown walks off to the left, while Snoopy looks at the food bowl and thinks "Not bad!"
- *Panel 4.* Now alone, Snoopy begins eating the food while thinking "The next step now is to begin lobbying for a national dog *month!*"

2. Permission to reproduce this strip was unobtainable, so I substitute a description of it. This strip can be viewed at http://www.gocomics.com/peanuts/1960/9/20.

In its initial newspaper syndication, this strip was published as a horizontal strip of four panels all adjacent to each other. In the collection *We Love You, Snoopy* (1962), it was reprinted in vertical format with each panel below the previous panel. In the collection *Peanuts Parade #7: The Mad Punter Strikes Again* (1976), it was reprinted in square format, with panels 1 and 2 above panels 3 and 4.

In a post to the comix-scholars listserv, Jeet Heer pointed out that Berlatsky's example doesn't disprove Chute's argument because *Peanuts* was deliberately designed so that it could be printed in either horizontal or square format, unlike other comics that are designed with only one publication format in mind. Schulz's comics can be converted from horizontal to square format without significantly altering the humor, but this is because they were designed that way (Heer n.p.). Most *Peanuts* strips consist of four panels of identical size, meaning that when they are reprinted in a square format, the visual flow of reading changes significantly, but no information is lost. According to *Peanuts* expert Nat Gertler,

> *Peanuts* was originally proposed as a three-panel daily strip. What the syndicate approved was a four-panel version, which allowed them to specifically market the strip as being arrangeable in a two-by-two square format, or even as four panels stacked vertically. While the restacking of the panels does have some impact on the eye flow, Schulz was aware of that when designing the strip. (personal communication)

Conversely, Fawcett Crest published a series of *Peanuts* paperback reprints in which panels were expanded, changed in size, or even dropped entirely. Sometimes this created interesting new meanings—Chris Pearce analyzes one example from one of these books, in which the panel composition is altered to suggest that "as everyone abandons Linus, the strip gets more and more narrow, until he's left by himself in the rain" (Pearce n.p.). Similarly, in the vertical version of the September, 20, 1960, *Peanuts* strip, the third panel has no border and is offset to the right, suggesting that the moment depicted in this panel takes longer than the moments in the other panels. This implication is absent in the horizontal and square versions of the same strip, where all four panels have identical borders. However, alterations like these often had the effect of radically distorting Schulz's intent and altering the flow of reading. When some French comics were converted from full-sized albums to pocket-sized books in the 1980s, a similar result occurred:

> It was impossible to reduce a complete page, because a lot of details would be lost and the drawings would become too small for the reader. Therefore, the comics were adapted: the original page lay-out was discarded and replaced by another division in rows. To do this, the initial panel dimensions had to be adapted and sometimes even the composition of the drawings had to be changed. (Lefebvre 95–96)[3]

For example, when Franquin's *Idées noires* was converted from album to pocket size, much of the humor was completely lost. However, the Schulz example suggests that this was not inevitable and that only some comics are intrinsically incapable of being "reflowed" effectively.

Heer went on to argue that Chute's position that comics can't be "reflowed" and Berlatsky's position that some comics *can* be—or the Schulz and Franquin cases—can be reconciled:

> All cartoonists . . . have to be thinking in spatial terms, whether they choose to be spatially flexible (as Schulz did) or spatially fixed (as McCay and Ware did). Spatial awareness is inextricable from comics, whatever the choice might be. (Heer n.p.)[4]

This tension between "fixity" and "flexibility" is a characteristic formal property of comics. Paradoxically, comics are irreducibly tied to the material form in which they are embodied. Chute is right to say that comics cannot be "reflowed" in the sense that, as I demonstrated in chapter 1, a comic republished in a different format provides a strikingly different visual experience. At the same time, a comic produced in one format is capable of being remediated for a different format.

We might think of fixity and flexibility as two options that cartoonists are capable of employing, though of course the fixity/flexibility distinction is more of a continuum than a strict opposition. Cartoonists who choose fixity seek to produce work that exploits the potential of a single format to its fullest extent, work that cannot exist outside of that format, at least not without the need for significant changes or losses of functionality. Examples include the works of Barry and Kindt discussed in the previous chapter, or the infinite canvas webcomics of artists like Scott McCloud.

---

3. As another example, in the late 1970s and early 1980s, Tempo Books, an imprint of Grosset & Dunlap, published a series of paperback books, reprinting old Marvel and DC comic books in black and white and with radically altered page layouts.

4. I thank Jeet Heer for permission to quote this e-mail.

Cartoonists who choose flexibility instead seek to create comics that can cross boundaries between formats and work acceptably well, although not identically, in either print or digital form. Comics that are "flexible" in this sense are similar to most prose texts in that they can be remediated from print to digital (or vice versa) without destroying the reading experience. However, with a "flexible" comic, the difference between its print and digital instantiations tends to be more visible than with a comparable work of prose literature.

The overarching argument of this and the next chapter is that print remains a central reference point for digital comics, whether those digital comics are "fixed" to the digital format or are "flexible" between digital and print. Thus, this chapter proceeds in two steps. First, I argue that even comics that are fixed to the digital format—or "digital-native" comics—are still frequently influenced by the legacy of print. Even when digital comics employ techniques specific to the digital medium and are therefore impossible to remediate into print, they still frequently use the cherished material properties of print. Contrary to McCloud's argument, digital-native comics are not completely intangible or weightless; for example, they often depend on touch as much as print comics do. My key reference point here is the *xkcd* comic strip "Click and Drag." Subsequently, however, I explain why, again contrary to McCloud, digital comics have not abandoned print. Digital-native comics that rely crucially on digital-specific features, and that cannot be easily remediated into print, have failed to become the dominant form of digital comics. The bulk of current webcomics can be published in print, and often are. In the second half of this chapter, I explore why this is the case.

Through both of these categories of examples, I suggest that McCloud's predictions have proven false because print remains vitally important even for born-digital comics (and vice versa). Even comics that start out in digital form remain tied to the medium of print, and print remains central to the way that webcomic creators and publishers imagine the medium of comics (while at the same time most print comics are produced with the knowledge that digitization is a possibility). The centrality of print-based thinking to webcomics may be viewed in negative terms, as evidence that digital comics remain shackled to an obsolescent analog medium. However, the continuing relevance of print can also be viewed in positive terms, as proof that print and digital can coexist harmoniously. A further question this raises is whether it's possible to produce comics that benefit from being read in *both* print and digital form, and the final chapter explores this further.

DIGITAL-NATIVE COMICS

Digital-native comics are comics that employ digital-specific features such as interactivity, synchronized sound, moving images, or the infinite canvas (which means essentially a page of a larger size than could be included in a printed book), meaning that they couldn't be published in print form without ruining the reading experience. These comics represent a significant segment of the digital comics landscape, although for reasons that will be dealt with later, they have not become as dominant as McCloud predicted in 2000.

McCloud suggests that the primary difference between printed and digital-native comics is that digital-native comics lack tactility. He takes it for granted that if there is a "fundamental need on our part to touch what we read" (*Reinventing Comics* 177), then digital comics don't satisfy that need. McCloud's response to this argument is to suggest that there is *not* a fundamental need to touch what we read, and that film and music are proof of this. His rhetoric further suggests that comics would be better if they didn't *need* to be touched. For McCloud, the physical form of the comic introduces arbitrary constraints on the reading experience—arbitrary barriers between the reader and the text—and digital comics remove these barriers. An example is McCloud's famous concept of the infinite canvas, in which a digital comic can extend indefinitely in all directions and "can take whatever size and shape a given scene warrants—no matter how strange—or how simple those sizes and shapes may be" (227–28). Part of the motivation behind the infinite canvas concept was to make the reading experience smoother. In advocating for the infinite canvas, McCloud observes that unlike earlier illustrated narratives, print comics fragment the reading experience. In a print comic, whenever the reader reaches the right edge of the page, he must shift his eyes back to the left side, as well as constantly turn pages (220). The infinite canvas removes such interruptions to the reading experience, resulting in a smooth, seamless reading experience. It eliminates what user experience and usability experts call *friction*, or "interactions that inhibit people from intuitively and painlessly achieving their goals within a digital interface." The infinite canvas allows the ideas behind the comic to travel from the artist's hand to the reader's mind with a minimum of interruption.

There are several possible objections to McCloud's argument against the relevance of touch in digital comics. First, McCloud underestimates the importance of touch in comics reading, but Saige Walton and Ian Hague have both demonstrated that touch plays a central role in comics: "Comics yield inherently tactile pleasures as much as they do visual/narrative ones. That tactility comes from a very real sense of their material handling; the density of their material weight . . . as it is turned at your fingertips" (Walton 101). In addition to actual touch, comics activate what Laura Marks describes as haptic visuality. For example, because comics represent the artist's handwriting, they enable a sort of imaginary tactile contact between the hand of the reader and that of the artist, and this is equally true in print comics and in digital comics. This argument will be taken up in chapter 5. More importantly, however, McCloud ignores the ways that tactile interactions help to shape the experience of reading comics, as I have discussed throughout this book.

The constraints associated with the physical form of comics, for example, tactility and the shape of the page, may be sources of friction, but that's not necessarily a bad thing. UX consultant Gideon Simons observes that "While friction is a negative agent for usability, for user experience friction can have both good and bad effects on the user. Good friction comes from things that may challenge your users and make them need to think more while using your product, maybe even make them do extra steps. — But at the same time imprint a stronger user experience" (n.p.). Similarly, in comics, friction arising from the materiality of the reading interface—such as friction caused by the shape of the page or the need for tactile interaction with the reading device—can make the reading experience more meaningful. In digital comics, some of the most exciting works seek to use the possibilities of the digital interface to create "good friction"—that is, to challenge the reader and interpose interesting barriers between the reader and the text—rather than remove friction entirely.

In the case of friction resulting from the need for touch, digital comics can remove the tactile aspects of comics reading. However, a second objection to McCloud's dismissal of the relevance of touch is that digital comics can do more than this: they can also provide for tactile interactions that are impossible in print. Ian Hague, the leading authority on non-visual sensory aspects of comics, observes:

> The weight of a digital comic remains constant throughout the reading, it does not shift from one hand to another, and the reader cannot feel how many pages remain[,] so there is not necessarily the sense of tactile engagement with the work as a progressively changing object that one experiences with the printed comic.
>
> This is not to say, however, that the digital comic is unable to accesss the reader's sense of touch while it is being performed. In fact, modern

> technologies in some instances offer modes of communication that are arguably more powerful than the relatively conventionalised tactile experiences that we find in the standard book form. (109–10)

In support of this argument, Hague observes that in comics that use the touch screen, the viewer is "implicate[d] in producing the image," and in comics that use force feedback technology, "vibrations are not just *represented* upon the page, they are actually present within the physicality of the reading experience" (111). Far from being completely devoid of tactility, digital comics actually enable tactile interactions that are not possible with print comics, thus expanding readers' understanding of what touch can mean in a comic.

The most persuasive example of how touch can expand rather than contract the tactile potential of comics is Chris Ware's iPad comic "Touch Sensitive," but this comic will be dealt with in the final chapter because it's an example of a comic that blends print and digital forms of materiality. Here I focus on another example: Randall Munroe's webcomic *xkcd.* Described as "a webcomic of romance, sarcasm, math, and language," *xkcd* is one of the small proportion of webcomics that are "self-supporting"—Munroe was formerly a NASA engineer but now makes a living from the sale of *xkcd* merchandise. Its primary target audience is engineers, mathematicians, and other geeks, and its jokes are often so complex and difficult that there's an entire blog devoted to explaining them. The characters in the strip are all drawn as stick figures, although this is not necessarily due to a lack of skill on Munroe's part.

Even before he started to experiment more radically with tactile interfaces, Munroe was a pioneer in the use of "alt text," or text which appears when the reader mouses over a webcomic. In *xkcd,* the alt text usually makes some sort of ironic comment on the subject matter of the strip. As a random example, strip #1534 makes the argument that "all beer tastes kind of bad and everyone's just pretending," and the alt text reads "Mmmm, this is such a positive experience! I feel no social pressure to enjoy it at all!" Because the alt text is invisible until the reader mouses over the comic, it can be read only by readers who already know it exists or who discover it spontaneously. It thus serves as a reward for experienced readers and helps to interpellate those readers as members of the *xkcd* community. Indeed, half the fun of alt text is knowing that it exists. In 2010 a Chrome extension was created that displays *xkcd*'s alt text directly below the image, thus removing the need to mouseover (the motivation was that some browsers only display alt text for a moment, making it unreadable). Commenting on this, Lowell Heddings wrote "Personally I think this ruins half of the fun of reading and finding the hidden text" (n.d.). Thanks to the influence of comics like *xkcd,* alt text has become one of the defining features of webcomics and has even spread to print comics. When writing the *Adventure Time* comic book, webcomic author Ryan North included a humorous message in barely legible text at the bottom of each page; this is essentially an attempt to replicate alt text in print. This practice was continued in other *Adventure Time* spinoff comics and in North's *Unbeatable Squirrel Girl* comic for Marvel.

Alt text is a digital-native feature, but it's also a tactile feature, in that it's activated by the contact between the comic and the reader's finger or pointing device. On a touchscreen device, the reader literally has to touch the comic in order to make the alt text appear. However, Randall Munroe's exploration of the tactile possibilities of webcomics did not end there. His most sustained exploration of touch, and perhaps his greatest and most ambitious work, is strip #1110, "Click and Drag." This strip begins with three panels in which a stick-figure character floats on a toy balloon and thinks "From the stories / I expected the world to be sad / and it was / and I expected it to be wonderful. / It was." In the fourth panel, which initially appears to be about twice the size of the first three combined, the character floats above a tree in the middle of a grassy field and thinks "I just didn't expect it to be so *big*." The alt text reads "Click and drag" (see figure 3.1).

If the reader accepts this invitation and starts clicking and dragging the panel, he soon discovers that the panel is a lot bigger than it looks. It extends seemingly forever to both the left and the right, and further exploration reveals that the panel also extends up and down; there's content hidden in the sky and below the ground. Whichever direction the reader goes, the panel is full of sight gags and humorous vignettes. Far to the left, the grassy field changes to water. In the water is a character riding on a boat who says: "I'm on a boat! I expected more from the experience! Instead, all I can think to do is tell people where I am! . . . I'm on a boat!" To the left of that is a pirate ship, then a "Bitcoin-only island nation," then a character swimming in the water and saying: "Marco! Marco!" Still further left, the reader discovers a shaft descending into the ground, and if she follows this shaft instead of continuing left, she discovers that there are all sorts of interesting things hidden below ground. If the reader makes it all the way to the left, she is rewarded by seeing two characters engaging in the following conversation: "We've walked pretty far. We must be on the other side of the world by now." "Let's see. We've gone . . . two miles." "Darn. You know, this is a nice spot. Let's just live here." By going right instead of left from the starting

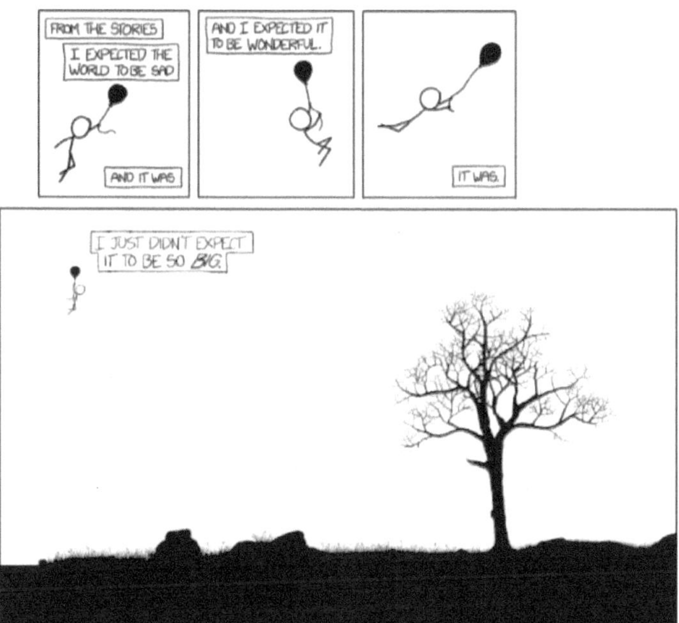

FIGURE 3.1. *xkcd* strip #1110, "Click and Drag," as it initially appears. Licensed under a Creative Commons Attribution-NonCommercial 2.5 License.

point, the reader can encounter all sorts of other wonderful and disturbing things, such as a giant jellyfish inexplicably floating in midair, or an unbelievably tall communications tower. If the reader has the stamina to make it all the way to the right, he finds the punch line of the entire strip: the character riding the balloon reappears and says: "I wonder where I'll float next."

This panel is unbelievably huge. According to statistics compiled by *explainxkcd.com,* it consists of "2592 sections of 2048 x 2048 pixels," of which 225 have actual content rather than being entirely white or black ("1110: Click and Drag"). Based on the scale of the figures, if the 225 tiles with unique artwork were reproduced at life size, they would cover an area of land the size of Princeton University, and if the whole comic were printed out, it would be about 46 feet by 18 feet ("1110: Click and Drag"). Various people have created versions of this comic in which the reader can zoom out and view more than one tile at once, but as the *explainxkcd* wiki points out, this defeats the purpose of the comic. "The best way to enjoy this comic is to play the game, explore the comic's world the way you're supposed to, get lost in the caves or in the sky, be startled by unexpected things or happy when finding some people after lengthy click-and-dragging through a repetitive landscape." "Click and Drag" is about the experience of exploration, of making serendipitous discoveries and diverging from the obvious path. The content in the comic is designed to surprise and delight (or horrify) readers who come upon it unaware. "Click and Drag" is also meant to impress the reader with its size. The fourth panel seems to go on forever, and on realizing just how big it is, the reader experiences the "sense of wonder" which has been described as one of the key aesthetic sensations produced by science fiction.

The power of this strip comes from the fact that it demands physical effort and tactile contact from the reader. In Hague's terms, "Click and Drag" "implicates" the reader in "producing" its images (110). The reader explores the strip by physically holding down the touchpad or mouse button and dragging his finger or hand. On a mobile device, the reader must place his finger directly on top of the comic and move it in the desired direction, frequently lifting the finger when he runs out of room. "Click and Drag" is unquestionably an example of the infinite canvas effect, but instead of producing a smooth, seamless reading experience, it interposes physical barriers between the reader and the text. In Marie-Laure Ryan's terms, it demands interactivity rather than immersion. In order to make sense of this strip, the reader has to be aware that he is producing it through physical effort.

Another effect of "Click and Drag" is to denaturalize the act of clicking and dragging. The click-and-drag functionality was invented in 1979, allegedly by Jef Raskin at Apple (Raskin n.p.). It replaced the click-move-click technique used at Xerox PARC, in which the reader would click on the object to be moved, then press the move key, and then click on the location where the object should be moved. Like many innovations introduced by Apple, click and drag was intended to make user interaction more intuitive and natural, and it's become a completely naturalized and invisible component of the graphical user interface. "Click and Drag," however, denaturalizes the click-and-drag process and reveals its physically effortful nature. It reminds the reader that clicking and dragging is a physical act that demands sustained effort—if the reader gets all the way to the right or left, he feels a genuine sense of accomplishment.

Other *xkcd* strips have experimented with other aspects of digital interfaces that are less obviously tactile. Munroe's other most famous work, "Time," consisted of a single panel that was replaced at regular intervals, initially every half hour but subsequently every hour; it took 120 days to complete. As the name indicates, the regular yet extremely slow progression of this comic was meant to make the reader feel a sense of time passing. Munroe's 2012 April Fool's Day strip, "Umwelt," displayed a different strip depending on factors such as the reader's physical location and the browser she used to view the strip. These strips represent the sort of born-digital comics that McCloud advocated in 2000. Nonetheless, even though *xkcd* makes innovative use of the unique capabilities of digital comics (and is aimed at an extremely digital-savvy audience), a strip like "Click and Drag" shows that Munroe and his readers remain committed to touch as a central component of the reading experience of comics. In a more abstract sense, touch remains central to *xkcd* because of Munroe's deliberately crude and slapdash-looking art, which reminds the reader of its origin in a human hand (see the earlier discussions of touch and haptic visuality).

The example of "Click and Drag" suggests that even when comics are tethered to the digital format and cannot be reproduced in print, reading comics can still be a tactile, physical experience. Even digital-only comics still need to be read through some sort of physical interface, and a skilled cartoonist can exploit the material affordances of this interface in exciting ways (we'll see more evidence of this in my discussion of Chris Ware's "Touch Sensitive" in the last chapter).

However, contrary to McCloud's predictions, many currently successful webcomics are not tethered to the digital format at all. Many, perhaps even most, current webcomics are texts that don't exploit the unique properties of digital media and therefore could be published in print form without significantly harming the reading experience. Indeed, webcomics often are ultimately published in print. The next section examines the reasons for this state of affairs.

THIS TANGIBLE, ATTRACTIVE PAPERY MECHANISM: OR, WHY DIGITAL COMICS ARE SO MUCH LIKE PRINT COMICS

Accurate statistics about webcomics don't exist because the market is too large; there is no clear definition of what constitutes a webcomic; and the webcomic industry, such as it is, is decentralized. However, it appears that the sort of webcomic McCloud advocates—one that uses digital-specific features and is not capable of being translated into print form—is the exception rather than the rule. Many successful current webcomics, possibly even a majority, are identical to print comics in terms of the formal devices and techniques they use. Such webcomics avoid the use of digital-specific features such as moving images, sound, interactivity, or the infinite canvas, and therefore they could be published in print form while preserving the reading experience. For these comics, digital platforms are useful primarily as a means of distribution and delivery. Digital delivery makes it possible to build an audience for comics that *could* be published in print but *wouldn't* be published in print for practical reasons. The fact that these webcomics can be published in print, however, means that they frequently do appear in print form after having demonstrated success in digital form. Webcomics have not transcended the print book; indeed, publication in print form remains important, because of both economic factors and the fact that contrary to McCloud's predictions, webcomic readers still feel a "fundamental need . . . to touch what [they] read" (177).[5]

In the first place, the popularity of print editions of webcomics is the result of economic factors. McCloud proposed that webcomics be funded by a micropayment model, in which each installment of a webcomic would cost only a few cents. The type of micropayment system McCloud proposed never became viable, partly for practical reasons (the costs associated with each micropayment transaction were typically greater than the amount of money being transacted) and partly because of consumer psychology. "Consumers were reluctant to pay even a tenth of a cent for something they believed should be free" (D. Mitchell n.p.). In the absence of a micropayment system, webcomics are typically funded through advertisements, merchandise sales, or crowd-funding platforms like Patreon and Kickstarter.

However, both of the latter two models of webcomic financing are dependent on the exchange of physical objects, and this means that many webcomics have a tactile, physical aspect: they are economically tethered to material objects. The sale of merchandise allows webcomic readers to show their support for their favorite webcomics by purchasing physical objects that are connected to the webcomic. This has proved to be a viable funding model on its own. In the case of *xkcd,* the T-shirts that say "Stand back, I'm going to try science" or "Science, it works, bitches" have probably been seen by many more people than have read the comic. Similarly, with sites like Kickstarter and Patreon, rewards are offered in exchange for specific amounts of donations, and these rewards are often physical. For a recent Kickstarter campaign for Zach Weinersmith's popular webcomic *Saturday Morning Breakfast Cereal* (*SMBC*), rewards included the following: a bookmark containing a "conversion chart for weird and/or worthless units"; a "handy little pocket notebook, the cover of which has 'SCIENCE: Ruining

5. This section is informed by Fattor's discussion of printed webcomics (21–26).

Everything Since 1543' written on it, along with a crossed out geocentric universe"; a "poster with a pictographic list of 18 things science has ruined since 1543"; and a shirt based on the poster (Weiner n.p.). As is obviously true of merchandise in general, these items are valuable because of their role as physical symbols of loyalty to the *SMBC* franchise. For *SMBC* in particular, the ownership of merchandise is especially valuable because the comic itself does not have a physical form; therefore, fans who want to physically symbolize their affection for the comic can do so by more than simply consuming the comic in its physical form. Collecting webcomic merchandise is thus a natural extension of the predigital practice of collecting comic books, which, as Matthew Pustz discusses, is an important practice even or especially among comics fans who are not speculators (79–83).

But at that point, the logical next step is to simply allow fans to read and to own the comic in physical form, by publishing print editions of webcomics, and McCloud could not have predicted how frequently this happens today. Many webcomics are currently published in print, even webcomics like *xkcd* that use specifically digital features, and sales of print editions of webcomics represent a significant source of income for webcomic artists. Webcomic collections like Allie Brosh's *Hyperbole and a Half* and Matthew Inman's *The Oatmeal* books have made the *New York Times* bestseller lists.[6] On the other end of the highbrow-lowbrow spectrum, respected alternative comics publishers have begun to offer webcomic collections, such as Drawn & Quarterly's edition of Kate Beaton's *Hark! A Vagrant.*

One obvious reason for the viability of print collections of webcomics is that they appeal to different audiences. Print editions of webcomics appeal to readers (stereotypically, older or more conservative readers) who don't read webcomics. Yet in many cases, print and digital editions of webcomics appeal to the *same* audience; that is, people who already read a comic digitally are often willing to pay for the privilege of owning a physical copy of it. Regardless of whether they read the comic in its digital form or not, readers of print editions of webcomics are paying to read a comic that they can already read free of charge online. This raises the obvious question: "Why pay for the book when the comic is free?" (Alverson n.p.)

A definitive explanation of why readers are willing to pay for print editions of free webcomics would require quantitative research, but logic and anecdotal evidence suggest some possible answers.[7] In the first place,

6. Admittedly, both of these works blur the lines between comics and other digital genres such as blogs and listicles.

7. Some of the information in this paragraph is based on an unscientific survey of my Facebook friends.

print editions of webcomics offer a tangible, physical reading experience. To borrow the standard cliché, printed webcomics can be read in the bathtub. Second, the digital nature of webcomics makes them impermanent. Like other electronic literature, webcomics are subject to degradation as links go offline and software becomes obsolete (see Montfort and Wardrip-Fruin). For Amanda Allen, one motivation for buying print editions of webcomics is that "I'm always paranoid that the webcomic may suddenly disappear" (n.p., quoted by permission). Third, print editions of webcomics fulfill the same role discussed above with respect to non-book merchandise: they offer a tangible way to show both emotional and financial support for the creator of the comic. For example, the goal of the *SMBC* Kickstarter described above was to fund the creation of the third print collection of the strip *SCIENCE: Ruining Everything Since 1543* (which I will refer to as *SCIENCE*).[8] As Hannah Fattor writes, "The presence and success of crowdfunding is a tangible expression of the symbiotic relationship between creator and fans. Though webcomics are freely available on the Internet, fans are willing to spend money to support an artist, and buying the book is a material expression of this support" (23). Fourth, print editions of webcomics can circulate as gifts in ways that are not possible with webcomics. Referring to *SCIENCE,* Zach Weinersmith writes: "Societal mores dictate that you can't give free webcomics as a real present to your favorite scientists, but you could give this!" (n.p.) On Facebook, two of my friends stated that they had bought print editions of webcomics as gifts. Finally, webcomics may provide added value relative to the print edition. As an incentive to Kickstarter backers, Weinersmith promised that *SCIENCE* would include additional content not available online:

> ***The more money raised in this Kickstarter, the more content goes in the book.*** Below this section is a map with lots of X marks on it. Those X marks represent a point at which you improve the book. Many of these stretch goals unlock exclusive, *never before seen* new comics. Even better, some of those goals will also unlock Tales of Science comics. These are illustrated, comic versions of AWESOME SCIENCE STORIES from a bunch of our favorite scientists. (Weinersmith n.p.; bold, italics, and capitalization in original)

Anecdotally, all of these factors help explain why I'm personally willing to buy books like the print edition of *Bandette,* discussed below. My bookshelves and my comic book boxes are a reflection of my identity as a

8. 1543 is the traditional starting date of the European Scientific Revolution because of the publication of Copernicus's *De revolutionibus orbium coelestium* in that year.

reader; looking at them gives me a sense of pride as they physically testify to the depth and breadth of my reading (I say with some lack of humility). For me, reading a webcomic doesn't "count" in the same way as reading a printed comic, even if the content is exactly the same in both cases. My personal experience is obviously not generalizable, but evidence suggests that many readers buy print editions of webcomics for similar reasons, even readers who don't feel the same sense of loyalty to the print medium that I do.

For all the above reasons, webcomics have the unusual property that they are available for free in digital form, yet readers are willing to pay to own them in physical form. This fact has even influenced the design of webcomics. A webcomic that uses the sort of digital-specific features McCloud advocates is less viable as a printed book than a webcomic that doesn't. This factor may help explain why many popular webcomics avoid digital-specific features and are formally and visually similar to newspaper comic strips, a phenomenon that could otherwise be uncharitably explained as the result of a lack of creativity among webcomic artists.[9] The more a webcomic looks like a print comic, the more effectively it can be translated to print.

To this extent, webcomics sometimes serve as a sort of developmental incubator for print comics. Publishing a comic on the web is far cheaper than publishing it in print. Therefore, if print publishers are not initially willing to take a chance on a comic, digital distribution can be used to establish an audience for the comic and to demonstrate the viability of publishing it in print. This factor is especially important for comics that appeal to very specific niche audiences, for example, the anonymous *Cardboard Crack* (which is about *Magic: The Gathering*), or Gene Ambaum and Bill Barnes's *Unshelved* (about librarians), or Josh and Rachel Anderson's *Worsted for Wear* (about knitting). Such works have a doubly narrow clientele in that they appeal to readers who are interested both in comics and in a specific type of subject matter, and in at least the latter two cases, the subject in question is something that doesn't appeal to the stereotypical comic geek. Therefore, a print publisher might not be willing to publish books

9. Another possible reason for the dominance of the strip format is that many webcomic authors grew up reading comic strips rather than comic books. In the '80s and '90s, when many current webcomic authors were growing up, comic strips were a much more egalitarian and popular medium than comic books. However, the limited space of the comics page has always meant there was little room for new talent. The rise of webcomics provided the vast population of comic-strip readers with the ability to create and publish their own comic strips. Proving this claim is outside the scope of the present chapter, but I hope to return to it elsewhere.

like these, and a traditional comic book store might not be willing to sell them. Yet thanks to digital delivery and Kickstarter, all three of these comics now exist in print form. Again, if print publication is the anticipated outcome of a webcomic, it makes sense to create it in a form that's easily adaptable to print. In an interview, the creator of *Cardboard Crack* (who requested anonymity) wrote:

> I put the comics in print well before SCG [StarCityGames] started offering them. It always seemed natural that I put my comics into books. It's a good way to make some money, plus my readers were asking for them. It's pretty hard to make money off a webcomic unless you have something physical to go along with it. Plus, it's pretty rewarding to be able to hold your work in a physical, tangible form. (personal communication)

In the particular case of *Cardboard Crack,* selling paper copies is a logical idea for other reasons. This comic appeals primarily to players of the trading card game *Magic: The Gathering,* sold through StarCityGames, a website whose primary business is selling *Magic* cards. *Magic* players, by definition, are already collectors of paper-based entertainment products, so this customer base is predisposed to want to buy printed editions of webcomics. Similarly, while Ambaum and Barnes did not decide to publish a print edition of *Unshelved* until the webcomic had already become popular (Ambaum, personal communication), the webcomic's subject matter meant that publishing it in print was an obvious choice. "Libraries and librarians are a beautiful built in audience to have—they buy lots of books, after all, for themselves and others." (Ambaum, personal communication) In both of these cases, the subject matter of the webcomic created an incentive for the authors to produce it in a format that could later be adapted to print. The use of digital-specific features would have been actively harmful to the financial success of these comics.

Yet fan demand for printed webcomics is such that even when a webcomic *does* use digital-specific features, it sometimes ends up getting printed anyway, despite significant loss of functionality. Hannah Fattor mentions the case of Ashley Cope, whose print comic *Unsounded* uses the infinite canvas. "The readers of *Unsounded* insisted that she print her comic (though she initially had no intention of doing so), but in this case the artistic experimentation in the webcomic was more daring than it appears in the resulting comic book" (Fattor 11). Creating the print version of *Unsounded* required some creative retooling. In the FAQs for the Kickstarter campaign that Cope launched to promote this book, Cope provides the following answer to the question "How will the pages with the overflowing borders be handled?"

> Every page was designed to work both on the web and in print. Though there's no way to replicate certain effects that are specifically meant for a browser window, every page will be carefully edited and retooled to work on paper. (Cope n.p.)

Even Andrew Hussie's *Homestuck*, a work that makes heavy use of animation and interactive features, has been published in print form. In the first print collection of *Homestuck*, Hussie writes:

> Homestuck in its native habitat is an all-out media blitz. The static panels here do not tip off its true nature. Many, if not most panels, are animated. Usually short looping GIF animations. Some pages are longer animations created in Flash, with music. Other pages are interactive, playable mini-games, also made in Flash. I don't claim these books to be an equivalent substitute for the series, as originally meant to be navigated. I see the books more as complementary material. Either as a gateway into the story for further reading online, or as an offline supplement to those who've already read it, and wish to peruse it more leniently, or studiously, by way of this tangible, attractive papery mechanism.[10]

For Hussie, the print edition of *Homestuck* is not an "equivalent substitute" for the web version; it doesn't reflect the way he intended the comic to be read. Yet it exists anyway because of fan demand. This example suggests that even when webcomics do take advantage of the factors that separate digital from print, they often get instantiated in print form anyway, sometimes against their creators' explicit intentions.

In short, contrary to McCloud's predictions, webcomics are not a purely ethereal, intangible medium devoid of physical properties. Even when webcomics use digital-specific features, they frequently make sophisticated use of tactile functionality. Moreover, thanks to the popularity of merchandise and print editions, webcomics circulate as objects, in the sense in which that word is used in object-oriented ontology, and belong to a network of relationships among physical entities.

---

10. I thank Franny Howes for supplying me with this quotation. This book does not include page numbers.

As a result, in the current webcomics scene, works that are fixed to the digital medium are less popular than works that are flexible, able to move gracefully between print and digital formats. Much of the contemporary architecture for the delivery of digital comics has been set up to facilitate the creation and distribution of such work. In the next chapter, I argue that the contemporary media ecology of comics enables comics to move flexibly from print to digital and back. I demonstrate through an analysis of one particular webcomic platform, ComiXology, and one particular comic produced through this platform, *Bandette.*

CHAPTER 4

GUIDED VIEW

How Comics Move from Print to Digital and Back

THE PREVIOUS two chapters discussed comics that are fixed to their original medium of publication, whether that medium is print (Barry, Kindt) or digital ("Click and Drag"). However, as Jeet Heer suggests, fixity is only one of two options that comics can employ. Comics can also be designed for flexibility—that is, comics creators can intentionally design their comics in such a way as to make them translatable into multiple publishing formats. Comics that are flexible, in this sense, can shift from print to digital platforms and back. Such flexible comics are similar to prose texts, the vast majority of which are capable of being converted from print to digital form, or vice versa, without significantly impairing the reading experience. However, comics are also different from print texts in that even if the reading experience of a comic is not ruined by the conversion from print to digital, or vice versa, the process of remediation always leaves visible marks. To successfully remediate a comic from one medium to the other, creators need to pay careful attention to the differences between the media, or else the result will be unsatisfactory or even unreadable.

This chapter explores some comics that accomplish this process of remediation effectively. For reasons of scope and expertise, I focus on one particular digital comics platform, ComiXology. This platform has been used to remediate comics in both directions, from digital to print and from print to digital. In more prosaic terms, ComiXology has been used both to distribute digital versions of comics that were originally published in print, and as an initial site of publication for born-digital comics that were later printed. I discuss examples of comics that have moved in both directions, from print to ComiXology and vice versa. These examples suggest that digital comics exemplify how a single text can be designed to take advantage of the material properties of both print and digital platforms.

THE PROBLEM OF DIGITIZING COMICS

Publishing a print comic in digital form, or vice versa, is typically a harder problem than doing the same with a prose text. On a basic level, all that needs to be done to convert a prose document into digital form is to type the text in the document into a computer. This was the original means by which Project Gutenberg, the oldest library of digital texts, was created. All the texts in its archive were generated manually from its creation in 1971 until 1989, when more sophisticated OCR technology became available. Obviously, "digitizing" a text in this way is not sufficient for scholarly purposes, and current DH text encoding projects are vastly more sophisticated. The Text Encoding Initiative (TEI) is a robust framework for translating print texts into digital form.

Still, digital encoding of comics presents problems that don't exist with text. In TEI, the dominant view of text is as an "Ordered Hierarchy of Content Objects" (OHCO). The OHCO model of text

> postulates that text consists of objects of a certain sort, structured in a certain way. The nature of the objects is best suggested by example and contrast. They are chapters, sections, paragraphs, titles, extracts, equations, examples, acts, scenes, stage directions, stanzas, (verse) lines, and so on. But they are *not* things like pages, columns, (typographical) lines, font shifts, vertical spacing, horizontal spacing, and so on. The objects indicated by descriptive markup have an intrinsic direct connection with the intellectual content of the text; they are the underlying "logical" objects, components that get their identity directly from their role in carrying out and organizing communicative intention. (Renear 224–25)

Marilyn Deegan and Kathryn Sutherland observe: "As an underlying theory of text, OHCO takes a view of text as a narrowly linguistic object abstracted from a physical container with a hierarchical structure that can be clearly understood and described: it supposes some kind of Platonic ideal of the text, a pure form that underlies actual representations" (85). Therefore, the OHCO model needs to be refined in order to take into account texts whose specific visual and material instantiation does matter, such as concrete poetry or medieval manuscripts. It is even more inapplicable to comics, where there is no "Platonic ideal" of the comic that can be separated from its visual and material form; that visual and material form *is* the comic. For example, as John Walsh observes: "In TEI the page is viewed as a 'milestone,' an empty marker within the flow of the text. In comics books (and similar documents), the page is not an arbitrary milestone, but a compositional feature—a composed container for 'panels' and text" (paragraph 14). Furthermore, some features of comics, such as word balloons that cross panel structures, are incompatible with a strictly hierarchical model of text (caption to figure 26). In short, notions of text designed for the digitization of print texts do not apply to comics.

Since comics cannot be encoded as texts can, the traditional means of distributing comics digitally is as image files (PDF, JPEG, or GIF). The first practical digital comics viewer, CDisplay, was released in 2000, but comics were being distributed digitally at a far earlier date, both via the Usenet binaries newsgroups and via storage media such as CD-ROMs. As early as 1989, a newsgroup existed for distributing scanlations of Rumiko Takahashi's *Ranma ½* ("History of Scanlation"). Image files are still the standard means for distributing pirated versions of print comics, and the .cbr and .cbz file formats were designed for the purpose of creating archives of such image files. There is also an active culture of "scanlators" who produce digital translations of Japanese comics that have not been licensed by English publishers, using photo editing programs to enter the translated text into scans of the original pages.

The trouble with reading comics as image files is that the size of the screen may not match the size of the page. One of the fundamental design elements of nearly every print comic is the page. According to Charles Hatfield:

> The page (or *planche,* as French scholars have it, a term denoting the total design unit rather than the physical page on which it is printed) functions both as sequence and as object, to be seen and read in both linear and nonlinear, holistic fashion. . . . There is a tension between the concept of

> "breaking down" a story into constituent images and the concept of laying out those images together on an unbroken surface. (48)

As Hatfield observes, the page as a compositional unit is not identical to the page as a physical object. Thierry Groensteen draws a distinction between the "usable zone" of the page and its "peripheral zone, or margin" (31), and he observes that the margin of the page can sometimes serve a compositional function and can even contain additional images and text, like Sergio Aragonés's marginal illustrations (32) (see figure 2.10). Still, in almost all print comics, each page (in the compositional sense) corresponds in size and shape to each page (in the physical sense) and can be seen in its entirety all at once. Exceptions—like the four-page splash from *MIND MGMT* #17, which can be fully viewed only by placing two copies of the comic book next to each other—are almost unknown.

By contrast, in digital comics, the size and shape of a page do not necessarily match the size and shape of the screen. In fact, they've almost guaranteed not to, since American comic book pages are typically published in portrait orientation, while computer screens are typically published in landscape orientation. Thus, a standard laptop or desktop screen cannot display a typical 6.625" by 10.25" comic book page at both its proper size and shape simultaneously. Standard .cbr and .cbz viewer programs (e.g., Simple Comic, which I have on my laptop) offer a variety of viewing options, but the two basic options are to view the entire page at once, which makes it too small to read, or to fit it to the size of the viewing window, which causes half the page to be cut off. Browser-based scanlation sites like mangafox.com offer even more limited options. Clearly, desktop computers and laptop computers are not intended to be used for reading comics.

This problem was solved by the widespread popularity of tablet devices starting in 2010. "The breakout success of tablets in the wake of the iPad finally provided digital comics with their ideal platform—and comics provided tablets and color e-book readers with their ideal content" (Salkowitz 211). Salkowitz even speculates that "comics might be the 'killer app' that drives market demand for tablets and high-end e-book readers" (38). However, tablet devices were initially only a moderate improvement over desktop computers as far as the experience of reading comics went. Even though the screen of an iPad or a Kindle Fire has dimensions reasonably similar to those of a comics page, the screen size is too small to read comics comfortably without zooming in.

Thus, the basic problem with translating print comics into digital form is how to make comics readable without undue effort on screens that weren't designed to display comics. This is a harder problem than displaying text on comics because a comic is not an Ordered Hierarchy of Content Objects which can be divorced from any particular instantiation—a comic has no existence independently of the specific visual form in which it is embodied. To make a comic digitally readable, one has to reproduce all the visual information in the comic and to present it in a form that can be read on a digital device. Currently the company that's had the most success at solving this problem is ComiXology, which forms my major case study in this chapter.

COMIXOLOGY

ComiXology was founded in 2007 by David Steinberger, John Roberts, and Peter Jaffe. Initially it was just a tool to allow users to manage their pull lists of monthly comic books (Kosturski n.p.). In 2009, ComiXology launched an app for viewing comics on the iPad. By the following year the company was being described as "the digital comics leader" because of partnerships with Marvel and DC (Rogers n.p.), and it had overcome competition from rivals Graphicly and iVerse (on which see Salkowitz 216). By the end of that year, the ComiXology app had been downloaded over a million times (Khouri n.p.). In 2013, ComiXology was the top-grossing non-game app for the iPad and the 11th highest-grossing app overall (MacDonald 2014 n.p.).[1] The following April, ComiXology was acquired by Amazon and promptly created massive controversy by disabling the option to purchase comics from within its iOS app. Customers instead had to visit ComiXology's website to buy their comics. This decision was made because "Apple's App Store policies demand that it receive a 30 percent cut of all in-app purchases and subscriptions" (D'Orazio n.p.). ComiXology's decision was widely criticized and was even seen as an existential threat to the company. Over a year later at this writing, ComiXology remains the dominant player in the digital comics market, though it now faces some competition. For example, Marvel's Netflix-style digital subscription service, Marvel Unlimited, is a separate entity from ComiXology.

ComiXology's success was due largely to its partnerships with almost all major comics publishers,[2] but the secret weapon in its arsenal was its

1. For more on the history of ComiXology up to 2011, see Salkowitz 216–19.

2. The major exception among commercial comics publishers was Dark Horse, which instead offered its comics through its own digital app. In 2015, Dark Horse's comics finally became available on ComiXology. Among art comics publishers, Drawn

proprietary Guided View technology, which Salkowitz describes as ComiXology's "special sauce" (217). Guided View enables readers to view comics pages on a panel-by-panel basis. When the user swipes left or right, the screen automatically zooms to the next panel in order. By tapping the screen twice, the user can exit Guided View and see the entire current page. While in Guided View mode, the user can also choose to view the entire page before and/or after turning to a new page.

What makes Guided View unique and effective is that it preserves but also radically changes the experience of reading comics. As Hatfield suggests in the above quotation, one of the fundamental tensions of comics reading is between the function of the panel as an isolated compositional unit and as an element of the larger unit of the page. Pierre Fresnault-Deruelle calls this the tension between the "linear" and "tabular" functions of the page (qtd. in Hatfield 48). With Guided View, these two functions of the page are severed from each other. While using Guided View,

> readers never see the entire page, which exists only as an organizational concept. On the iPhone, the program window and the screen edge are coterminous, and unlike Marvel's digital subscriptions, the app has no page-view function, so the "page" is entirely notional and the frame is the major unit. (Wershler-Henry 133)

Even in the ComiXology Kindle app, which does have a page-view function, the size of the screen makes it inconvenient to read the entire page when it's displayed all at once. Therefore, the viewer must choose between reading each individual panel on its own or viewing the page as a complete but illegible compositional unit. This transformation doesn't destroy, but does radically alter, the experience of reading a comics page. In 2012, when I used Guided View for the first time, I wrote that "when read one panel at a time instead of one page at a time, a comic becomes a sort of very slow movie" (Kashtan 2012, n.p.). This resembles Drew Morton's description of the *Saw* motion comic as "a PowerPoint slideshow presentation of a comic book, condemning it to the formal purgatory between the comic book and animation" (15). However, ComiXology purports to be not a hybrid of comics and animation but a digital format for viewing comics. The point of Guided View is simply to make comics readable in digital form when they wouldn't be otherwise.

& Quarterly was a notable holdout until it announced a partnership with ComiXology in September 2015.

If Guided View achieves this goal with reasonable effectiveness, then one reason is the amount of care that goes into choosing the panel borders. In order for a page to be translated into Guided View form, a new set of decisions must be made that were not necessary when the comic was published in print form. Specifically, someone (or something) has to decide where to put the panel transitions. ComiXology's patent application for the Guided View technology suggests that the conversion of a page to Guided View could be done algorithmically with no human intervention: "The border of a panel could be determined by automatically detecting the edges of a panel and creating a shape around the panel and/or finding the best fit for a rectangle around the panel." However, ComiXology seems to have chosen not to use this option. Instead, Guided View transitions are defined by ComiXology employees (an option also described in the patent). In 2013, the official ComiXology Tumblr page wrote:

> We have a great team here that specifically works to shape Guided View for each comic we have in our library. As we prepare a book for sale, a member of our team will go through and use our technology to add our cinematic experience to the issue. The length of the book itself, language, and style can change how long that process can take.
>
> We're super lucky in that the team responsible for adding Guided View not just loves comics, but they also love creating comics. When they aren't doing Guided View, they're writing, drawing, inking, and/or coloring their own comics. (Comixology n.p.)

This post is careful to emphasize that Guided View decisions are not made on an arbitrary basis; rather, these decisions are made thoughtfully and carefully, and by people who are intimately familiar with the comics reading process. If performed algorithmically, or by people without comics experience, the conversion from print to Guided View could wreck the reading experience, but ComiXology is careful to avoid this.[3] Instead, Guided View results in a reading experience which is radically unlike the experience of reading a printed comic, yet not inherently worse. Noel Murray observes that in the first two pages from Matt Fraction and David Aja's *Hawkeye* #6,

3. In 2010, ComiXology even announced that their "Guided View Authoring Tools" would be made available to authors and creators, but for unclear reasons this project never got beyond the beta stage.

> the white space is gone from the Guided View version, as is the vertical portion of the page two schematic. But the drama of that first page (and thus the second page's comedic switcheroo) is even stronger when read on the phone, at least to my eyes. The progression of the action is clearer, and even more intense, when the reader's only seeing two or three panels at a time. (n.p.)

In Murray's view, Guided View enhances certain aspects of page composition at the same time that it detracts from other aspects: "I'd never contend that Guided View is superior to reading a print comic [. . .] But sometimes changing the frame for a piece of art can change the way we look at it" (n.p.).

Still, not all pages are equally convertible to Guided View. Because of the shape of the iPad or Kindle screen, Guided View works best with panels that are roughly rectangular. For example, the first comic I read on ComiXology was Alex Robinson's *Box Office Poison*. This comic is ideally suited to Guided View because of its use of rectangular panel grids (often 4 by 2 grids in particular, a design feature probably borrowed from Dave Sim's *Cerebus*). With such pages, the conversion to Guided View requires relatively little effort (see figure 4.1).

The transition to Guided View becomes much more difficult with pages that have diagonal or other irregular borders or that don't have panel borders at all. Some pages of Box Office Poison are full-page compositions without panel borders, and with pages like these, Guided View "panel" borders must be drawn on a much more impressionistic basis. Part of the experience of reading a composition like the one that appears on pages 292 and 293 is deciding *how* to read it—where to start and where to end, what to look at first and what to save until later (see figure 4.2).

With ComiXology, however, those decisions are made on the reader's behalf by the Guided View Editor, resulting in a less individualized reading experience. For example, in Guided View, pages 292 and 293 are broken down into four "panels." In order, these are (1) the first two panels on the top left, (2) the entire two pages at once, (3) the bottom right-hand panel on page 292, and (4) the bottom two panels on page 293. As figure 4.3 demonstrates, none of these four sections of this two-page spread is rectangular in shape. Thus, for example, when the fourth of these panels, that is, the bottom of page 293, is viewed in Guided View, a large chunk of the section above it is necessarily also included, with the result that the top half of the screen is filled with a giant disembodied arm. Moreover, when the entire two-page spread is viewed in Guided View, some parts of it, including the lower left-hand panel of page 292 and the top two panels

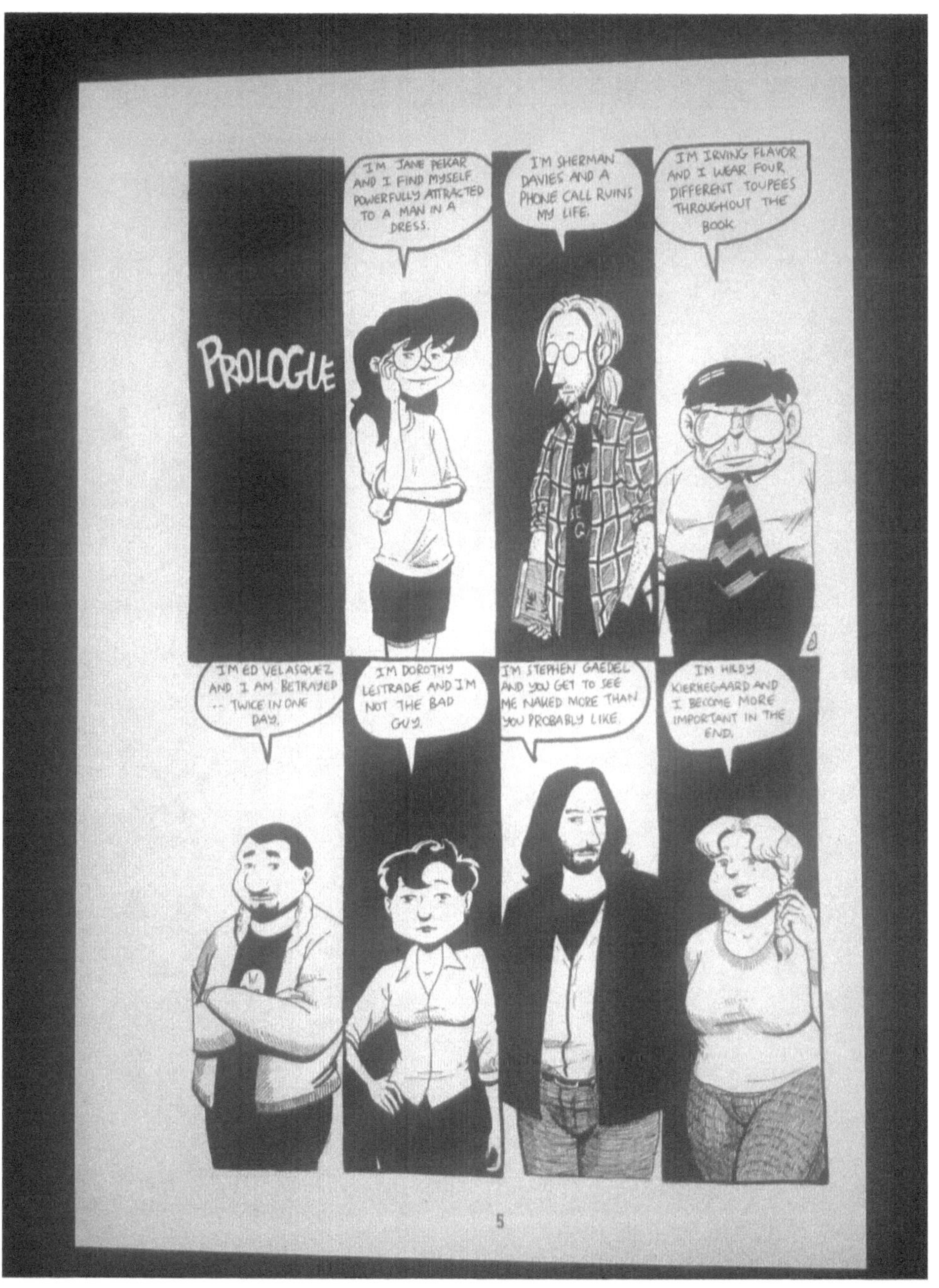

FIGURE 4.1. Page 5 of *Box Office Poison,* as displayed on the author's Kindle Fire. The page works perfectly with Guided View because it has panels that are the same shape as the screen.

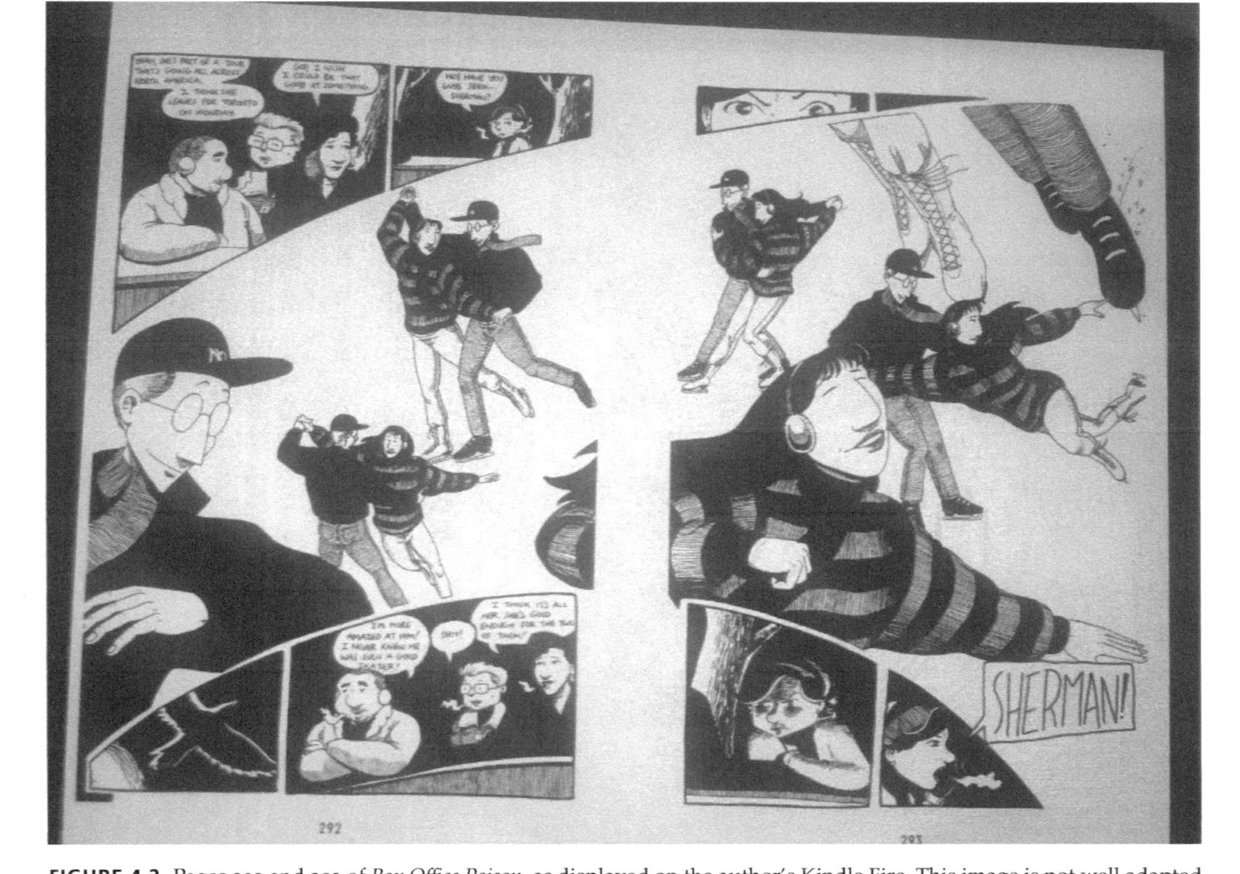

FIGURE 4.2. Pages 292 and 293 of *Box Office Poison,* as displayed on the author's Kindle Fire. This image is not well adapted to Guided View.

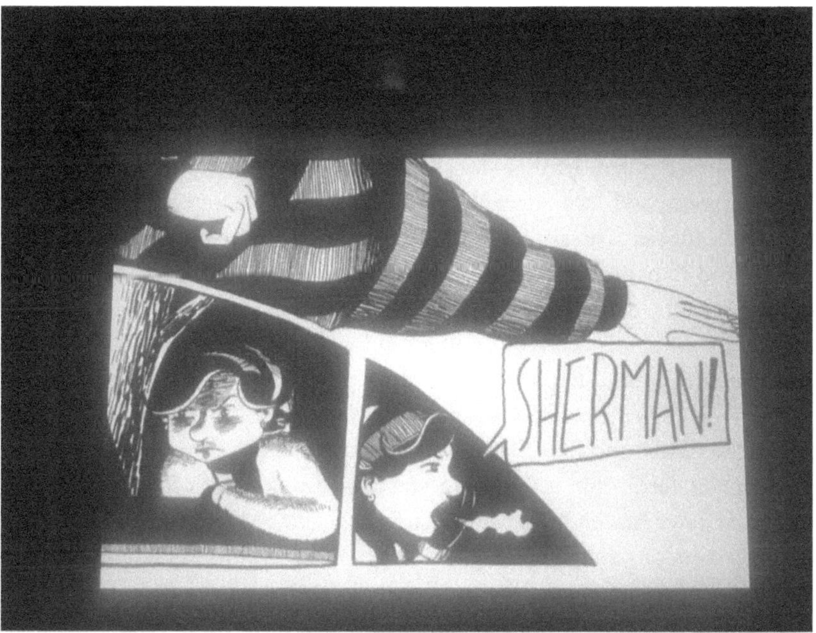

FIGURE 4.3. The bottom of page 293 of *Box Office Poison,* as displayed on the author's Kindle Fire. This represents the lower right-hand corner of figure 4.2. Notice how the two bottom panels don't fill the entire screen, and a large section of the panel above them is included by necessity.

on page 293, can be seen only when the entire page is viewed as a unit. Similarly, on pages 278 and 279, only the inset panels get Guided View "panels" of their own, and the parts of the page that aren't included in any of the inset panels are visible only when the camera zooms out to display the entire two-page spread.

The Guided View process breaks down completely when pages are formatted in a way that makes sense *only* in print. Cases where this happens are when the start and end points of a page are intentionally unclear, as with the famous Möbius strip page from Alan Moore and J. H. Williams III's *Promethea,* or when pages are meant to be read out of order, as with *Fantastic Four* #352. (The latter comic is not available on ComiXology, but it appears to have been published on Marvel Unlimited without any attempt to replicate its unique "time-travel" functionality.) In *Batman* #5 (2012), pages are intentionally printed upside down and sideways to reflect Batman's confused state of mind. When this issue was released on ComiXology, the company's official Twitter account wrote: "Batman #5 contains upside-down and sideways pages. To maximize the reading experience you may want to lock the orientation on your device" (ComiXology 2012).

One example of a recent comic that required unusual effort to translate into digital format, and that even then failed to work properly in that format, is Dan Slott and Mike Allred's *Silver Surfer* #11. This issue is the most notable recent example of a print comic that's "fixed" to the print format, in that it uses print-specific features that are difficult to replicate in digital form. In this story, the Surfer and his human companion, Dawn Greenwood, are attempting to find a new planet to house a group of alien refugees. Their travels take them through a region of space called the Giraud Expanse (named after legendary French cartoonist Jean Giraud, a.k.a. Moebius, and therefore a reference to the Möbius strip structure of the story), where the convoy is attacked by hostile aliens. The Surfer seeks to escape the Giraud Expanse by "folding time," at the same time the aliens seek to use their "Chrono-Cannon" to defend themselves from what they see as the Surfer and his allies' unprovoked aggression.

In print form, this issue has a structure unlike any other comic book before or since has had. The entire story is a giant Möbius strip. Each page has two tiers of panels, one right-side up and the other upside down. For the first half of the comic, the right-side up tier of panels is on top. At the center of the comic, the right-side up panels cross diagonally over the upside down panels, and from this point on, the upside down panels are on top. The main part of the comic can therefore be divided into four sections—upper right-side up, lower right-side up, upper upside down and lower upside down—which I will label sections A, B, C, and D for ease of reference.

The story begins with an introductory monologue delivered by "the Never Queen, the embodiment of all possibility." The reader then starts with section A. At the center of the issue, the upper tier of panels crosses over the lower tier, and the reader has to start reading again at the bottom of the page. This corresponds with the point in the story where the Surfer attempts to "fold time" at the same time that the aliens fire their chrono-cannon, sending the Surfer and his allies back in time (see figure 4.4).

At this point section B begins and the story starts over. The reader reads about the same events again, but from Dawn Greenwood's perspective this time. This time, when the climactic moment is reached, the reader has to flip the comic book over and start reading backwards and upside down, and the story reverts back to the starting point yet again, only now it's told from the perspective of the Surfer and Dawn's alien companions. This is section C. On reaching the center of the comic again, the reader moves diagonally down (or up) to the bottom tier of the upside down panels and begins reading about the same events a fourth time, this time from the per-

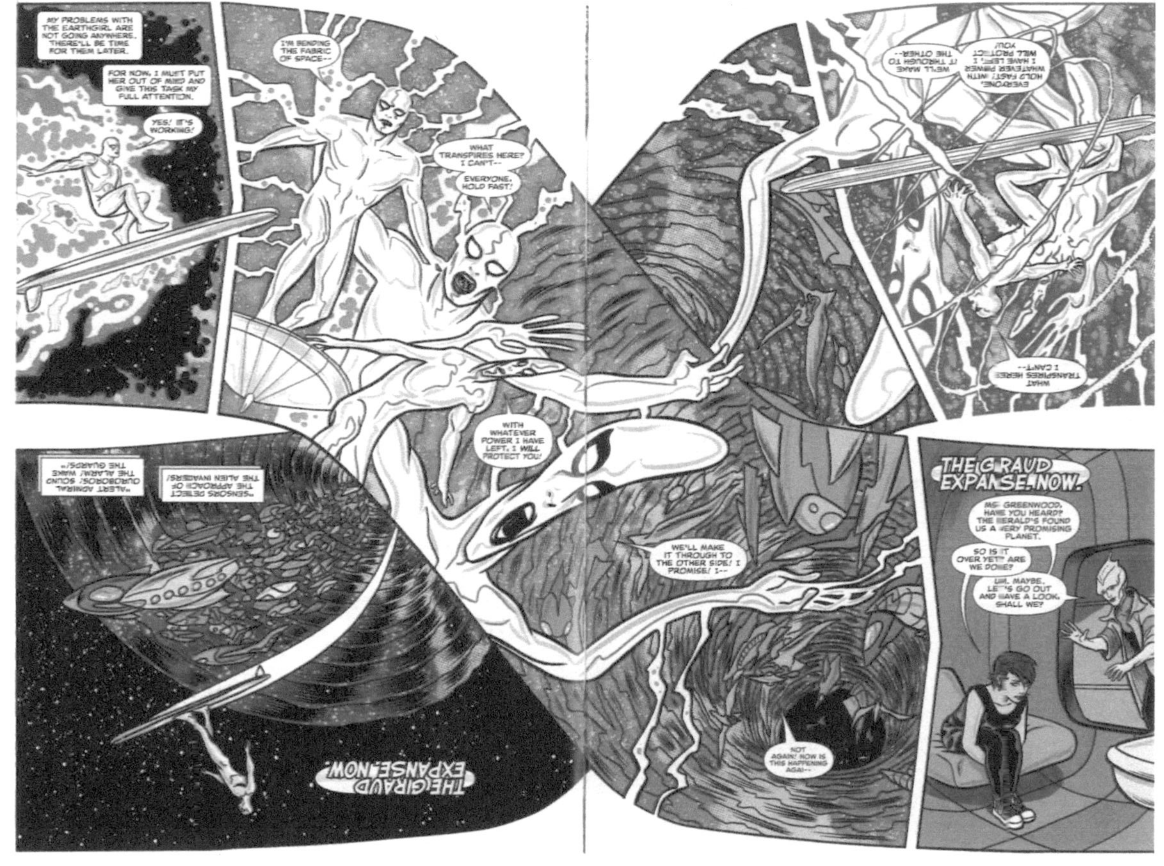

FIGURE 4.4. The point in the print version of *Silver Surfer* #11 where the sections of the narrative intersect.

spective of the hostile aliens. This is section D. At the end of this tier of panels, the reader has to turn the comic book right-side up again, and the entire story starts over again with section A, in an infinite loop.

The question that confronts the reader of this comic is the same question that confronts the Surfer himself: how to break out of this endless cycle and reach the end of the story. On page 23, the point where the reader has to flip the comic upside down and start reading backwards, the Never Queen offers a clue. She says: "There is a way off this endless path. Exert your free will. Grab hold of all you accept as real, then reach beyond. . . . Be the one who turns this page in the story of your life." To finish this comic book, the reader has to take this advice literally. Turning page 23 reveals that this page can be folded over on top of page 24 (as with Al Jaffee's *Mad* magazine"fold-ins"), revealing a new continuation to the story—which I will call section E—in which the Surfer successfully folds time (see figure 4.5).

The Never Queen says: "Yes, you have worked it out, Norrin Radd [the Surfer's real name]. Do what must be done, and yet know this. . . ." If the reader continues past this panel, she can proceed forward in time to the end of the story, in which the Surfer successfully leads the convoy out of the Giraud Expanse and to a new homeworld. Yet if the reader wants to see the end of the Never Queen's just-quoted sentence, she has to flip the comic upside down to find another panel in which the Never Queen says: "With every choice comes a price. Such is the nature of free will." This panel belongs to a final upside down tier of panels, which I will call section F. It takes place before the rest of the issue and reveals the dark secret behind the story's events. The convoy's leaders, Krattaka and Founder Keen, had been conspiring with the hostile aliens to get rid of certain weak and sick members of the convoy, whom they blamed for the convoy's inability to settle on any of the planets they explored.

In its print form, *Silver Surfer* #11 is one of the most successful formal experiments ever attempted in a Marvel or DC comic. It uses the comic book format in a radically innovative way which is also beautifully integrated with the story. In particular, the fold-in is a feature that takes advantage of the three-dimensionality of the print comic. The fold-in works only because the pages of the comic are separate and yet physically attached to each other, which makes it possible for the reader to place one page on top of another so that both pages are partially visible at the same time.

How well does this experiment work in digital form? As it turns out, not so well. One of the keys to the print version of *Silver Surfer* #11 is the arthrological dimension of the page. When reading the right side up tier of panels, the reader is constantly aware of the existence of the upside down

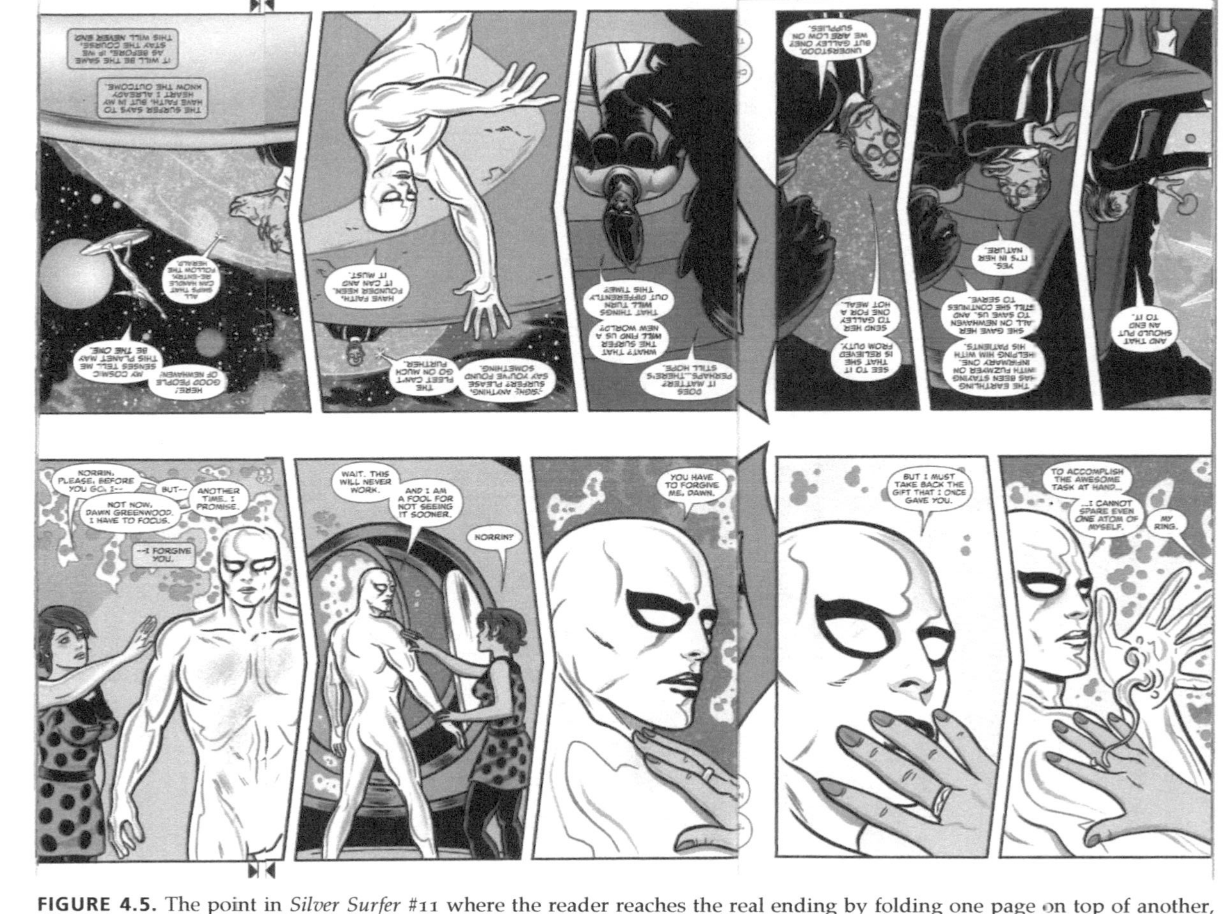

FIGURE 4.5. The point in *Silver Surfer* #11 where the reader reaches the real ending by folding one page on top of another, as with Al Jaffee's "Fold-Ins" in *Mad* magazine. The thin strip in the middle (showing part of the Never Queen's face) is not supposed to be visible, but is visible because the two pages don't line up perfectly.

tier of panels above or below and knows that once he gets to the end of the comic, she will have to flip it over and start again. When reading the upside down panels, the reader is constantly reminded that he has already read the right-side up panels on the same pages. On each page the past and the present are simultaneously visible, and this reflects the plot of the story, in which the normal forward progression of time is derailed. Again, the figure-8 visual structure of the story reflects the circular structure of the narrative. All these arthrological elements are missing in the ComiXology version of the issue, where only one tier of panels is visible at a time (see figure 4.6). When section A ends, the story continues diagonally on the next page, but there's no indication of why the panels have moved from the top of the page to the bottom. When section C ends, there is a giant gap in the middle of the page, where the transition from section A to B originally was in the print version.

Still more frustratingly, the interactive, puzzle-like element of the story is missing because the reader does not have to fold the page in order to complete the story. After the reader finishes reading sections A through D, the story begins again with section A. This time, however, when the reader reaches the panel where the fold-in occurs in the print version, the story simply proceeds to the panel after the fold-in, with no additional intervention required from the reader. The panel where the Never Queen congratulates the Surfer (and implicitly the reader) on "working it out" is missing and is replaced by a new panel not present in the print version. In this panel the Never Queen instead says: "A new *choice* has been made. And with it . . . new pathways are revealed. With new *tolls* that must be paid." The story then proceeds to section F. After this sequence there's another new panel that appears only in the digital version, in which the Never Queen says: "You know what must be done, Norrin Radd. Cast all else aside! Create a new possibility! Will it into being!" Following this panel, the story concludes with section E.

In its digital version, this comic is no longer an example of what Espen Aarseth calls *ergodic literature,* in which "nontrivial effort is required to allow the reader to traverse the text" (Aarseth 1). In the print version, when the Never Queen urges the Surfer to "reach beyond" and "be the one who turns this page in the story of your life," these exhortations are directed at the reader as well as the Surfer. In order for the Surfer to figuratively turn the page in his life, the reader must literally turn the page of the comic. In the digital version, the Never Queen utters the same exhortation, but it's directed only at the Surfer and not at the reader. The reader doesn't need to figure out that she needs to turn the page and fold it in after finishing Sec-

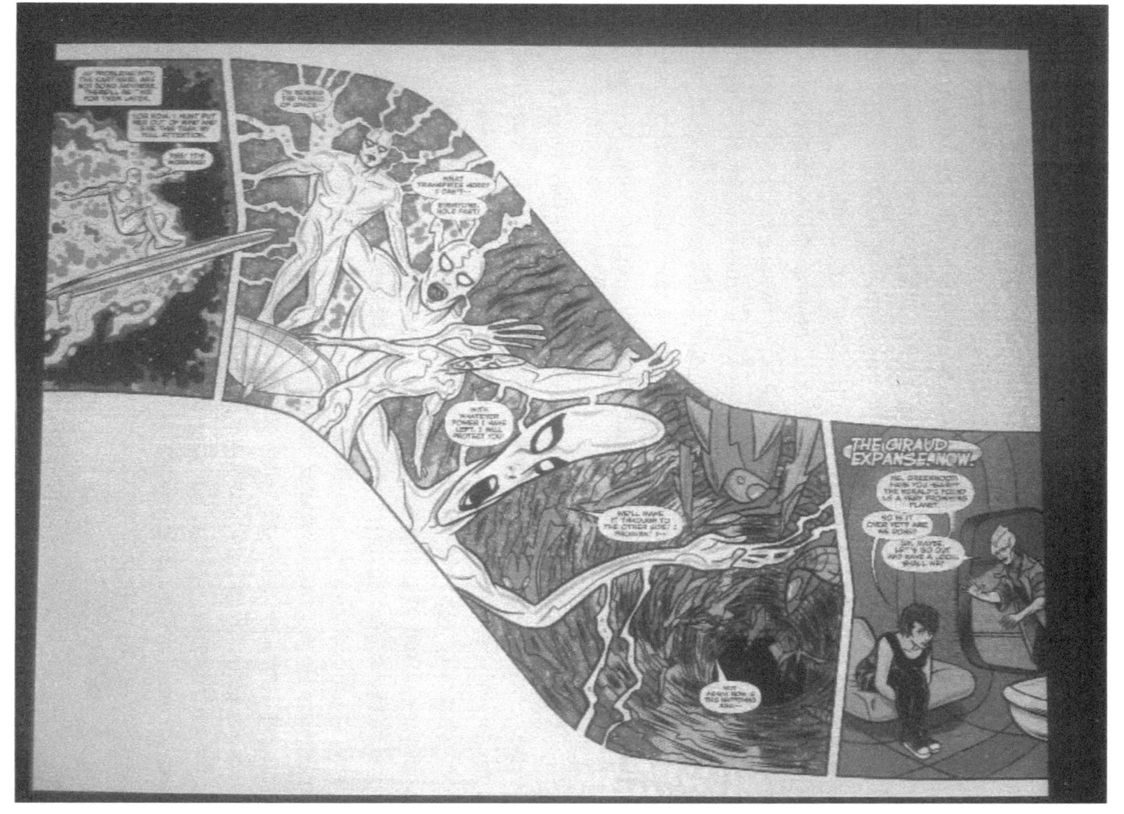

FIGURE 4.6. The centerfold of the digital version of *Silver Surfer* #11, as displayed on the author's Kindle Fire. Compare figure 4.4.

tion B for the second time, because the order of panels in the digital version is predetermined, whether the reader uses Guided View or reads the comic one page at a time.

The digital version of *Silver Surfer* #11 therefore lacks much of the functionality of the printed version and offers a comparatively impoverished reading experience. It would have been possible to do a better job. There was no obvious reason why the digital version had to limit the reader to seeing only one section of the comic at a time; sections A and D, for example, could have been present at the same time. The challenge here would have been structuring the Guided View layout of the story in such a way as to allow the reader to read the same pages multiple times. On a tablet or phone, it would be easy to turn the comic upside down when necessary. The one part of the story that would be impossible to replicate in digital form is the element of folding the page over, since the "pages" of digital comics are, in Wershler-Smith's words, "entirely notional"—a print comic consists of separate physical reading surfaces attached to each other, while a digital comic consists of only one such surface. However, if there's one thing that digital platforms are good at, it's interactivity, and surely some means could have been devised for replicating the page-folding functionality in digital form. It seems likely that the reason this wasn't done was because it was not cost-effective—there was no financial incentive to produce a more faithful digital version of *Silver Surfer* #11, especially since readers who only read the digital and not the print version would have been unable to tell the difference. (For an example of the sort of effort required to translate a print-specific comic into digital form in a more sensitive way, see the section on Jason Shiga's *Meanwhile* in chapter 5.)

This example suggests some of the ways in which Guided View can fail to accurately translate the experience of reading a given printed comic. Still, as a tool for translating print comics into digital form, Guided View represents the current state of the art. Digitizing a print comic involves some necessary compromises, and ComiXology has been careful to make these compromises in an informed and sensitive way.

THE OTHER DIRECTION: FROM COMIXOLOGY TO PRINT

However, ComiXology distributes not only digital versions of print comics but also original content. While ComiXology has not become a creator of original content along the lines of Netflix, it has become a platform for the distribution of new comics that are initially created in digital form. In 2013, ComiXology announced the launch of the ComiXology Submit service, which allows independent creators to host their work on the site in exchange for a 50–50 split of revenues between the creator and the company. There are even digital publishers, most notably Chris Roberson and Allison Baker's Monkeybrain, that distribute their work only through ComiXology and not through print. Unlike other digital comics platforms like Madefire, ComiXology does not offer digital-specific features like motion, sound, or interactivity and can therefore only distribute comics that are reasonably compatible with print. For example, Mark Waid and John Rogers's digital publisher Thrillbent, which has experimented with digital-specific comics, publishes some of its comics through ComiXology, but only if they don't require digital-specific functionalities that ComiXology lacks. Thus, comics initially published through ComiXology can easily be remediated into print form, and many of them have been. Several of the comic books originally published via this service were subsequently or concurrently self-published in print through Kickstarter (e.g., Janelle Asselin's anthology *Fresh Romance* and Art Baltazar and Franco Aureliani's Aw Yeah! Comics), or else were picked up by print publishers (e.g., John Allison and Lissa Tremain's *Giant Days*). As is the case with webcomics in general, ComiXology acts as a distribution channel for works that a print publisher may not have been willing to take a chance on, enabling the subsequent print publication of those works after their digital versions have found an audience.

Monkeybrain Comics is an important example of how this strategy works. It was founded in 2012 by the husband-and-wife team of Chris Roberson, a writer of comics and science fiction, and Allison Baker, a TV and film producer. They both had previous print publishing experience: they had previously founded an independent publishing house, Monkeybrain Books, in 2003. However, Roberson and Baker chose to launch Monkeybrain (Comics) not as a print publisher but as "a home for quality creator owned comics made available in digital format via the Comics By ComiXology platform" ("About" n.d.). ComiXology is effectively the exclusive distributor for Monkeybrain Comics, although there was apparently never an exclusive contract between them. Roberson and Baker chose to focus on digital publishing for several reasons.[4] In 2012, Borders Books had just gone out of business, and Diamond had a monopoly on the com-

4. Much of the following information comes from a Skype interview with Chris Roberson and Allison Baker. I'm indebted to them for their time.

ics distribution market, so digital offered the advantage of less restricted distribution channels. Furthermore, digital publishing involves much less capital risk and is scalable, in that it doesn't require additional capital investment if a title becomes successful (Roberson and Baker, interview). An additional advantage of Monkeybrain is that it can publish works that might not be feasible as print titles. Roberson wants Monkeybrain's creators to follow their "idiosyncratic, personal creative visions" (interview), and this often results in works that don't fit into established comic book genres and that print publishers would be initially unwilling to take a chance on. However, Monkeybrain holds only the digital rights to the comics it publishes. The creators of Monkeybrain comics keep their copyrights and are free to simultaneously publish their work in print form with other publishers (interview). For example, *Edison Rex* (by Roberson and Dennis Culver) and *Amelia Cole* (D. J. Kirkbride, Adam P. Knave, and Nick Brokenshire) have been published by IDW in trade paperback form, and *Bandette* (Paul Tobin and Colleen Coover) and *High Crimes* (Chris Sebela and Ibrahim Moustafa) have been published by Dark Horse as deluxe hardcovers.

Bandette, Monkeybrain's biggest success story, is an instructive example of the development of a project that can move from print to digital form and back. Its creators, Paul Tobin and Colleen Coover (another husband-and-wife team), were both comics industry veterans; Tobin wrote multiple titles for Marvel's all-ages imprint Marvel Adventures, while Coover was previously best known for her lesbian erotic comic *Small Favors* and her backup stories in various Marvel titles. The title character of *Bandette* is a masked, costumed teenage French thief, who leads an army of "Urchins" and battles rival thieves like Monsieur and Absinthe. It was developed specifically as a project for Monkeybrain after Roberson and Baker approached Tobin and Coover and asked them to create one of the company's flagship titles. However, like other Monkeybrain titles, *Bandette* is highly personal and idiosyncratic and might therefore have been difficult to sell to a print publisher. As the above summary indicates, *Bandette* has many of the trappings of the superhero genre, though it's a somewhat marginal example of that genre: in the first place, its protagonist is a criminal, and in the second, it has an extremely lighthearted and humorous tone and is appropriate for children, unlike most current Marvel and DC comics. Even then, its resemblance to a superhero comic meant that Tobin and Coover might have had difficulty finding a publisher for it if they had initially developed it as a print comic. According to Baker and Roberson, independent publishers (at least in 2012) thought of superhero comics as the primary domain of DC and Marvel, and they would have been unwilling to even read a submission that looked like a superhero comic. Therefore, *Bandette* was a prime example of a project that was more appropriate for Monkeybrain than for a print publisher.

When *Bandette* debuted on ComiXology in 2012, its exemplary level of craft and its lighthearted, positive tone made it a major critical success. It debuted in 2012 and was nominated for four Eisner Awards the following year, winning the award for Best Digital Comic. In 2015, *Bandette* picked up three more nominations, including one in the prestigious Best Continuing Series category. This success was notable given that the Eisner Awards are decided primarily by readers of traditional print comics. Digital comics have received occasional Eisner nominations at least since 2003, when Justine Shaw's *Nowhere Girl* was nominated for Best New Series, but nearly every other work on the 2013 and 2015 Eisner ballots was published in print form before or concurrently with its digital release. *Bandette* is therefore a crossover success that appeals not only to webcomics readers but also to fans of print comics who may be reluctant to read webcomics. It's able to reach the latter audience because of its creators' preexisting excellent reputation among comics fans and because of its adoption of publishing tropes specific to print comics. On ComiXology, *Bandette* is released in the form of "issues" that cost 99 cents and include about 22 "pages" plus a "cover." Thus, *Bandette* looks and feels like a pamphlet-sized comic book and costs about one-third as much. *Bandette* also appeals to fans of print comics because of its deployment of nostalgia and self-conscious references to other comics. Its characters are visually based on classic movie actors like Audrey Hepburn, Peter Falk, and Cary Grant (Tobin and Coover 2015, 131–32), and it's aware of its debt to the Franco-Belgian bande dessinée tradition. One of its primary characters, Inspector B. D. Belgique, looks like a character from Franquin's *Gaston Lagaffe* and has a name that means "Belgian comics."

Another factor that contributes to the success of *Bandette* is that it's ideally adapted to the constraints of the ComiXology platform with its Guided View interface. Each page of *Bandette* consists of three tiers of panels with rectangular borders, which means *Bandette* can be effortlessly displayed in Guided View. In an e-mail interview, Colleen Coover said: "The only creative decision that I made specifically in terms of art was to stick to a strict three-tier layout for my pages—it makes adapting the page to phone-sized panels easier for ComiXology," although she added that "even that is probably a choice I would have made for print, because I love using restrictions in my work" (personal communication). Still, *Bandette* reads much better in ComiXology compared to other Monkeybrain comics that use more radical page layouts, for example, *Aesop's Ark*. The use of three-panel strips also intensifies *Bandette*'s resemblance to classic French comics, which were typically formatted as a series of horizontal strips. This was deliberate: in a March 2014 interview with Bruce Lidl, Tobin stated: "We love the three-tier approach to comics, at least for this project, because it's not only handy for digital, but also an homage to the comics we're emulating to a certain degree . . . *Tintin*, for instance" (Lidl n.p.).

Given its success in digital form and the lack of formal barriers to remediating it into print, it was perhaps inevitable that *Bandette* would be published in print form. Two hardcover *Bandette* collections were published by Dark Horse in 2013 and 2015, with further volumes certain to follow. As discussed in the previous chapter, print editions of digital comics are economically viable for several reasons, including portability, tactility, and the desire of fans to support creators. However, compared to most print editions of digital comics, the *Bandette* volumes offer even more added value. Both volumes of *Bandette* are handsome books that use publication design to enhance the reading experience. According to Coover,

> the editor from Dark Horse, Brendan Wright, worked closely with us on making sure that the book was designed to our satisfaction. The designer of the first volume, Irina Beffa, came up with these bright, yellow, Saul Bass–style title pages that really get the interior pages to pop. Even the paper stock was a matter we discussed at some length. (personal communication)

In each volume, each issue is preceded by a reproduction of its original digital cover and one of the title pages that Coover mentions (see figure 4.7).

As Coover indicates, these title pages resemble the cinematic title sequences created by the legendary graphic designer Saul Bass; thus, they accentuate *Bandette*'s resemblance to a classic Hollywood film. The color scheme used for the chapter title pages is also used for the title page of the entire book and for the introduction. The book even makes minimal use of the sort of blending between book and story that Matt Kindt exploits in *MIND MGMT*. On the first right-hand page is a bookplate that reads "THIS BOOK ~~BELONGS TO~~ acquired by:" followed by a blank space for the reader's name (Tobin and Coover 2013, inside front cover). "Acquired by" is handwritten in lowercase, and a picture of Bandette's mask appears above this text (see figure 4.8). The implication is that like most of Bandette's pos-

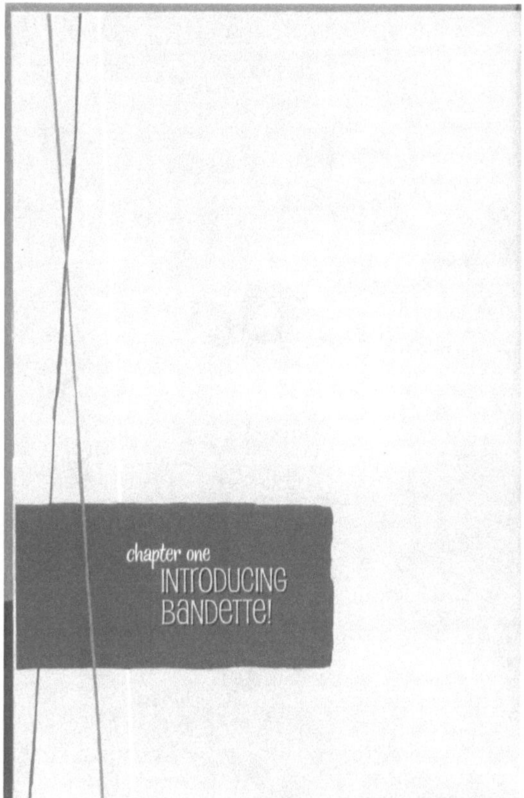

FIGURE 4.7. One of the decorative chapter title pages from *Bandette Volume 1*. Note the resemblance to an old film title card.

sessions, this book is stolen property, and the further implication is that this book is just as precious as any of the valuable items that Bandette steals during the story, despite its modest $14.99 price point.[5] The mere fact that the book includes a bookplate (albeit a fake one) further testifies to its value. According to Wikipedia, the bookplate—"a small print or decorative label pasted into a book, often on the inside front cover, to indicate its owner"—is almost as old as the printed book, dating back to a time when books were valuable and rare commodities, and bookplates are an important tool for tracing the provenance of rare books ("Bookplate").

Besides its creative publication design, this book also offers extra content that's not included in the ComiXology digital editions of *Bandette*. In

5. The inclusion of this bookplate was a last-minute decision by Coover (Lidl n.p.).

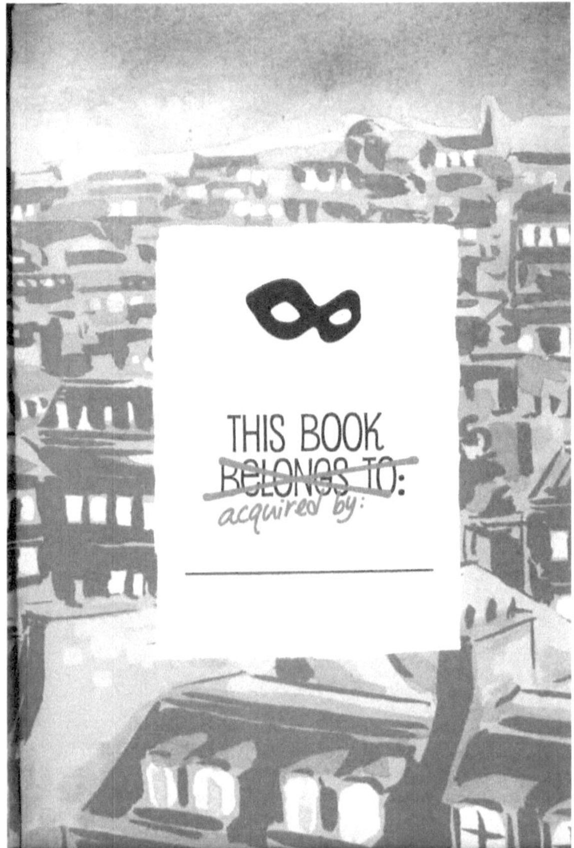

FIGURE 4.8. Bookplate from the inside cover of *Bandette Volume 1.*

addition to the first five digital issues of *Bandette,* volume 1 reprints eight two- or three-page "Urchin Stories" that were previously published only on Monkeybrain's website. Each of these stories, written by Tobin and drawn by a guest artist, focuses on one of the minor characters from the series. Volume 1 of *Bandette* is the first place where these stories appear together with the main series. Besides that, the book contains other features not previously published anywhere: a prose story written by Tobin with spot illustrations by Coover, focusing on Bandette's love interest, Daniel; a list of all the items stolen by Bandette in the book; Tobin's script for the first three pages of issue 1; and an article by Coover about her production process, which "expands on the *Bandette* process posts from Colleen's blog" (Tobin and Coover 2013, 132). These bonuses offer readers an incentive to buy the *Bandette* hardcover even if they've already read the comic in digital form and are not sentimentally attached to the print medium.

In short, *Bandette* is a prime example of a comic that effectively manages the transition from print to digital form. The print edition is intended to complement rather than replace the digital edition, and the two editions appeal to different readers but also to the same readers at different times. In the above-quoted interview, Lidl asked: "What is your impression of the hardcover purchasers? Are they primarily the same audience as the digital purchasers, but now looking to own a tangible artifact? Or is it a whole new audience that was not interested in the comics as digital purchases?" Tobin responded:

> Both. We've had plenty of readers contact us and say that they loved the digital comic so much that they were thrilled to have a hardcover, and then there were others who wrote to say how happy they were to have the hardcover, because reading comics digitally either didn't appeal to them or that they just didn't have access. I think it was the right way to go for us; it's not even a "best of both worlds" situation, because it's "both worlds" straight up. (Lidl n.p.)

The print version of Bandette thus appeals both to readers who did read the digital version and to readers who didn't, but for both groups of readers, its advantage is that it's not just a physical, tangible artifact, but one that is thoughtfully and sensitively designed. However, the print version does not replace the digital version because it's published on a biennial basis, while digital issues of *Bandette* come out much more frequently. Dedicated *Bandette* fans may be willing to pay 99 cents every few months to keep current with Bandette's adventures, rather than waiting two years for the next hardcover.

Bandette is readable in both print and digital formats, largely because it's designed that way. It's an example of a flexible comic that can move from digital to print without losing the qualities that make it appealing. At the same time, neither the print nor the digital version of *Bandette* is a strict improvement on the other. The print and digital versions of Bandette haven't cannibalized each other by competing for the attention of the same readers; instead, each has driven sales of the other.

The lesson here is that even comics developed for one medium (print or digital) can be effectively remediated into the other medium, as long as this is done carefully. A thoughtless conversion in one direction or the other can destroy the reading experience, but a thoughtful conversion can result in a comic that readers want to purchase in one medium even if they already own it in the other medium. But this suggests a further step. What about a comic that's meant to be read in *both* print and digital form at once—a comic where the print and digital versions are so different that it's worthwhile to read and compare them, or where the print and digital versions go together and are each meaningless without the other? That's the question I explore in the final chapter.

CHAPTER 5

BETWEEN PANEL AND SCREEN

Comics That Are Print and Digital at Once

THE PREVIOUS four chapters considered digital and print comics separately, examining how print comics have responded to digital technology and how digital comics have remediated the characteristic forms of materiality of print comics. These chapters accepted the standard assumption that print and digital books represent two divergent lines of development that will continue to evolve along nonintersecting paths. In contrast, this chapter discards this assumption, suggesting that the print/digital opposition is unproductive and that the two media need to be conceived of in complementary rather than oppositional terms. Electronic books can benefit from taking advantage of the tactile, physical forms of materiality associated with the print book. Conversely, if the print book simply emphasizes its own physicality and tactility, it will become an increasingly arcane and inaccessible art form. In order to maintain its viability as a popular medium, the print book must somehow incorporate the efficiency, accessibility, and interactivity of the digital book.

We therefore need to ask not which side will ultimately win the struggle between the physical book and the digital book, but how the two media can productively complement each other. Comics provide a model of how this can be done effectively. The comics industry has found that the two media are not necessarily competitive in an economic sense. At the "Digital vs. Print: Friends or Foes" panel at Comic-Con, the consensus of the panel was that the two media can coexist and that sales of one can actually drive sales of the other. Comics like *Bandette* can be published in digital form with the intention of subsequently appearing in print after they have proven their marketability. On the flip side, in 2011, DC started offering select comics as "print/digital combo packs": for $1 more than the price of the print comic book, the reader received both a print and a digital copy (R. Johnston, "DC Announces Digital Print"). In March of 2012, Marvel started providing a free digital download code with all its print comics that were priced at $3.99 or higher. A Marvel executive described this decision as motivated by the desire for print/digital synergy:

> "At Marvel, we're always looking for ways to bring the worlds of print and digital media together to deliver the best comics experience for our fans," said Peter Phillips, SVP & GM, Marvel Digital Media. "With this next step, fans will soon be able to buy their comics from their favorite retailers but also enjoy them on their mobile devices and tablets, all at no extra charge. Welcome to the Revolution." (MacDonald 2012)

Heidi MacDonald suggested that this decision was a way to soften the blow of the $3.99 price tag. It also presumably functions as a loss leader, encouraging purchasers of print comics to explore Marvel's digital offerings. Compared to Marvel and DC, print publishers and booksellers have been slower to adopt the model of print/digital bundling. In early 2013, Lauren Indvik suggested that Amazon was unlikely to start offering free digital copies of books purchased from its site, as it does with CDs, because it had no economic incentive to do so. Offering free digital copies of CDs was a way for Amazon to compete with Apple's iTunes for digital music sales, but in online book sales, Amazon had no one to compete with (n.p.).

Beyond thinking of print and digital comics as complementary in economic terms, however, we should think about how they can work together in a physical sense. How can comics be created in ways that straddle the print/digital divide? How can comics creators produce works that exist in both media at once?

One way to think about print/digital synergy in comics is to realize that the print and digital versions of a single comic need not simply be facsimiles of each other. Instead, the two versions can be formatted differently for different media, so that they offer dissimilar reading experiences. Comics produced in this way would offer a form of what Henry Jenkins calls *transmedia storytelling,* or "a process where integral elements of a fiction get dispersed systematically across multiple delivery channels for the purpose of creating a unified and coordinated entertainment experience" (n.p.). Readers would be encouraged to follow such a comic across two media simultaneously, because the print and digital versions would each offer reading experiences that the other didn't. This strategy, in which the print and digital versions of a comic are significantly different texts, has been adopted in a limited fashion by works such as Chris Ware's *Building Stories* and Jason Shiga's *Meanwhile.* Each of these comics exists in both print and digital form, and in each case, although the print and digital versions are self-sufficient works that can stand alone, they also benefit from being read together. What matters in the experience of reading these comics is the productive *difference* between their print and digital versions; thus, the print and digital versions of each text are not mutually exclusive but complementary, and they benefit from being read together. I begin by discussing *Building Stories,* a book (or booklike object) that is heavily committed to the medium of print and offers a pessimistic account of the digital future. However, a small but significant chunk of *Building Stories* was first published in digital format, and it leverages the unique properties of the iPad to offer a reading experience that differs significantly from that provided by the print version. *Meanwhile* offers a useful counterpoint to *Building Stories* because its iOS app version is conceptualized as a self-sufficient but significantly different artifact from the print version, and both are equally valid but different ways of accessing the text.

An even more radical possibility is to imagine a comic that combines print and digital modes of reading and offers a reading experience possible with neither medium on its own. Currently the most successful attempt to realize this strategy is not a comic but a book of concrete poetry, Amaranth Borsuk and Brad Bouse's *Between Page and Screen.* This book is sold in print format but is unreadable without the aid of a webcam. The comics industry is already starting to adopt this form of print/digital integration, which has become known as *augmented reality,* in a limited way, and, as I will suggest at the end of the chapter, comics are ideally positioned to offer a fully integrated blend of print and digital forms of reading.

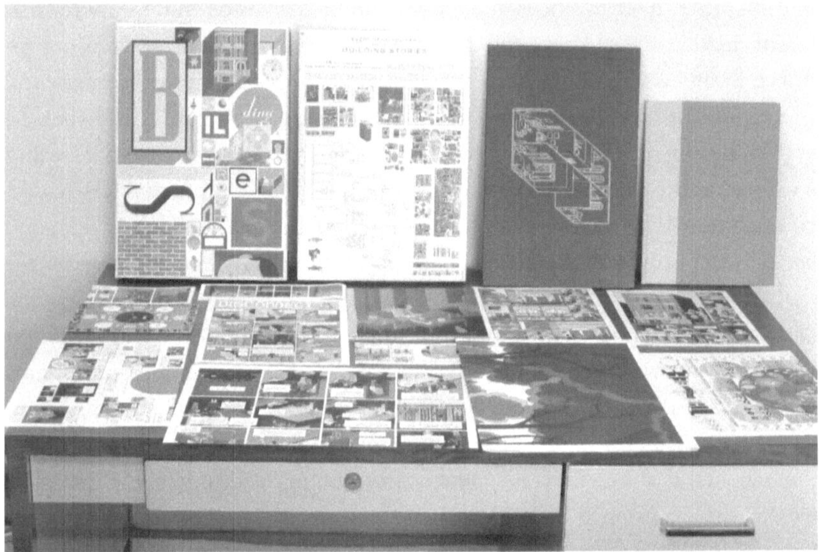

FIGURE 5.1. Everything included in a copy of *Building Stories.* Photo by author.

"AND IT HAD EVERYTHING IN IT": *BUILDING STORIES* AS A BOOK OF THE FUTURE[1]

Building Stories is a box containing fourteen printed comics of various sizes, ranging from tiny, vertically formatted tracts to a giant newspaper section (see figure 5.1). The fourteen comics, which may be read in any order, tell interconnected stories that take place in the Chicago area and mostly revolve around an unnamed woman with a prosthetic leg (whom I will call Protagonist). *Building Stories* was the most critically acclaimed graphic novel of 2012, winning four Eisner Awards and prompting a significant amount of critical commentary. Much of its interest comes from the way it interrogates the contemporary condition of the printed book. Rick Moody described *Building Stories* as "a very clever and moving statement about what a book is now" and as a deliberate rejection of the impoverished material parameters of the e-book. (I refer to *Building Stories* as a "book" under erasure; later I will deal with the question of whether it qualifies as a book at all.)

1. Material in this section was previously published as "And It Had *Everything* in It: *Building Stories,* Comics, and the Book of the Future," *Studies in the Novel,* vol. 47, no. 3 (2015): 420–47.

Most critics have seen *Building Stories* as the ultimate proof of the standard binary opposition between books and e-books. As a book that could only ever exist on paper, *Building Stories* seems like a conclusive demonstration that the printed book is far more materially rich than the digital book could ever be (though it also pushes the limits of the form of the book, to the point that it creates uncertainty as to whether it even is a book). It can therefore be read as a passionate plea for the survival of the printed book or, less charitably, as a monument to biblionecrophilia. *Building Stories* encourages this reading by depicting the digital and mobile devices that threaten to replace books as destructive of personal connection. Thus, I begin by suggesting that *Building Stories* seems to reject digitization in the strongest possible terms, both through its physical structure and through the claims it makes about media. However, I will then read *Building Stories* against the grain, suggesting that it depends crucially on the same digital technology that it critiques and that its use of the comics form helps to resolve this apparent contradiction. Thus, this chapter unpacks Hillary Chute and Patrick Jagoda's brief observation that "though *Building Stories* is virtually a manifesto for the book as a material object, it also promotes forms of decision making, spatial navigation, narrative architecture, and interactive play that are common to new media forms such as video games" (n.p.), showing how *Building Stories* exemplifies the power of comics to bridge gaps between print and digital culture.

When asked about his attitudes toward digital reading devices, Ware cited the tactile and material aspects of printed books as justification for their continued existence: "Books offer a sort of reassuring physical certainty for the ineffable uncertainties of life. . . . I think there are plenty of things that books can do that e-books can't" (Burchby n.p.). Elsewhere, he elaborated:

> Additionally, there's something already so weightless and ineffable about what writers and artists do that I think it almost needs the certainty of paper and print as a sort of poetic contradiction to make it work. I generally feel cheated and disappointed in any e-purchase I make for that very reason; in art school terms, the form and the content just seem too much the same. (Larimer n.p.)

For Ware, the physical form of the book serves to concretize the abstract object that constitutes the literary text. "Texts" are abstract, free-floating entities that can be instantiated in many ways; the e-book leaves these entities in their natural disembodied state, while the printed book gives these entities a local habitation and a name. *Building Stories* can most easily be read as embodying Ware's belief in the superiority of printed books over digital books and as lamenting the seemingly imminent death of the printed book. This reading is suggested both by *Building Stories*'s physical form and by the way it depicts questions of mediacy and materiality.

In the first place, *Building Stories* is a book that celebrates its own materiality and that could exist only as a physical book. The book's physical design is so striking that the reader cannot possibly be unaware of it, and the book clearly could not be replicated in digital form without radically changing the reading experience. As Peter Sattler observes:

> The most palpable effect of these various sizes is, well, that they remain *palpable.* The variable printing formats compel you to share a space with them: they refuse to disappear as you read them. They are propped stiffly before your gaze one moment and extend between your outstretched arms the next. Ware's multipage folio obscures your lap and flops around in an ungainly way, while his "Golden Book" chapter fits comfortably in your hands, but demands to be pulled close before it can be read. (n.p.)

Moreover, as Sattler implies, many of the sections are designed to resemble specific types of comics or illustrated texts, for example, Golden Books or Jack Chick tracts. Even before reading the sections, therefore, the reader unconsciously associates them with the types of comics they resemble. Furthermore, *you* stay with the book as much as it stays with you. Some of the sections are fragile enough that they quickly start to display evidence of the reader's handling. My copy of it in the large newspaper section (which I will refer to as "god . . . ," after its first word), has a hole in the spine of one page due to repeated page-turning (see figure 5.2). After I unfolded the board game section, I couldn't refold it properly. Moreover, readers are likely to remember *Building Stories* in tactile as well as visual or semiotic terms: "If you read my contribution to *The Comics of Chris Ware*—the final entry in that collection—you probably remember the essay as much by its position within the book as by its contents" (Sattler n.p.). In remembering *Building Stories,* I recall scenes not according to what they looked like, but according to which pamphlet they appeared in. This effect is exacerbated by the book's lack of page numbers or section titles. Because only some of the individual components have identifying names, it is difficult to identify which component one is talking about; it is much easier to simply *point* to or hold up the component one has in mind. This book wants to be shown, held, and seen, rather than talked about in its absence.

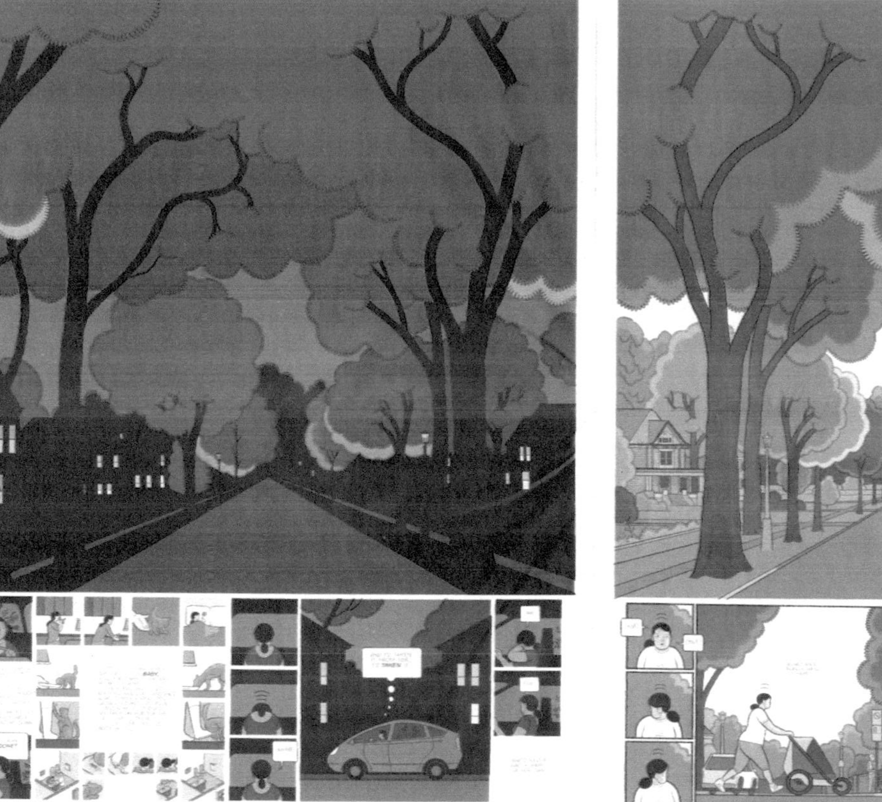

FIGURE 5.2. Evidence of physical damage incurred while reading my copy of *Building Stories*. Note the hole at the center of the two-page spread.

Building Stories is not only a beautiful artifact but also a highly inconvenient one. Its sheer size poses storage problems: in my previous apartment, my copy of *Building Stories* was too tall to fit on any of my bookshelves. I have so far declined to teach *Building Stories* partly because of the physical difficulty of carrying the book to class. I could ask my students to bring only certain sections of the book to class every day, not the entire box, but this violates the principle that the class should have access to the entire text under discussion. The book's size and complexity contribute to its $50 price tag, another reason why I hesitate to teach it. *Building Stories*'s format also makes it difficult to work with; when writing this section, almost every time I remembered a scene I wanted to discuss, I had to hunt through multiple different sections of the book in order to find it.

None of this is accidental. One of the most frequently cited advantages of e-books relative to printed books is their superior convenience. An e-reading device weighs far less than a printed book while storing far more data. Some advocates of the printed book have argued that its inconvenience is an advantage. In June 2013, when Stephen King announced that his novel *Joyland* would be available only in print, Esther Cepeda wrote that

> reading "Joyland" will be a minor inconvenience. . . . My choices will be to either haul myself out to a faraway bricks-and-mortar bookstore or wait for a mail shipment.
>
> I'll cope while letting King's latest novel transport me to the not-so-distant past when I used to be able to read for hours without the unwanted interruptions of email dings, Facebook alerts, Twitter mentions, calendar notifications, text messages, and my nearly pathological desire to share a beautifully crafted sentence or two with my social media networks. (n.p.)

Cepeda's argument is an example of what Edward Tenner calls "the prestige of inconvenience": "Just as luxury watches remain in demand while most people carry cellphones that give the time with virtually observatory-standard accuracy, the Web will never destroy older media because their technical difficulties and risks help create glamour and interest." (n.p.). Print books are valuable precisely by virtue of the qualities that make them inconvenient—their weight and size, their tactile materiality—because these qualities make the reading of a printed book a materially rich experience. *Building Stories* is the ultimate demonstration of this; through its inconvenience, it makes the reader aware that reading is a physical, embodied process.

Thus, *Building Stories* resists digitization; it could not be translated into an electronic version without radically altering its reading experience. An initial close reading of *Building Stories* suggests that its resistance to digitization is intentional—that it is intentionally Kindle-proof in Hallberg's sense. In *Building Stories,* digital technologies are destructive of traditional forms of embodied interaction, while printed books generate materially rich reading experiences and foster personal interconnections. This implies that *Building Stories* is a monument to biblionecrophilia, a work that pleads for the survival of the printed book and expresses anxiety over its disappearance.

As Georgiana Banita observes, "What will probably draw most attention in *Building Stories* is the alienating interaction of its protagonists with various kinds of electronic devices and gadgets" (2012 n.p.). Even in sections of *Building Stories* that take place early in the Internet era, digital technologies seem to be replacing more personal forms of interaction. For example, in the "I Just Want to Fall Asleep . . ." hardcover book, which takes place in the late 1990s or in early 2000, Protagonist, working at a flower store, observes that the ability to order digitally has lowered customers' inhibitions:

> With 1-800-FLOWERS (and especially with the new web orders) shamelessness seems to know no bounds, though . . . I guess people like the anonymity of the Internet, but doesn't it occur to them that *someone* is going to print out their message and put it in an envelope?[2]

Protagonist's customers don't care if she sees a message like "Best fuck ever!" because they don't have to interact with her personally. The obvious irony here is that the practice of gifting flowers is a cherished mode of embodied interaction. The gifting of flowers is a standard way to begin or commemorate a successful date or dinner party. Indeed, Protagonist believes flowers have feelings and can react to harsh treatment, and she therefore feels reluctant to sell flowers to people she dislikes. But the Internet has reduced this mode of embodied interaction to a faceless, anonymous exchange.

Again, later in the same section, Protagonist tries to Google her former boyfriend Lance but finds only other people who share his name. Instead of the connection she wants, Google links her with strangers, failing to

---

2. Because *Building Stories* doesn't include page numbers and the individual sections have no official titles, it is difficult to cite individual pages. In all quotations from *Building Stories,* emphasis and ellipsis are in the original unless indicated otherwise.

distinguish the person she is looking for from everyone else of the same name. Finally, in the "September 23, 2000" section, Protagonist's future husband, Phil, comments: "Oh, *God,* the *Internet* . . . don't get me started . . . before we know it we'll all be wearing giant computer helmets and having sex through *serial ports*. . . ." For Phil, the Internet is a disturbing specter because it represents a future where in-person interaction is no longer possible.

Elsewhere in *Building Stories* we find that this prediction has come true. The comic book pamphlet involving the couple living below Protagonist (which I unfortunately have to refer to as "Shit," from its first word) includes a scene taking place in Chicago in 2156. The natives of this future dystopia wear full-body suits and fishbowl helmets to protect themselves from heat and pollution, plus "XL-9000 Intercoupler" devices attached to their genitals, and use the computer displays in their helmets to send and receive requests for anonymous virtual sex. Here, in-person interaction has been replaced by digital pseudo-interaction. In sections that take place in the present, we see how this dystopian future will come into existence. The "Disconnect" section begins with Protagonist visiting a grocery store and thinking "Disconnect these people from their cell phones and I swear they'd all starve to death [. . .] I'm sorry, but I *relish* the time I get alone, even if it is just spent shopping. . . . I'm not going to waste it talking or 'texting'. . . ." The word *disconnect* here means the opposite of what it sounds like—Protagonist means that digital devices connect people when they prefer *not* to be connected, so in this context disconnection is a *good* thing, and the problem with digital devices is that they create a condition of permanent, intrusive connectedness. When using cell phones, people are connected to hundreds of faraway strangers but can't see what's in front of their faces.

Ware suggests that at the same time that digital technologies foster a spurious sense of connection with strangers, they also *dis*connect their users from those closest to them. On the third tier of the same page, Protagonist and Phil, now married with a child, are sitting across from each other, each working on a laptop (see figures 5.3 and 5.4). Despite being physically copresent, they are less connected to each other than to whomever they are talking with online. A nearly identical panel appears in "god. . . ." Here Phil seems distracted by whatever he is doing on his laptop: when Protagonist suggests setting up their friends Cary and Stephanie with each other, Phil replies dismissively. Digital pseudo-connection makes Phil uninterested in face-to-face, embodied connection, even with his wife.

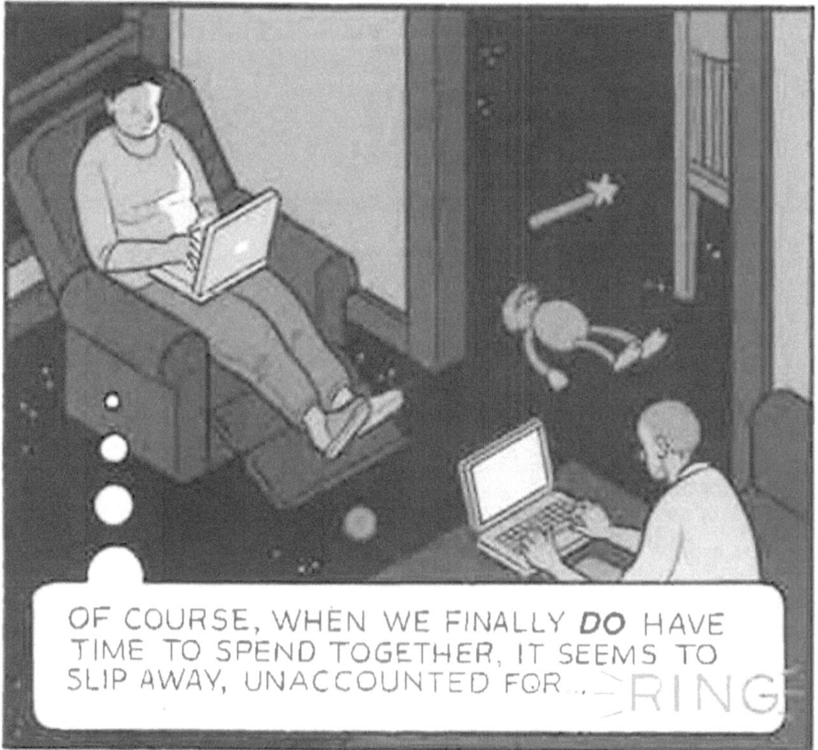

FIGURE 5.3. Detail from *Building Stories.*

Furthermore, Ware insists on the remoteness, lack of affect, and excessive speed of digital modes of communication, such as e-mail and text messaging. In "Disconnect," a panel in the shape of an iPhone depicts a message from Phil saying that he can't get home in time to take their daughter Lucy trick-or-treating. Protagonist angrily replies that in that case they will leave on a planned trip to her mother's house without him. Phil misses the angry undertones of her message, merely replying in typically clipped and unemotional style: "Roger. Will call in am. Be careful! Love, p." Here Ware illustrates another common critique of digital communication: its purely textual nature deprives it of the emotional nuance of face-to-face or even telephonic conversation. Similarly, in "god . . .," after Stephanie's suicide, Protagonist rereads her old e-mails to Stephanie and is shocked at their "quick, curt" tone, in contrast to the "lucidity," "wit," and "genuine insights" of Stephanie's e-mails to her. Initially, Protagonist had thought of these e-mails as "rambling, oppressive screeds, suffocating for their length

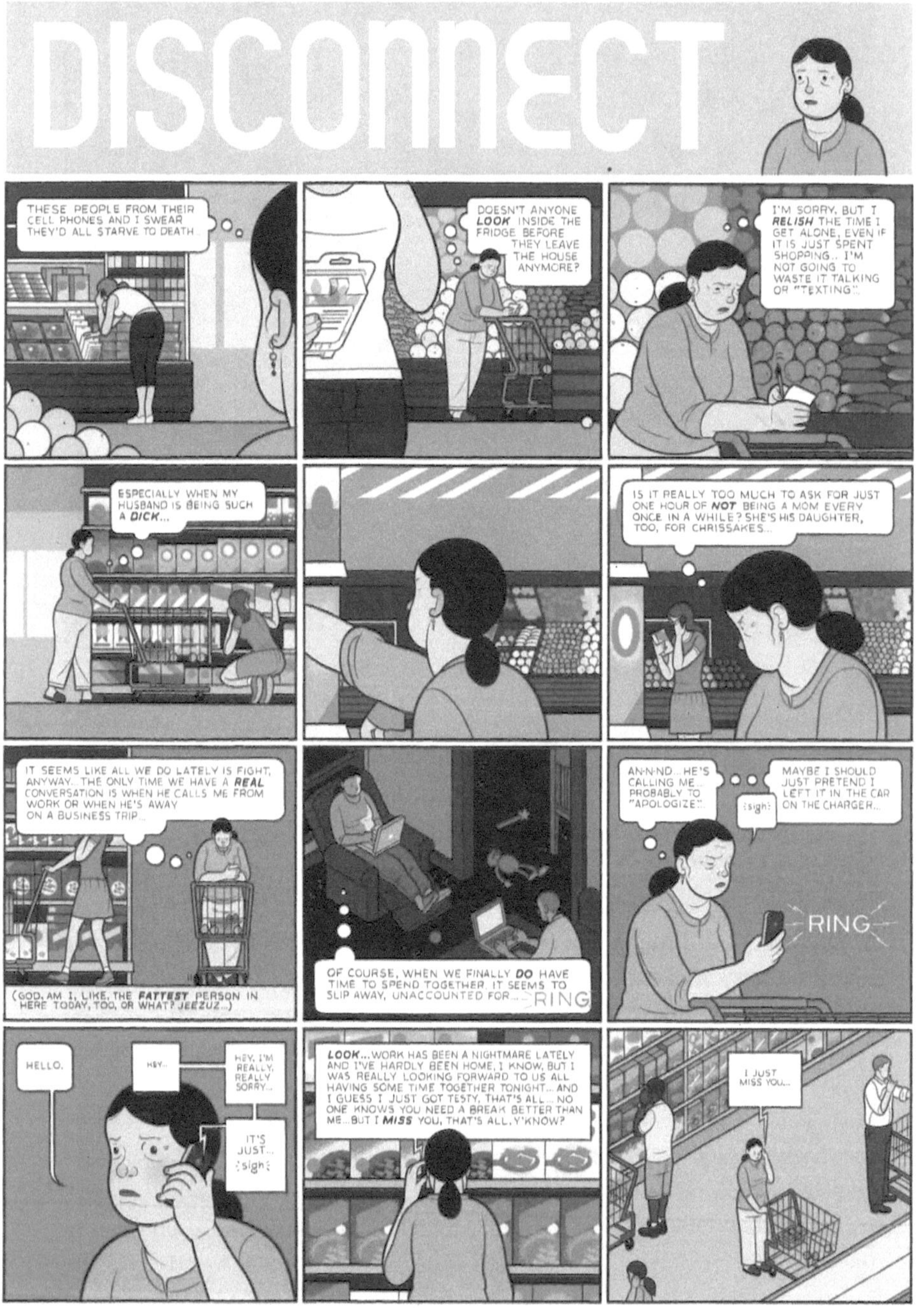

FIGURE 5.4. Original page from which figure 5.3 is taken. In deference to Chris Ware's wishes, I reproduce this page so that the panel can be seen in context.

and neediness." This is an example of the "too long; didn't read" phenomenon, in which Internet users are unwilling to expend the time and mental effort necessary to read long texts. On the next page, Protagonist discovers that Stephanie's parents have canceled her funeral by means of an "unctuous and patronizing" e-mail that "was basically a 'fuck you' to all of us who had tried to make up for *their* lack of warmth over the years." Adding insult to injury, Protagonist initially fails to see the e-mail because it ends up in her spam filter.

Even when digital communication leads to actual in-person connections and embodied interactions, it often seems to do so in an unsatisfying way. At the end of "Disconnect," Protagonist's ex-boyfriend Lance sends her an "(uncapitalized, unpunctuated)" e-mail inviting her to his theatrical performance. This leads to one of the few satisfying narrative resolutions in the book, as seeing Lance onstage allows Protagonist to get over her unrequited love for him. Yet when they meet in person afterwards, neither of them can think of anything to say, and Protagonist's final judgment of the experience is that it was "stupid."

Ware's critique of the Internet's pseudo-connective nature also extends to social media. When Protagonist suggests setting up Stephanie with Cary, Phil scornfully replies, "Why are you trying to play matchmaker, anyway? Isn't that what Facebook is for?" This implies that Facebook has replaced more personal ways of encountering romantic partners. Later in "god . . .," after Stephanie's suicide, Protagonist reads Stephanie's Facebook page, where her final posts, which received no comments, are followed by a succession of insincere-sounding memorial posts. These posts' authors ignored Stephanie while she was alive and only bothered to post memorials on her Facebook page because it required no effort. Though "a couple of friends actually posted vivid reminiscences which choked me up," this merely makes Protagonist feel ashamed of not being able to write her own memorial post. After the funeral is canceled, Protagonist has the idea of organizing an alternative funeral but discovers that Cary has already suggested this idea in a Facebook message posted at the exact moment that Protagonist had the idea. This leaves Protagonist feeling that Cary has usurped her right to organize the alternative funeral simply because he was quicker to post the idea to Facebook. Moreover, she knows precisely when Cary's message was posted because Facebook obsessively marks the timestamp of each post. This, along with Facebook's adoption of a format for user pages known as "Timeline," suggests that Facebook is all about time, but only in the sense of Walter Benjamin calls "homogeneous, empty time" (261). Facebook's time is a simple duration that proceeds at the same rate for anyone, whereas the reading of books offers a time experience that is teleological (defined in terms of progress through the book rather than abstract duration) and specific to the individual reader; the time of reading is what Wai Chee Dimock has called "deep time."[3] In summary, *Building Stories* presents Facebook as an excessively fast, superficial, insincere medium of communication, an inadequate substitute for embodied interaction.

In its depiction of digital communication, *Building Stories* participates in a widespread contemporary discourse that denigrates such communication as excessively quick, insincere, and superficial. Sherry Turkle, for example, argues: "Digital connections and the sociable robot may offer the illusion of companionship without the demands of friendship. Our networked life allows us to hide from each other, even as we are tethered to each other. We'd rather text than talk" (1). For Turkle, the mode of interpersonal connection enabled by digital communication is less genuine than that offered by embodied interaction. Some empirical research appears to support this generalized view of digital and social media. For example, a 2012 study found that "since Facebook users are far more likely to depict the happiest times of their lives through carefully curated photos rather than catalog depressing events, many users are more likely to believe that happiness is a constant in their friend's [*sic*] lives" (Flacy n.p.). This implies that Facebook encourages its users to portray themselves in a sanitized, falsely cheerful light, editing out the more negative aspects of their lives, which presumably would be more likely to emerge in face-to-face conversation.[4]

Digital skeptics often point to handwriting and print as models of preferable modes of communication that encourage individuality, depth of thought, and sincerity, in contrast to the groupthink, shallowness, and superficiality that they attribute to digital and social media:

> While . . . electronic media offer the considerable advantages of diversity and access, print culture affords irreplaceable forms of focused attention and contemplation that make complex communications and insights possible. To lose such intellectual capability—and the many sorts of human continuity it allows—would constitute a vast cultural impoverishment. (Gioia vii)

---

3. Mollie Dezern helped me develop the ideas in this paragraph.

4. In June 2014, the news broke that Facebook had collaborated on a controversial study in which users' news feeds were altered to display disproportionately positive or negative messages. This study suggests that the emotional climate of Facebook is not only artificial but also subject to deliberate manipulation.

Similarly, Nicholas Carr has argued on neuroscientific grounds that "deep reading" is necessary for developing depth of character. Moreover, for traditionalist critics, the physical cohesiveness and unity of the printed book, which is a single portable object distinguishable from other such objects, testifies to its author's unitary and distinct selfhood. As John Updike said in 2006, in a speech which Ware later cited approvingly:

> Books traditionally have edges: some are rough-cut, some are smooth-cut, and a few, at least at my extravagant publishing house, are even top-stained. In the electronic anthill, where are the edges? The book revolution, which, from the Renaissance on, taught men and women to cherish and cultivate their individuality, threatens to end in a sparkling cloud of snippets. (Updike n.p.)

For Updike, the edges of the book symbolize the edges of the unitary humanistic self of its author. In contrast, tools like Facebook promote "the digital flattening of expression into a global mush. . . . People are encouraged by the economics of free content, crowd dynamics, and lord aggregators to serve up fragments instead of considered whole expressions or arguments. The efforts of authors are appreciated in a manner that erases the boundaries between them" (Lanier 47). Moreover, the physical materiality of the printed book makes it useful as a means of fostering personal interconnections. Books, like flowers, must be exchanged hand to hand and therefore act as physical symbols of interpersonal interactions, whereas digital devices only foster a false sense of connection.

Building Stories participates in this discourse because it portrays chirographic and print media as facilitators of identity, idiosyncrasy, and selfhood. Handwriting and hand drawing in *Building Stories* are associated with self-expression and creativity. In the Golden Book volume, Protagonist draws a picture while waiting for the plumber (then scribbles over it in anger). In "god . . ." she symbolically abandons her dreams of being an artist by throwing away her old notebooks. In "Disconnect," Phil performs a rare act of kindness by letting Protagonist sleep in, leaving her a handwritten note explaining that he has already gotten Lucy ready for school, together with a note in Lucy's childish handwriting that reads "I love you Mommy!" Here, handwriting has connotations of creativity, authenticity, and (positive) childishness. Similarly, when books or bookstores appear in *Building Stories,* they often serve to facilitate interpersonal connection. When Protagonist suggests setting up Cary with Stephanie, an out-of-context panel depicts a flashback of Protagonist pulling a book off a bookshelf and telling Cary: "You aren't going to believe this." In "I Just Want to Fall Asleep . . . ," Protagonist encounters her former babysitting charge, Jeffrey, while browsing in a bookstore. These scenes support a reading of *Building Stories* as "biblionecrophilic" because they contrast the embodied interaction characteristic of the printed book with the disembodiment and depersonalization characteristic of digital media.

Building Stories's most significant scene involving books initially seems like another exercise in biblionecrophilia. However, a close reading of this scene reveals the ways in which *Building Stories* is not simply a lament for the death of the book; it also offers productive ways of thinking about the future of the book in the digital era. This scene is therefore the starting point for an alternative reading that views *Building Stories* as a prototype of the book of the future.

On the back cover of "Disconnect," Protagonist tells a now-adult Lucy about a dream in which she is "browsing . . . but not on the Internet, in one of those big chain bookstores that don't exist anymore. . . ." This gloomy prediction may have been based on the collapse of Borders in 2011 and seems even more prescient now, given the continuing uncertainty over the fate of Barnes & Noble. While browsing, Protagonist encounters a book she never knew existed—a type of serendipitous discovery that can happen much more easily in physical bookstores than on Amazon.com, and that therefore represents one of the major arguments for the continuing existence of brick-and-mortar bookstores. The book proves to be "*my* book [. . .] and it had *everything* in it . . . my diaries, the stories from my writing classes, even stuff I didn't know I'd written . . . everything I'd forgotten, abandoned or thrown out was there . . . everything . . . and you know, it wasn't so bad. In fact, it was kind of *good* . . . interesting. . . ." Although Lucy calls the dream "retarded," it represents the closest *Building Stories* comes to a narratively satisfying resolution. Protagonist's book, however, isn't a traditional codex book: it "wasn't really a *book,* either . . . it was in *pieces,* like, books falling apart out of a carton, maybe . . . but it was *beautiful* . . . it made *sense.* . . ." That is to say, her book is *Building Stories* itself.

Perhaps this suggests that in a world where digital culture has destroyed traditional print culture—including its major commercial and social space, the bookstore—the only type of book that "makes sense," that can still exist, is a book like *Building Stories.* To understand this claim, we must read *Buliding Stories* against the grain and realize that while it expresses deep nostalgia for the traditional printed book, it also productively combines print and digital organizational logics of materiality. *Building Stories* can bridge the print/digital divide because it employs the medium of comics, which, while firmly rooted in its print origins, also has deep affinities with digital and hypertextual forms of materiality. Thus, *Building Stories* suggests that the book of the twenty-first century may have less in common with the traditional print novel than with the graphic novel.

The first way in which *Building Stories* productively hybridizes print with the digital is that its physical form is shaped by digital production processes. *Building Stories* could never have existed in its present physical state in the absence of digital technology. An example of Chris Ware's emotional investment in nondigital forms of materiality is his commitment to doing artwork on paper: "I am very old-school—pencil, ink, and brush on Strathmore 500 Series Bristol board. Can't think any other way" (Larimer n.p.) Yet in the same interview, Ware admitted that "I do a small amount of editing once I scan it into the computer sometimes." Moreover, Ware's distinctive style of coloring would be impossible without digital technology. "Even a quarter of a century ago, the kind of color production essential to Ware's work would have been prohibitively expensive" because "digital front-end printing has introduced much higher levels of quality control for color matching and calibration as well as finely tuned registration" (Drucker 2008, 43–44). Elsewhere, Ware explains how computer coloring made his rich use of color possible:

> I really wanted to learn how to get or at least simulate the beautiful colors of the early newsprint comics. Of course, back in the early 20th century, the separations were acid-etched by artisans, sometimes individually for each metropolitan edition of each paper, and I was of course completely unable to come even close to this sort of subtlety with dot screens [. . .] But with the advent of computers and digital file preparation, printing is now more than ever able to recreate that intense color and I've been nothing but pleased for years now. (Irving n.p.)

Despite being nostalgic for a lost era of manual, "artisanal" coloring, Ware is satisfied with the digital tools that have rendered such handcraft obsolete. Finally, *Building Stories* itself was printed digitally.[5] "Digital technologies are now so thoroughly integrated with commercial printing processes that print is more properly considered a particular output form of electronic text than an entirely separate medium" (Hayles 2008, 5). This is only marginally less true of comics than printed books—even if the artwork for a given comic is drawn by hand, that artwork passes through a variety of

5. Chip Kidd confirmed this in an informal interview with me in May 2014.

stages of digitization before reaching readers. "Art boards used to be manually corrected, with layers for lettering and coloring. 'Today it all goes electronically as a digital file to the publisher'" (Rhoades 143, quoting Allison Gill). *Building Stories* was produced with the same digital production methods that are now the industry standard. In addition, the inside of the top of *Building Stories*'s box reads "Printed in China," indicating that the book is a product of the sort of network of globalized capitalism that is facilitated by digital technologies.

Building Stories thus owes its existence to digital production processes, even more so than a comparable prose novel: because its narrative is conveyed largely through images, it demands the most advanced technology for coloring and image reproduction. In this sense, *Building Stories* suggests that comics are ideally positioned to take advantages of the unique affordances of both print and digital technology.

Second, *Building Stories* uses comics to combine the affordances of print and digital technology through its use of a hypertextual mode of narrative organization. In both its physical structure and its mode of narration, *Building Stories* resembles a work of hypertext fiction. Thus, it applies a structural logic derived from electronic literature to the medium of print. This works because of the basic similarity between hypertext and comics, both of which depend crucially on fragmentation.

I have described *Building Stories* as a book under erasure, but *is* it a book at all? When I showed my copy to the students in my freshman composition class "The Future of the Book," they thought not. Earlier in the semester, based on Ulises Carrión's statement that "a book is a sequence of spaces" (1), I had defined a book as a collection of discrete writing surfaces physically attached to each other. For my students, *Building Stories* didn't meet this definition because its sections are physically independent and therefore lack the unity and cohesion that characterize the printed book. Furthermore, *Building Stories* doesn't follow a single "sequence of spaces." Its sections can be read in any order, and it doesn't privilege any of the possible reading orders over any of the others, through either authorial instructions or page numbering. Nor does it have a clear starting or ending point. When Philip Nel taught *Building Stories,* he arbitrarily had his students read the sections in the order in which they were packaged in the box. It would be equally valid to read the sections in order from largest to smallest or to generate a reading order randomly. All that gives *Building Stories* any sort of cohesion is the box, without which it would simply be a collection of fourteen loosely related but independent comics.

Because *Building Stories* can be read in any order, it follows a logic of organization and narrative structure that has more in common with hypertext than with the printed book. This is ironic insofar as hypertext literature was celebrated precisely because it freed literature from the material constraints of the codex book:

> Hypertext fragments, disperses, or atomizes text in two related ways. First, by removing the linearity of print, it frees the individual passages from one ordering principle—sequence—and threatens to transform the text into chaos. Second, hypertext destroys the notion of a fixed unitary text. (Landow 54)

For Landow, the notion of a book as a cohesive, singular, and textually stable entity was an artifact of print culture. In manuscript culture, all manuscripts were unique objects, and no two readers had the same reading experience (55). Hypertext turns reading back into a unique experience which differs between readers and even between reading sessions. Hypertext fictions like Michael Joyce's *Afternoon* and Shelley Jackson's *The Patchwork Girl* consist of many "lexias" (individual units of text), each of which is linked to many others.[6] Since only one path can be taken from each lexia at any given time, each hypertext offers many possible reading orders. Moreover, whereas the printed text typically offers a cohesive, unitary reading experience, hypertext fictions are collections of fragments, each clearly demarcated from the others:

> As a result of the frothy digital middle of the computer's structure, fragmentation and recombination are intrinsic to the medium. These textual strategies can of course also be used in print texts. . . . But unlike print, digital texts cannot escape fragmentation, which is deeper, more pervasive, and more extreme than with the alphanumeric characters of print. (Hayles 2000, para. 7)

A work like *The Patchwork Girl* emphasizes the affinity between the fragmentation of the text and that of the narrative. Its protagonist, a female Frankensteinian monster, is composed of fragments of various bodies, making hypertext appropriate for telling her story. "As the unified subject is thus broken apart and reassembled as a multiplicity, the work also high-

6. Terry Harpold has criticized Landow's use of Barthes's term *lexia* (Harpold 143–52).

lights the technologies that make the textual body itself a multiplicity" (para. 30). In such texts, fragmentation of the linear reading experience is a crucial means of creating meaning.

The fragmentation characteristic of early hypertext is also present in more recent forms of digital media. Contemporary social media have been both praised and blamed for fragmenting the book into a collection of fragmented texts, thus metaphorically fragmenting the singular humanist subject:

> Once a book has been integrated into the new expanded library by means of this linking, its text will no longer be separate from the text in other books. . . . Once digitized, books can be unraveled into single pages or be reduced further, into snippets of a page. These snippets will be remixed into reordered books and virtual bookshelves. . . . Indeed, some authors will begin to write books to be read as snippets or to be remixed as pages. (Kelly n.p.)

A literal example of this is Total Boox, an e-book app where instead of buying a whole book at once, readers pay for each page they read. Total Boox severs the link between individual pages and the substantial form of the book, shifting the emphasis from books as self-contained entities to individual pages.

However, claims that hypertext explodes the unity and sequentiality of the printed book must be modulated by the realization that the traditional codex book already encourages fragmentation and multilinearity. Rita Raley observes that hypertext has always "had the question of its ontological difference from analog text as one of its core themes" (para. 1). She cites texts ranging from the *I Ching* to Italo Calvino's novels as analog texts that prefigure hypertext (para. 3). Indeed, print novels may be *more* nonlinear than hypertexts:

> In a codex novel, you may turn to any page at any time, directly from any other point. In a hypertext such as *Victory Garden,* to get to a specific passage you must typically follow an arbitrary path involving other specific passages before you get what you want. In other words, hypertexts without free text search capabilities are more, not less, linear than the codex (Aarseth 63).

For instance, Michael Joyce's *Afternoon* uses "guard fields" which prevent the reader from accessing some lexias until others have been read.

Thus, hypertext can deprive the reader of the freedom to choose a reading sequence, one of the codex book's defining properties (the codex book's random-access nature was its major affordance relative to the scroll). Similarly, the structure of independent lexias with links between them is often seen as the defining property of hypertext. Yet this linking structure is also present in books that contain internal cross-references, like Bibles and encyclopedias.

This context enables us to appreciate one of the key ironies of *Building Stories*: it is more hypertextual than actual hypertext. *Building Stories* reimagines the codex book through the lens of hypertext. It takes the fragmentary, multilinear structure that hypertext borrowed from the codex book and feeds that structure back into the codex book, resulting in an artifact that combines properties of both. Hypertextual narrative and visual structures are common in Ware's earlier work:

> *Jimmy Corrigan* recalls the de-temporalized simultaneity of the rhizome-concept as articulated . . . by hypertext as a mode of sequential and parallel differentiation . . . In this system, any point may be connected to any other point. Ware's comics resemble this model of connectivity in the allusive form of its non-linear, boundary-less narrativity that lacks temporal finitude and closure. (Banita 2010, 182–83)

Building Stories, however, employs hypertextual structures to a degree unprecedented in Ware's earlier work (see figure 5.5). First, *Building Stories* is a collection of fragments that are united into a cohesive whole only by being encased in the same box. Earlier precedents for this sort of structure include Marc Saporta's *Composition No. 1* (1962) and B. S. Johnson's *The Unfortunates* (1969). Yet unlike these books, *Building Stories* is fragmentary at an additional level in that it is a comic rather than a prose novel. Fragmentation of the page is an essential element of comics. McCloud's famous definition ("juxtaposed pictorial images in deliberate sequence") emphasizes the independence as well as the copresence of the individual panels, and for McCloud, the gutter, the gap between panels, is as important as the panels themselves (1994, 9). Even compared to other comics, *Building Stories* employs particularly fragmented, noncohesive panel structures. Many pages, especially the large splash pages in the newspaper sections, consist of collages of discrete elements and can be read in multiple orders. Thus, *Building Stories* fragments the linear reading experience as effectively as any hypertext fiction, if not more so.

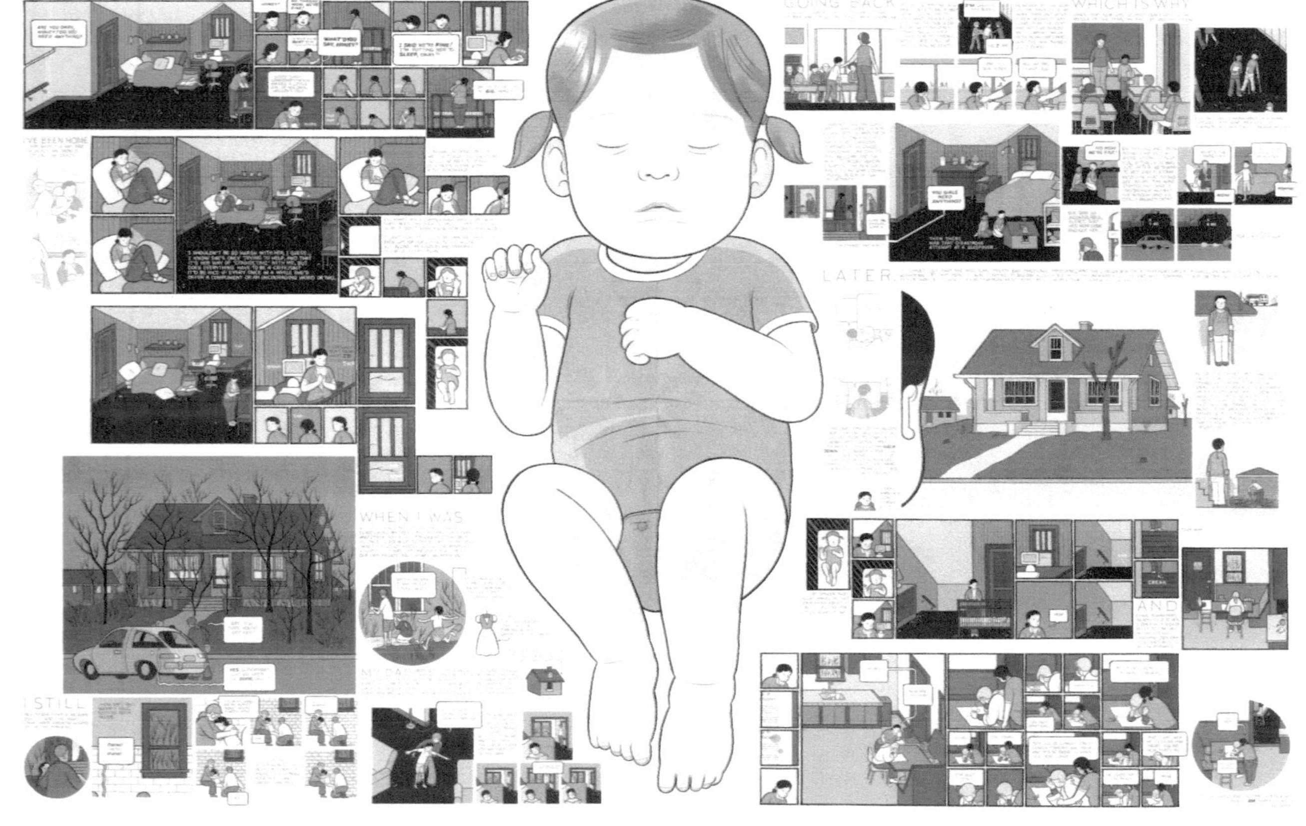

FIGURE 5.5. Two-page spread from *Building Stories*; an example of a page that demands a hypertextual mode of reading.

Yet as with hypertext, *Building Stories* is also about drawing connections between fragments. While *Building Stories* doesn't employ explicit hypertextual links, a major attraction of the process of rereading it is the spontaneous discovery of connections between sections. For example, in "September 23, 2000," Protagonist accidentally clogs her toilet by flushing a tampon. In "god . . . ," Phil tells Protagonist: "Look . . . asking you not to flush tampons down the toilet is *not* an attack on your character!" Ware leaves it up to the reader to notice the connection between these two tampon flushing scenes, but the unexpected discovery of connections like this is delightful. Moreover, the reader's understanding of this connection changes depending on which section is encountered first. If the reader reads "September 23, 2000" first, then the second instance of tampon-flushing, in "god . . . ," serves to show that Protagonist has not learned to give up this bad habit. If the reader encounters the sections in the reverse order, then the tampon-flushing incident in "September 23, 2000" explains how this bad habit originated. Similar internal links include Phil's prediction that "we'll all be wearing giant computer helmets and having sex through serial ports," which later literally comes true; or Lucy's question, "Mama, do *bee* families have children just like people families do?" in "god . . . ," which is answered affirmatively in "Branford, the Best Bee in the World"; or the two nearly identical panels showing Protagonist and Phil working on their laptops (see figure 5.3). An annotated edition of *Building Stories* might use marginal symbols to indicate these and other cross-references. Even the references to printed books in *Building Stories* are spread throughout various sections rather than appearing in one place; thus, even when *Building Stories* praises the unity and cohesion of the printed book, it does so in a disunited, noncohesive way. One of the major tasks the reader performs in reading *Building Stories* is to notice connections between sections and combine them into a cohesive map or web of the narrative. The book's ambiguous title gestures to this: if *building* is an adjective, the title means "stories of buildings," but if *building* is a verb, the title names the activity of constructing stories, which both the reader and the characters engage in.

Such nonlinear connection-building is a central narrative logic of comics. For Thierry Groensteen, "Comics is not only an art of fragments, of scattering, of distribution; it is also an art of conjunction, of repetition, of linking together" (22). *Arthrology* is Groensteen's name for "the way panels . . . [are] linked in series (continuous or discontinuous) through non-narrative correspondences, be it iconic or other means." Arthrology both links individual sequences of panels together (restricted arthrology) and also creates larger networks that extend across multiple pages or an entire work (general arthrology). In *Building Stories,* Ware's use of arthrology allows the reader to draw connections between images and texts appearing in disparate parts of the same pamphlet or in different pamphlets.

Thus, *Building Stories*'s multilinear and fragmented structure means that it activates a mode of reading that, while derived originally from the codex book, is now more commonly associated with digital texts. As Banita notes, there is a basic irony here given Ware's disdain for digital strategies of reading: "It is thus paradoxical that Ware's work should be influenced by the very technologies he set out to denounce through his insistence on the deceleration of perception" (2010, 183). For Banita, this paradox is resolved by Ware's emphasis on materiality: "What sets his work apart from digital design, however, is the intractable materiality of the medium as an object [that] can be seen, held, toyed with, and finally collected." However, if "the intractable materiality of the medium" means the close connection between the printed book and the embodied self, then *Building Stories* questions this connection. If the book is a surrogate for the author's body, then this suggests that embodiment itself is technologically mediated (recalling Bernard Stiegler's suggestion that technology and the human evolve in tandem). Indeed, *Building Stories* often gestures to the technologically mediated nature of human embodiment. In "I Just Want to Fall Asleep . . . ," Protagonist muses:

> I've heard it all, thousands of times. . . . "Look at her leg" . . . "Do you think her leg is fake?" . . . "That's not *really* her leg" [. . . .] What do they really *mean,* anyway? "My leg" . . . of *course* it's mine . . . just the same way those were "her" shoes or "her" purse [. . .].[7]

Protagonist asserts that her prosthetic left leg is just as much "hers" as her right leg. She has had six different prosthetic legs, since she needs a new one every time her body changes significantly, but she suggests that this is only an accelerated version of the body's normal processes: "And how many years is it before your cells completely replace themselves, anyway? Seven or something like that? So I guess I've had *ten* legs now, if you count all of those. . . ." This version of the Ship of Theseus paradox suggests that the link between selfhood and embodiment is not obvious—that the body itself is in some sense a prosthetic attachment to the self. And if the body has such a

7. I have a friend who used to show people what he called his "grandmother's skull"—which, it turned out, was not the skull *of* his grandmother but a human skull that had *belonged* to his grandmother.

fraught relationship to selfhood, then the relationship between the self and the technology of the printed book must be even more contested.

A better way out of the paradox Banita detects is to suggest that *Building Stories* is a hybrid print-digital text, a printed book which couldn't have existed without the influence of digitization, and that it resolves the apparent contradiction between digital and print through its use of comics. As an art that developed from print but employs logics of fragmentation and linking often associated with digital media, comics combines the continuity of analog media with the discreteness of digital media. This is another way in which *Building Stories* suggests the potential of comics for imagining a book of the future that would be both printed and digital at once.

Building Stories, however, is already such a book in a literal sense, in that part of it exists in separate digital and print forms. A small but vitally important section of *Building Stories* is a born-digital text, having been published for the iPad before reappearing in print form. This section of *Building Stories* takes on added significance when read in both print and digital versions at once; it is a liminal text whose true significance rests neither in its print form nor in its digital form but rather in the space between the two. Thus, it represents a prototype of future texts that might depend on print/digital synergy.

The last seven pages of "Shit," which focuses on the woman who lives below Protagonist, were originally published as "Touch Sensitive," a comic created for the *McSweeney*'s iPad app. Because the two principal characters in this section have no names, I will call them Wife and Husband. The "Touch Sensitive" section is principally about the deterioration of their marriage, which is indicated by the fact that Husband never touches Wife affectionately anymore. In an interview, Ware explained how "Touch Sensitive" "tried to use touch-sensitivity as a poetic metaphor for how we manipulate our memories and move things around in our minds, about how the act of touching in a relationship gradually goes from one of tenderness and affection to one of anger and dominance" (Irving n.p.). Accordingly, in "Touch Sensitive," touch is an event that is perpetually deferred. Satisfying experiences of touch only happen unexpectedly and always involve the wrong people. The story begins with Wife wondering:

> How long has it been since he touched me in a way that didn't betray the obvious repulsion he feels, anyway? . . . I mean, if all we are is bundles of energy . . . what *is* a 'hug,' anyway? And how can we ever *really* touch each other?

When Wife is sexually and emotionally aroused by a touch, it makes her ashamed because it comes from a man other than her husband. In the 2156 scene, this impossibility of satisfying touch has become a universal condition. The characters in this sequence cannot make physical contact because of ubiquitous pollution, so they compensate, probably inadequately, by engaging in constant virtual sex. On the last page, Husband's desire to reestablish contact with Wife is again frustrated as she refuses to take his phone call. "Touch Sensitive" is ultimately about how the longing for satisfying, unmediated touch is never fulfilled.

The iPad version of "Touch Sensitive" actually forces the reader to enact this pessimistic view of touch, because it requires tactile interaction in order to be read. Swiping from right to left advances the story by adding or modifying panels. Some panels also feature animation and other effects not included in the print version; for example, when Wife thinks about another man, swiping the screen makes her face and groin turn red. In this format, "Touch Sensitive" enacts the same sort of illusory touch-without-touch that the 2156 sequence critiques. The reader's touch makes events happen but gives the reader no tactile feedback; the screen offers a completely smooth surface, and the player can't feel the texture of the buildings, the characters' skin or clothing, or anything else. "Touch Sensitive" frames the iPad as a precursor to the XL-9000 Intercoupler, a device that offers the illusion of a tactile relation without any genuine skin-to-skin contact. This reading recalls David Parisi's argument that the Nintendo DS handheld video game system, which features a touch screen, offers an impoverished model of touch because it provides no tactile feedback:

> The promise to touch the game is never fulfilled—the finger never reaches through the screen to touch what is on the other side. . . . Rather than putting us "in touch" with the world, where touch involves a process of mutual exchange between perceiver and perceived, the DS advances a model of touch absent of feeling in which the perceiver is merely a manipulator, a controller. (319)

This critique also applies to the iPad, and "Touch Sensitive" thus critiques the very technology with which it was created, pointing out the inability of digital devices to permit tactile interaction.

The first time I read it, the iPad version of "Touch Sensitive" even offered a literal case in which touch failed to enable complete satisfaction. The 2156 sequence seemingly ends with a panel in which an anonymous female character says, "You just don't understand *anything*, do you?" The previous panel depicts a pair of subway doors with a "Loading" icon in front of them. I initially thought the "Loading" icon was a purely cosmetic detail. However, in a conference paper, Paddy Johnston pointed out that if the reader waits a few seconds, the "Loading" icon changes to a "Ready" icon (see figure 5.6). Touching this icon brings up a sequence that appears at the end of the print version of "Touch Sensitive" but is otherwise absent from the digital version. In this scene Husband, regretting his boorish behavior, runs to catch the subway while trying to call Wife on his phone. Failing to do either, he collapses in exhaustion, saying, "I'm such an idiot." As Johnston observes, this added sequence "changes the tone of the whole comic completely," suggesting that there still was a possibility of genuine contact between Husband and Wife, even if that possibility is now gone. Because I missed this scene (as Johnston also initially did), I thought "Touch Sensitive" ended less hopefully than it in fact did. On learning of the existence of this scene, I felt that my initial encounter with the text was incomplete—that I didn't achieve the sort of connection with the text that I was supposed to. Thus, "Touch Sensitive" is about the unsatisfying, incomplete nature of tactile experiences. It analogizes the excessively slick, smooth, nonreciprocal tactile interactions that the iPad provides and the unsatisfying, disturbing tactile contacts that Wife experiences.

However, "Touch Sensitive" also suggests that unsatisfying, unidirectional tactile experiences are endemic to print as well as digital media and that comics are a clear demonstration of this. A major component of the reading experience of comics is the reader's awareness of the trace of the artist's hand. The reader of a comic is continually aware that the text she is reading originated in the artist's act of inscription. I suggest, however, that the touch of the *reader*'s hand is an important factor in the comics reading experience. "Reading is an activity involving and requiring *manual dexterity*—that is, skilful handling by our fingers and hands. . . . Haptic perception is of vital importance to reading, and should be duly acknowledged" (Mangen 405). In comics this is especially true: the reader's hands are constantly active, flipping pages and repositioning the book for better light. Moreover, the graphic surface of the page is more important and visually interesting in comics than in all but the most visually experimental works of fiction, and this implies that the reader's physical contact with that graphic surface is also far more important. (This discussion should be qualified by my earlier comments on haptic visuality.)

In particular, the surface the reader touches is a surface that bears the imprint of the artist's hand, though that imprint is filtered through a variety of medial layers. When I read Jack Kirby's comics, for instance, there

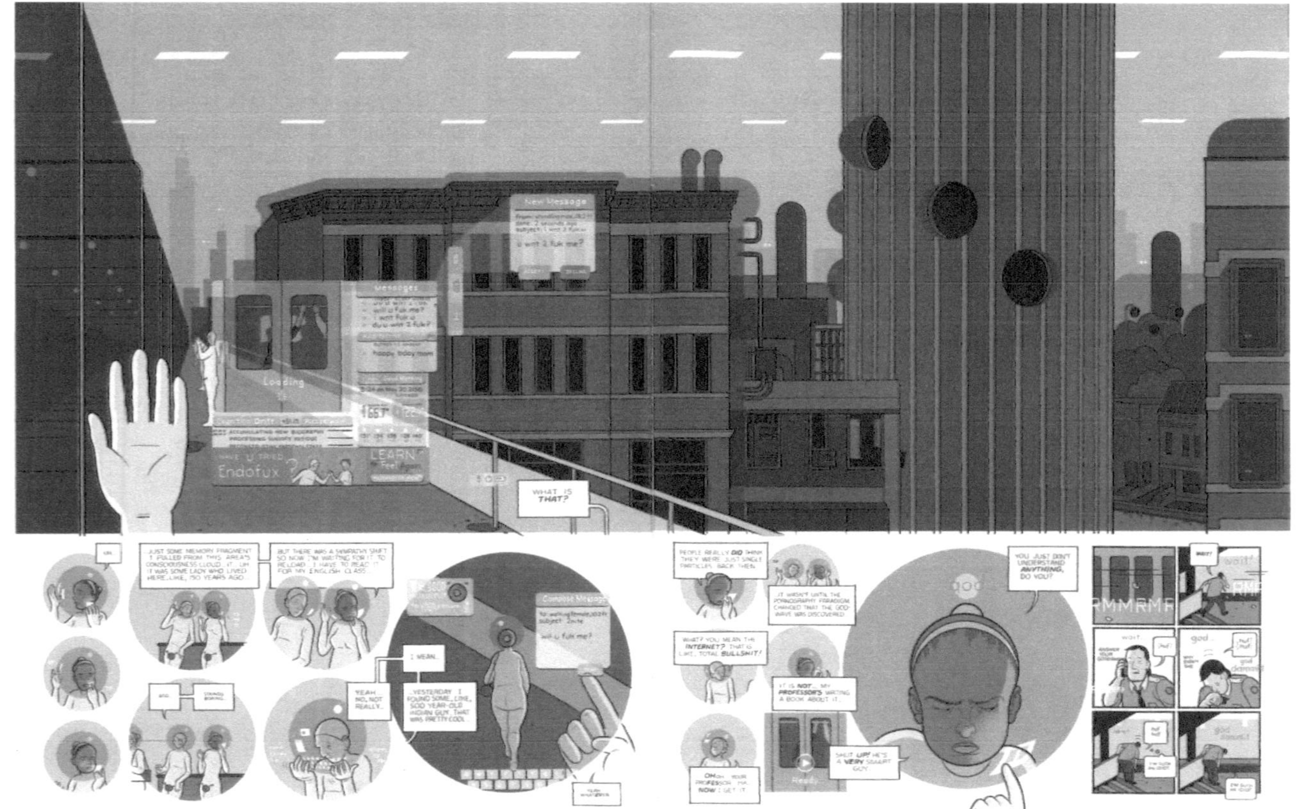

FIGURE 5.6. The 2156 sequence from *Building Stories.* Note the "Ready" message at the bottom, just to the right of the centerfold. In the digital version, this image initially says "Loading" instead of "Ready."

is a certain phantasmal sense in which I am *touching his hand.* This contact between reader and author is ghostly or symbolic rather than real, considering all the layers of mediation that intervene between the artist's and the reader's hand, but this makes it still more poignant—Kirby died before I ever met him, so reading his comics is as close as I will ever get to shaking his hand. This notion of reading as tactile contact is not unique to comics. As Whitman wrote (and as previously quoted in chapter 1), "Camerado, this is no book / Who touches this, touches a man. / (Is it night? Are we here alone?)" (382). But in comics, this sense of mutual contact is intensified by the indexical relationship between the artwork of the comic and its artist's body. The printed text of Whitman's book bears no visual resemblance to Whitman's handwritten manuscript, so what the reader touches is not a direct trace of Whitman's body. Conversely, because *Building Stories* bears the visual trace of Chris Ware's drawing hand, it seems to offer the reader a more genuine opportunity to make contact with its author's body.

Yet in comics the touch always stops at the surface of the page. The reader cannot reach *through* the page to touch the artist's hand; the reader touches the surface of the page, not its depth. Therefore, touch in comics is purely one-directional, offering only an illusion of reciprocity. To this extent, print comics have no significant advantage over digital comics in terms of tactile richness. Although the pages of a print comic offer more tactile richness than the screen of a digital device, neither print nor digital comics allow any tactile interaction between reader and author. Indeed, "Touch Sensitive" demonstrates that digital comics have one significant advantage over print comics in tactile terms: in digital comics, touch can produce concrete results. Touch in print comics is inert: nothing happens on the surface of the page in response to the reader's touch. In "Touch Sensitive," however, touch causes panels to appear and vanish, as well as producing changes in existing panels. "Touch Sensitive" turns touch into a way of shaping and producing the comic, rather than just a way of accessing a static text. Indeed, touch even permits the reader to alter the outcome of the story. If we reconsider the aforementioned six-panel sequence that appears only if the reader touches the "Play" icon, we can interpret it more optimistically than I did above: it proves that the outcome of "Touch Sensitive" depends on the reader's actions. The reader has the ability to change the ending of the story by deciding what to touch and what not to touch.

Thus, the insubstantiality and immateriality of the digital version of "Touch Sensitive" is balanced by its superior tactile richness. Ware was dissatisfied with "Touch Sensitive" because it felt immaterial to him:

> I wrote the strip about how touching goes from affection to aggression in a lot of relationships. I thought, well, I'm going to be using something, a device, that is touch sensitive. . . . It came out right, but when the final thing was done it just felt so insubstantial. It's like you're buying compressed gas or something. It just doesn't feel, really honestly it doesn't.
>
> I much prefer a tangible physical thing. There's something about the ideas and thoughts and feelings and uncertainties that go into books that demand a certain opposite and opposing structure to contain them. It's almost like an aesthetic necessity that the books have, they have to confine and protect these ineffable things in a way. (Reid n.p.)

Ware is correct that "Touch Sensitive" lacks the (literal) weight and presence of *Building Stories.* Reading the digital version of "Touch Sensitive," the reader lacks the sense of holding a unique physical artifact with a distinctive look and feel. However, "Touch Sensitive" compensates by empowering the reader's touch in a way that printed books cannot.

What this shows us is that neither the print nor the digital version of "Touch Sensitive" is the genuine, authentic version. To fully comprehend what this text says about touch, we need to examine both the print and digital versions and to observe the productive difference between the two. The true meaning of "Touch Sensitive" emerges only when we realize how the tactile experiences provided by the digital version are in some ways superior and in other ways inferior to those provided by the print version. Thus, instead of seeing the digital version of "Touch Sensitive" as a failed experiment, as Ware does, we should understand it as a text with its own form of materiality. Neither the print nor the digital version of the "Touch Sensitive" section is the primary, authentic version. Both are components of a single hybrid print-digital text, a text whose true identity resides in the space between print and digital versions. To this extent, the "Touch Sensitive" section of *Building Stories* may be read as a prototype of the book of the future, because it combines print and digital codes of materiality in order to create effects that are reducible to neither on its own—and it achieves this effect because it employs the art form of comics, which, despite its origins in print, is surprisingly adaptable to the digital context.

Admittedly, to read "Touch Sensitive" in this way is to read it against the grain. Ware's own published interviews reveal that he does in fact view it as a failed experiment and that for him the printed version does take priority over the digital version. Moreover, there are various technical reasons why "Touch Sensitive" is of limited usefulness as a prototype of the hybrid print-digital book. Its print version, as discussed above, is highly inaccessible and difficult to acquire. The same is true of the digital version, which is exclusively available for the iPad.[8] Only a limited number of readers, therefore, will have the ability to read either version of the text at all, and only an even more limited number will be able to compare the two. Furthermore, "Touch Sensitive" is only a small fragment of a larger work, and it therefore offers limited guidance as to how to create an entire comic that hybridizes print and the digital. For a better example of how this might work, we turn to my second case study: Jason Shiga's *Meanwhile.*

CHOOSE YOUR OWN MATERIAL RHETORIC: *MEANWHILE* AS HYBRID PRINT-DIGITAL TEXT[9]

Another possible model for how comics can straddle the print-digital divide is offered by Jason Shiga's *Meanwhile.* This comic was originally published in print form and was later adapted into an iOS app, which contains the same visual and textual content as the print version but was specifically redesigned to be readable (or playable) on the iPhone or iPod, and thus offers a radically different reading experience relative to the print version. As discussed earlier in the book, when print comics are adapted for digital reading devices, the digital version is usually just a scan of the print version. This approach, however, was unworkable in the case of *Meanwhile* because of its extreme dependence on the specific affordances of print, and adapting the book into an iOS app demanded radically reimagining it. Thus, *Meanwhile* is not simply a printed comic that has been adapted from one medium to another; it is a transmedia artifact, a single text or textual experience that exists in multiple media forms at once. *Meanwhile* suggests a model in which texts can be developed separately for print and digital interfaces, with each version of the text taking advantage of the unique capabilities of its medium.

Jason Shiga's comics are noted, in the first place, for their use of gamelike, ludic, and mathematical elements. Born in Oakland, Shiga received an undergraduate degree in pure mathematics from the University of California at Berkeley, giving him a disciplinary background that is perhaps unique among current cartoonists. His works often focus on problem solving through logical deduction. For example, in his 2002 book *Fleep,* the pro-

8. Since I have a Kindle instead, I was able to read "Touch Sensitive" only by borrowing a friend's iPad.

9. A radically different version of this section is currently under review as a journal article.

tagonist, Jimmy Yee, is trapped in a phone booth surrounded by concrete and is also suffering from amnesia. Purely through logical reasoning he figures out where he is, who he is, how he got there, and what to do next. Shiga's latest work, *Demon,* features a protagonist of the same name who uses logic to work out the implications and affordances of his power to possess the closest body when he dies.[10]

In the second place, Shiga has a longstanding interest in the materiality of the book and in unusual publishing formats. Shiga got his start in the industry by publishing minicomics, that is, self-published, do-it-yourself comics that are printed by hand, usually at copy shops, and distributed at conventions or at local comic book stores. Making minicomics is a profoundly physical experience; it requires the author to photocopy, staple, and assemble each comic by hand and to personally distribute each comic to local stores or to individual readers. Shiga's experience with this physically demanding medium seems to have given him the desire to experiment with the physical form of the comic. His minicomics include *The Last Supper,* an origami comic where the direction in which you unfold it determines the progression of the story, and *Hello World,* which is cut into two horizontal layers, an upper layer that tells the story and a lower layer that keeps track of the items the protagonist is carrying. More recently, Shiga returned to self-publishing when he was unable to publish *Demon* otherwise. Due to its extremely lurid content, his agent advised him against submitting it to a publisher, and his printer refused to print it due to the "demographic and age" of their employees (Shiga 2014). Therefore, Shiga published *Demon* simultaneously as a webcomic and as a series of "booklets which I made myself, by buying a 500lb risograph duplicator, driving it down from Sacramento in my wife's Rav4, getting completely covered in ink and odd bruises every month, and then collating and stapling every single one of them by hand!" (Shiga 2014).[11]

---

10. All of Shiga's recent works feature a protagonist named Jimmy Yee, and all the Jimmy Yees look identical. However, they can't all be the same character because at least one of them is killed during the book in which he appears.

11. Ironically, Shiga funded this process through Patreon, making *Demon* an example of positive synergy between digital and print methods of production and distribution. Moreover, *Demon* was so successful in minicomic and webcomic form that it drew attention from multiple publishers, and in August 2015, Shiga announced that First Second had agreed to publish *Demon* as a series of four paperback volumes. This makes *Demon* another example of how comics can proceed from webcomic to print form, as discussed in chapter 4.

Meanwhile, Shiga's best-known graphic novel, seamlessly combines his interest in puzzles and in materiality.[12] *Meanwhile* first appeared in as a self-published, black-and-white comic in 2001 and was reprinted in a color hardcover edition in 2010, earning it a much wider audience. *Meanwhile* is a self-described Choose Your Own Adventure comic in which the reader is invited to make decisions on behalf of the protagonist. It presents a branching narrative about a boy, Jimmy, who has to choose whether to order vanilla or chocolate ice cream. The former decision ends the story at once; the latter decision leads to a further set of increasingly complicated choices, which the reader must negotiate successfully in order to reach a satisfactory (though depressing) conclusion to the narrative.

Meanwhile is a deliberate homage to the gamebook genre, which Shiga grew up reading. Demian Katz has defined the gamebook as "any book in which the reader participates in the story by making choices which affect the course of the narrative." Typically, the gamebook is a printed book containing a second-person narrative in which the reader is the protagonist, and it consists of numbered pages or sections, each of which ends by asking the reader to make a choice. The reader expresses this choice by choosing among two or more sections to read next. A further distinction can be made between gamebooks like the classic *Choose Your Own Adventure* series (1979–98), which contain no gamelike elements other than asking the reader to make choices, and gamebooks like Steve Jackson's *Fighting Fantasy* series, which include detailed rulesets that govern elements such as combat, making them similar to tabletop role-playing games (RPGs).[13] For example, Joe Dever's *Lone Wolf* books, which I grew up with, include combat sequences that are simulated by choosing random numbers from a table at the end of each book. The former type of gamebook often features multiple outcomes, both successful and unsuccessful, while the latter type typically includes just one successful outcome, with all other outcomes culminating in the player's death.

The gamebook boom of the late twentieth century began with the *Choose Your Own Adventure* series, created by Edward Packard in the early 1970s and published by Bantam Books from 1979 to 1998. (I will use the abbreviation CYOA, without italics, to refer to the gamebook format in gen-

12. Shiga has also produced works that fall into neither category and are more concerned with Asian American identity, including the Xeric Grant–winning *Double Happiness* (1999) and *Empire State* (2011).

13. Katz further subdivides this second category into gamebooks that use the rules of an existing role-playing game, for example, *Tunnels and Trolls,* and gamebooks that come with their own set of rules, for example, *Fighting Fantasy.*

eral.) However, the notion of the gamebook goes back much earlier. Borges's "The Garden of Forking Paths" (1941) may be seen as a manifesto for the genre, and Julio Cortázar's *Hopscotch* (1963) and Raymond Queneau's "Un conte à votre façon" (1967) are experimental literary texts that prefigure many features of the gamebook genre. Moreover, the gamebook has clear affinities with other genres such as hypertext fiction, text adventure games, and modern video games. However, the rise of digital equivalents to CYOA books contributed to the collapse of the genre in the late 1990s. Between 1995 and 1998, the *Choose Your Own Adventure, Fighting Fantasy,* and *Lone Wolf* series all ceased publication. According to Joe Dever, this "was mainly due to the inexorable rise of console gaming. . . . Penguin were the first to take fright at a drop off in sales and decided to axe the Fighting Fantasy series. Other publishers took note and chose to follow their lead" (personal communication).[14] The disappearance of the gamebook genre was an early example of how digital media have supposedly begun to render the medium of the printed book obsolete.

Before the publication of *Meanwhile,* attempts to extend the gamebook genre to comics were very rare. In our interview, the only pre-*Meanwhile* example that Jason Shiga mentioned was Dan Slott and Mike Kazaleh's story "Masters of Time and Space" from Marvel's *Ren & Stimpy Show Special* #3 (1994). Two examples that postdate *Meanwhile* are "The Many Lives of Lizzie Hexam" by Mike Carey, Peter Gross, and Ryan Kelly (*The Unwritten* #17, 2010) and *Adventure Time* #10 by Ryan North, Shelli Paroline, and Braden Lamb (2012).[15] CYOA comics have also been attempted in digital form; examples include Scott McCloud's webcomic *Choose Your Own Carl* (1998–2001), an expansion of a short strip published in his earlier *Understanding Comics,* and DC's *Batman: Arkham Origins* iPad comic (2013).

Of the comics mentioned, *The Ren & Stimpy Special* #3 and *Unwritten* #17 are simply CYOA stories that use pictures instead of words. Like classic gamebooks, they consist of numbered sections, each of which ends with an instruction to choose which section to read next. The only difference is that each section consists of one or more comics pages rather than a passage of text. Neither work attempts to push the boundaries of the gamebook genre

14. Quoted with permission. I'm grateful to Mr. Dever, who unfortunately passed away while this book was in preparation, for his assistance.

15. I thank Jarod Roselló and Seth Johnson for some of these references. Another comic intended to be read in a nonlinear order is Walt Simonson's *Fantastic Four* #352, though it doesn't include any choices. Gamebook comics have also been published in France, for example, Makaka Editions's *La BD dont vous êtes le héros* ("The Comic Where You Are the Hero").

by including features possible only in a comic. The other works listed here go somewhat further in that direction, but *Meanwhile* is unique in that it uses comics to radically rethink the moribund gamebook genre.

Shiga read *Choose Your Own Adventure* books as a child but became interested in Steve Jackson's *Fighting Fantasy* books at the age of twelve or thirteen, and the latter were the primary influence on *Meanwhile* (personal communication). Unlike the *Fighting Fantasy* books, *Meanwhile* does not include an RPG-like ruleset or an element of random chance. However, it does contain gamelike elements insofar as completing the book successfully requires an element of strategy. At the beginning of the story, Jimmy, the player character, meets a mad scientist who allows Jimmy to play with his three inventions: a doomsday device that can destroy the world, a time machine that can send the user back in time, and a device called the SQUID that allows the user to relive the memories of another person. The remainder of *Meanwhile* is a giant puzzle that requires using these devices in tandem with each other to reach the one ending that provides a satisfying resolution to the narrative (though this ending is not particularly happy) and that reveals the truth about Jimmy, the Professor, and their world.

Initially, both the time machine and the SQUID have a ten-minute limit: the time machine can only take Jimmy back in time ten minutes (and it takes ten minutes to warm up after being used), and the SQUID can only recover ten minutes worth of memories. However, both devices have ten-minute access codes that remove the ten-minute restriction, and to find these access codes, the player needs to have Jimmy use the two devices in combination. If Jimmy uses the time machine to go back ten minutes and *then* uses the SQUID on the professor, the player gets access to the professor's memories starting *twenty* minutes ago, and these memories include the access code to the time machine. Similar strategic decisions are necessary in order to find the access code to the SQUID. Thus, to complete *Meanwhile* successfully, the player must use the same type of thinking that would be required to solve a text adventure or graphical adventure video game, using logical deduction to overcome seemingly insurmountable obstacles. *Meanwhile* even includes elements that remind the player of the button-pushing interfaces of video games. It requires the player to manually input the access codes to the SQUID and the time machine by selecting the correct options from a menu.

In general, *Meanwhile* uses tropes conventional to the gamebook genre, and it uses the random-access nature of the printed book as a means of creating meaning in the same way that the traditional gamebook does. However, it also expands on the traditional gamebook by adding additional design innovations, many of which are possible only because *Meanwhile* is a comic rather than a prose novel. Therefore, it takes advantage of the unique affordances of the comics medium to rethink the gamebook genre and, by extension, the medium of the printed book.

In traditional CYOA books the reader traverses the book by turning from one numbered section or page to another. This same format is used in some CYOA comics, like *The Unwritten* #17. By contrast, in *Meanwhile* the reader/player traverses the book by following lines, or "trails," that lead from one panel to another (see figure 5.7). In panels that offer the reader a choice, multiple outgoing trails are available. Some panels can also be reached by multiple paths and therefore have multiple incoming trails—much as in Borges's hypothetical novel *The Garden of Forking Paths,* where each scene can be accessed in a variety of different ways. Through its use of trails, *Meanwhile* provides the reader with a visual mechanism for expressing choices. *Meanwhile*'s use of trails also creates a greater sense of unity between sections of the narrative. In a traditional CYOA narrative, each section is physically demarcated from all the others. By contrast, in *Meanwhile,* each panel of the story is physically connected to all the others, meaning that the story is a giant web, network, or "garden of forking paths" in a visual as well as a metaphorical sense. Its use of trails may further be seen as an example of arthrology, as defined earlier in this chapter. The trails that link individual panels are an example of Groensteen's restricted arthrology, which operates at the level of individual panels and sequences. Yet each panel in *Meanwhile* is at least indirectly linked by trails to every other panel in the book (with a few notable exceptions I will mention later), making *Meanwhile* perhaps the most arthrological comic imaginable.

Meanwhile also displays general arthrology or braiding, which links together panels belonging to different sequences, both on the same page and on adjacent pages. An unusual feature of *Meanwhile* is the copresence on each page of panels belonging to different, noncontiguous parts of the narrative. For example, the panels that show Jimmy's initial visit to the bathroom in the professor's castle are embedded within other panels from another part of the story that show Jimmy visiting the same bathroom. This page includes two nearly identical panels that show Jimmy flushing the toilet while looking at a physics textbook that rests on the toilet tank, yet these two panels are not directly connected by any trail. Reading this page for the first time, the reader wonders what sort of circumstances might result in Jimmy's ending up in the same bathroom again: What is he doing there, and to whom is he referring when he says, "Heh heh, he'll never find me in here"?

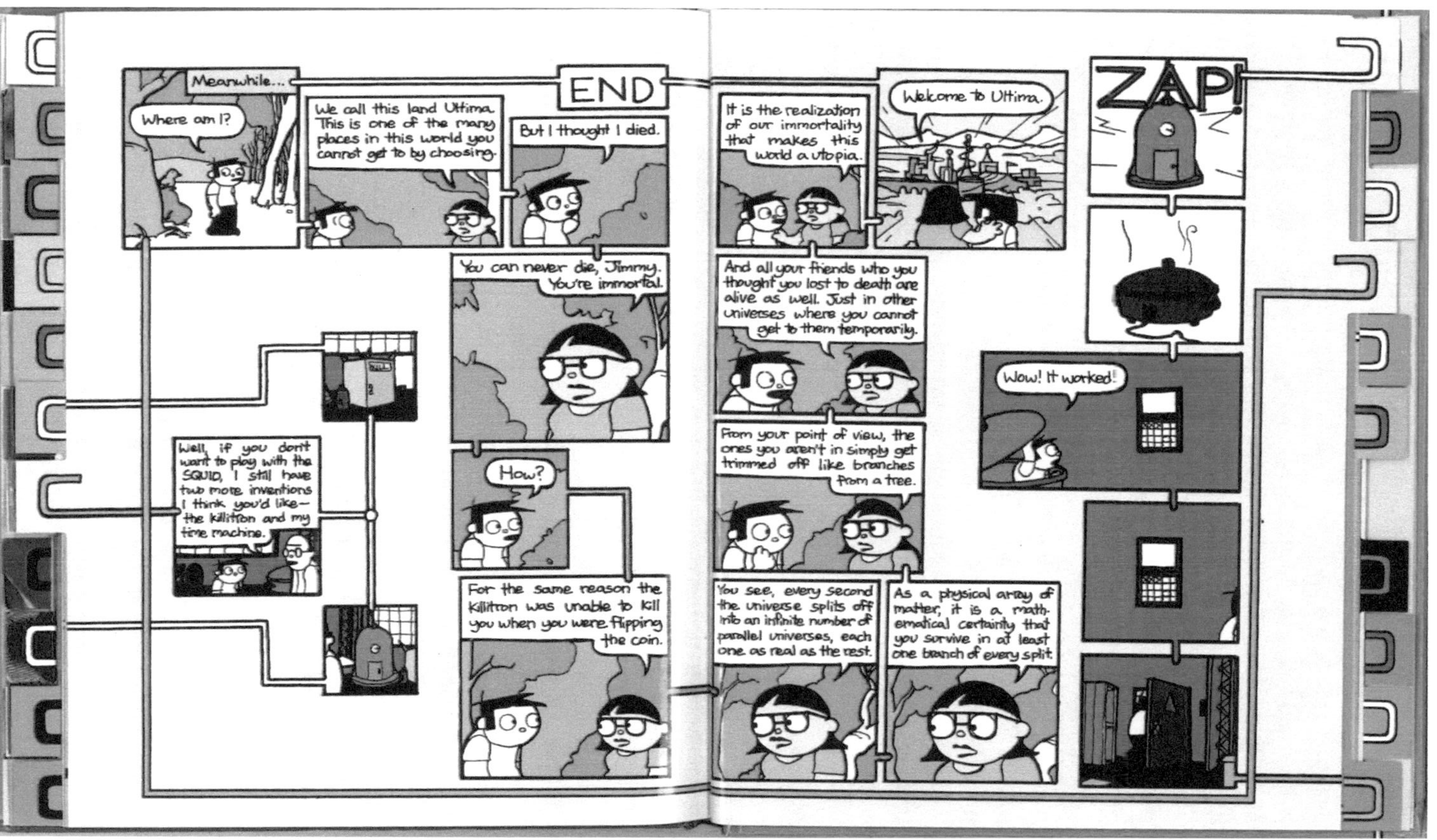

FIGURE 5.7. Example of *Meanwhile*'s use of trails and tabs. Note the "Ultima" section, which has no tabs leading in or out.

To notice this sort of thing, the reader has to violate the standard protocol of comics reading, which dictates that the reader is supposed to pay attention only to the panel he or she is reading at the moment. Yet this rule is invariably violated in practice. Among cartoonists it is a commonplace observation that when the reader turns the page, he always sees whatever is on the next right-hand page. Therefore, Mark Crilley suggests: "Put the big reveal in the first panel of a left-hand page. Readers can't see it until they turn the page[,] so they'll get the ultimate shock. If you put the surprise panel anywhere else, the readers will see it too soon and the dramatic opportunity will be lost" (112). Rather than trying to work around readers' natural tendency to look at panels they're not supposed to be looking at, *Meanwhile* plays with this tendency, offering readers tantalizing glimpses of possible futures or pasts.

Meanwhile even encourages these experiences of accidental discovery because it includes a section that cannot be reached through the normal course of the narrative and can be detected only if the reader notices it while reading other sequences on the same pages. At the top of one page of *Meanwhile*, Jimmy arrives at the utopian land of Ultima. This section, however, is inaccessible from anywhere else in the book because there are no trails leading into or out of it. The Ultima section actually calls the reader's attention to its inaccessibility, because it includes a character who tells Jimmy: "This is one of the many places in this world you cannot get to by choosing." Similarly, in a section depicting a conversation between two different time-displaced versions of Jimmy, one panel depicts Jimmy saying "Ultima." Again, there are no trails leading from this panel in any direction, so the player cannot reach it legitimately, although in both the print and digital versions of *Meanwhile*, the Ultima section can be reached by entering an incorrect access code.

Ultima is a reference to Edward Packard's 1982 *Choose Your Own Adventure* book *Inside UFO 54–40*, in which pages 101 to 104 feature an ending to the story in which the protagonist reaches a utopian planet also called Ultima.[16] This section is inaccessible from anywhere else in the book—it begins "You did not make a choice, or follow any direction" (101)—and the reader can discover the Ultima section only by turning to one of its pages en route to another section. The Ultima section in *Meanwhile* is different from the "Ultima" section in *Inside UFO 54–40*, however, because it exists on the same page as other sections that can be reached normally. The reader can

16. *Ultima* is also the name of a long-running video game series created by Richard Garriott, whose first installment was released in 1981. This use of identical names appears to be coincidental.

discover it incidentally while following the normal course of the narrative, simply by following another branch of the narrative that traverses the same page. Like "Easter eggs" in video games, the Ultima sequence rewards the player for being attentive—for paying attention to the entire page rather than concentrating on the narrative thread she is following at the moment.

Through its use of arthrology, *Meanwhile* uses comics to rethink the genre of the gamebook. Insofar as the gamebook is a means of exploiting the specific material properties of the codex book, *Meanwhile* thus also represents an innovation with respect to the format of the printed book. To see why, we have to examine a further unique property of *Meanwhile*: its combination of trails with tabs.

The use of trails to connect panels was pioneered by Scott McCloud and was originally associated with webcomics. In his fall/winter 2000 *I Can't Stop Thinking!* strip, which popularized the term *trails,* McCloud argues that the use of trails allows for the creation of infinite-canvas webcomics that are not bound to the print format but can take any "shapes" that "the stories dictate." However, in *Meanwhile,* Jason Shiga adapts the device of the trail to the physical book. Whenever a trail goes off the left- or right-hand edge of the page, it continues off the page onto a tab which extends from another page located vertically lower.

The use of tabs both discourages cheating and increases the physical richness of the experience of reading *Meanwhile.* In a standard gamebook, when choosing one of two options, the reader can remember the number of the page that contained the choice, allowing him to later go back and choose the other option. In *Meanwhile,* this doesn't work because there are no page numbers. The only way to tell pages apart is by their color, and some pages have the same color as others. To be able to return to a previous page, the reader has to mark the page with a finger or sticky note, which turns the process of reading *Meanwhile* into a physically meaningful (because physically awkward) experience.

However, the real importance of *Meanwhile*'s use of tabs is that they take advantage of the fact that a printed book is a three-dimensional object that has height as well as length and width. By exploiting its own three-dimensionality, *Meanwhile* counteracts the common tendency of books to represent themselves merely as vehicles for a stream of text that is effectively two- or even one-dimensional, that is, purely linear. According to Jan Baetens, "The book itself induces an undeniable *vectorization* of discourse; the book consecrates a linear, or more exactly monovectorized, reading, that distinguishes (and sometimes discriminates) a start and an end, an *incipit* and an *explicit,* a first and last of the cover" (quoted in Groensteen

147, emphasis in original). A standard un-illustrated prose book consists of a continuous stream of text, interrupted at various points by page, chapter, or section breaks. In digital reading environments, even the page breaks sometimes vanish. For example, Apple introduced a scrolling interface into the 2012 version of the iBooks app, thereby allowing the reader to read a book as a continuous stream of lines rather than as a collection of page images.

Yet *Meanwhile* reminds us that books have three dimensions rather than two or one and that this was the original affordance of the book relative to the scroll:

> Whereas the scroll was well suited to accessing a sequential group of pages, the codex was better for random access among passages throughout a book. For Christian purposes, the codex was clearly superior. In the church, the codex facilitated flipping easily from one scriptural passage to another, a process that would have necessitated a clumsy and time-consuming rolling and unrolling of a 35-foot scroll.[17] (Mathisen 145)

If random access is the primary technological affordance of the book relative to the scroll, then gamebooks are an effective way of exploiting this affordance. The gamebook depends crucially on the ability to read the book out of order and would be impossible with a sequential-access medium such as a scroll or a VHS cassette.

In its dependence on nonlinear orders of reading, the gamebook resembles other genres of books that are meant to be read out of order, such as dictionaries or books of scripture. The closest equivalent to *Meanwhile*'s tabs are the thumb indexes found in large dictionaries, which allow the reader to effortlessly flip to a specific letter of the alphabet. However, unlike reference works, gamebooks are meant to be read in a *specific* nonlinear order, and this is the case with *Meanwhile*. The reader is supposed to follow the tabs rather than flipping through the book at random. Nonetheless, *Meanwhile* anticipates the possibility that readers might not follow the order of the tabs, and Shiga includes Easter eggs that can be discovered only by reading out of order. For example, the book includes a two-page splash depicting Jimmy riding a giant squid. The squid section is unreach-

---

17. In Judaism, scrolls are used for public Torah readings in synagogues. On holidays, two or, rarely, three nonadjacent passages from the Torah are read during the same service. If the synagogue has multiple Torah scrolls, each passage is read from a different Torah scroll, to save the effort of rolling the scroll to the location of the second passage after reading the first one.

able from any other page, since it has no tabs on either side, and it has nothing to do with anything else in the book, except that one of the professor's devices is called SQUID. A similar reward for nonlinear reading is the Ultima section, discussed above.

However, *Meanwhile*'s encouragement of nonlinear reading only goes so far, because it also includes safeguards that discourage cheating and force the reader/player to play the game fairly. Shiga anticipated the possibility that a reader might cheat by flipping through the book cover to cover until she found the activation code to the SQUID. To prevent this, the book includes two nearly identical two-page spreads in which Jimmy finds the activation code to the SQUID. One of these can be reached legitimately and includes the real activation code, while the other cannot (the trail that appears to lead into it is fake) and includes an incorrect code. By including this page, *Meanwhile* ensures that the player is rewarded for playful and creative reading but not for cheating. The digital version, discussed later, also includes an incorrect activation code to the time machine, although if this was included in the print version, I couldn't find it.

In short, *Meanwhile* is an example of what comics can tell us about the future of the printed book. *Meanwhile* uses the arthrological potential of the comics medium to revitalize the genre of the gamebook, a genre that originated as a means of exploiting the unique affordances of the printed book but declined in importance due to competition from digital media. The subsequent history of *Meanwhile* shows that Shiga's effort to rethink the gamebook was successful. *Meanwhile* is Shiga's best-selling and most widely discussed work[18] and earned such accolades as an inclusion on the ALA's 2011 Top Ten Graphic Novels for Teens list. Its biggest audience has been children, which is somewhat surprising given its rather bleak and disturbing content, but also logical considering that the children's book market has historically been more receptive than the adult book market to books with creative and unusual formats. *Meanwhile* therefore demonstrates how print books, in seeking to adapt to competition from digital media, can take inspiration from comics. Furthermore, in the vocabulary of chapter 2, *Meanwhile* is a print-specific comic that demonstrates one effective way of using print comics to respond to the crisitunity caused by digital media.

However, the story of *Meanwhile* does not end here, because one of its readers was Andrew Plotkin, a prominent author of text adventure games.

18. In addition to Lombard-Cook, *Meanwhile* was also the subject of a paper read by Jeremy Douglass at MLA 2014.

Meanwhile appealed to Plotkin because it combined his longstanding interests in both gamebooks and digital adventure games:

> When I first saw the print form of *Meanwhile,* it was the original self-published black-and-white edition. . . . I was delighted because Jason had managed to come up with something new in the form. By using the structure of repeating events (thematically supported by the story elements of time travel and memory-reading), he put together a CYOA book which supported the kind of experimentation that characterizes adventure game puzzles. (Plotkin, personal communication)

Having just become interested in iOS programming, Plotkin felt that "the idea of translating the book into a program was an interesting design challenge" (personal communication), so he approached Shiga with a proposal to create an iOS app version of *Meanwhile.* If you think Shiga should have said no, because *Meanwhile* is a totally print-specific artifact that could never have been replicated in digital form, then read the next paragraph. If you think he should have said yes, then read the paragraph after that.

Shiga refused Plotkin's offer, saying that there was no way to replicate the experience of *Meanwhile* in an e-book form. Therefore, no digital version of *Meanwhile* was ever published, and *Meanwhile* does not help prove this chapter's thesis that comics can suggest ways of productively hybridizing print and digital media. The end.

Shiga accepted Plotkin's offer, and the digital version of *Meanwhile* was released in November 2011. It proved surprisingly easy to produce because in 2004, Shiga had prepared an "exploded" version of the book in which the entire book was laid out on a five-foot square sheet (see figure 5.8).

The iOS version of *Meanwhile* is visually based on this single-sheet version, but it enables the reader/player to make selections by tapping the screen. It also includes additional functionality such as a "back" button, which rewinds the story to the previous choice point, and a "so far" button, which allows the reader to review the story up to the current panel and revisit earlier choice points (as well as seeing the codes for the SQUID and time machine, if she has found them). The reader can also toggle between "story" mode to "browse" mode, in which the touch functionality is disabled and the reader can scroll anywhere in the story and zoom in or out.

The iOS app version of *Meanwhile* is not in fact the first digital version. In about 2005, Shiga had already released an earlier webcomic version of *Meanwhile* which was a digitization of the original 2000 minicomic version.

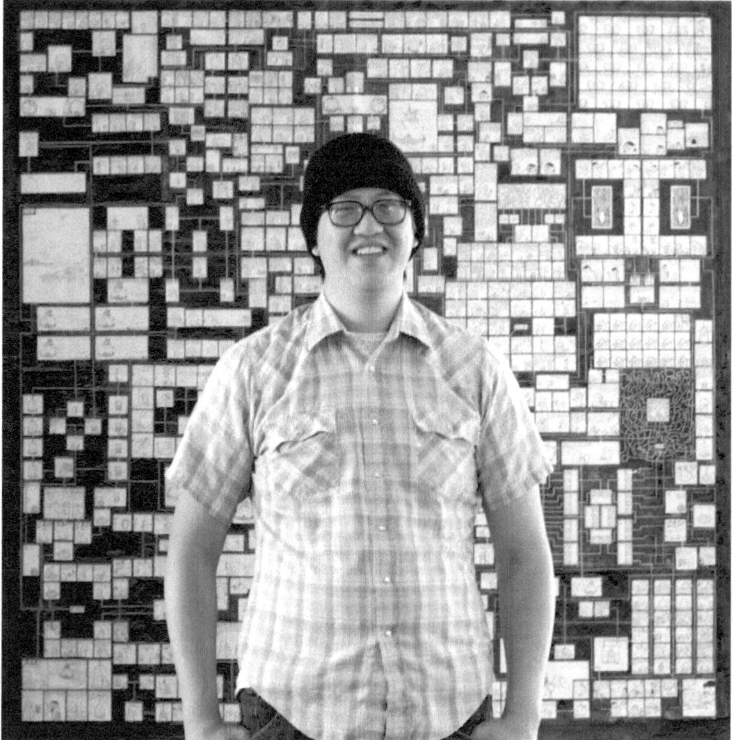

FIGURE 5.8. Jason Shiga standing next to the single-sheet version of *Meanwhile.* Photo courtesy of, and reproduced by permission of, Jason Shiga.

In the 2005 *Meanwhile* webcomic, each tab is replaced by a clickable link.[19] This incarnation of *Meanwhile* is a simple digital facsimile of the print version, except that it permits the reader to cheat by clicking the back button. In this it resembles the majority of web versions of print comics, which are simple digital scans of the print versions rather than genuine attempts to replicate the functionality of the original comic.

According to Shiga, Plotkin's original idea for the second digital version of *Meanwhile* was to create a more literal version of the book (personal communication). However, the digital version of *Meanwhile* that was ultimately released is not a simple scan of the original but a true adaptation: a new version of the text designed to exploit the affordances of the iOS platform. In an e-mail interview with me, Plotkin wrote that "the two forms

19. This version of *Meanwhile* is no longer available in its entirety on the Internet, but parts of it can be viewed through the Internet Web Archive at http://web.archive.org/web/20130828142612/http://www.shigabooks.com/interactive/meanwhile/01.html.

are each meant to stand on their own. I designed the app to be the best *Meanwhile* app it could be, and I'm sure Jason designed the book the same way. They're not intended to lean on each other." Thus, the iOS *Meanwhile* does not seek to precisely replicate the experience of reading the print version. It dispenses with the tabs, which would be impossible to simulate digitally because they depend on the three-dimensionality of the printed book. Instead, it substitutes the functionality of touching the screen, which only works on a touch-screen device; as discussed in the above section on "Touch Sensitive," in texts on mobile devices, the act of touching can have visual consequences.

The introduction of the touch interface and the other digital functionalities significantly changes the experience of reading *Meanwhile* in many ways. First, when the reader is in "story" mode, the panel she is currently reading is lit up, while the other panels are grayed out (see figure 5.9). This deemphasizes the importance of the adjacent panels and encourages the reader to pay attention only to the active panel. While reading in this mode, the reader is less likely to notice the Easter eggs (the Ultima section and the squid-riding panel), even though these are present. Conversely, by adding the "back" and "so far" buttons, the digital version makes it easier for the reader to experiment and explore different story threads. In the print version, taking back a choice is cumbersome because the reader has to follow the trail all the way back to the point where the choice is made. Therefore, the reader is encouraged to follow the current story thread to its logical conclusion rather than going back and trying a different one. The only way to easily access a prior choice point is to use a bookmark or a finger to mark the point where the choice was made. By contrast, in the iOS version the reader can get back to any prior choice point with only a few touches.

Finally, the material phenomenology of the app version is different from that of the print version. The *Meanwhile* app has no thickness; locations in the story are identified by their position on the two-dimensional canvas, not by the side of the page they occupy or the location of that page in the book. The app version doesn't offer the experience of feeling the weight of the book, the hardness of the cover, or the glossiness of the pages. In exchange, the reader has more direct tactile contact with the text than he does in the print version.

Further differences pertain to the audiences that the print and digital versions are aimed at. As suggested above, the primary target audience for the book version of *Meanwhile* is children. *Meanwhile* is distributed by Abrams Books's young adult and middle grade imprint, Amulet Books,

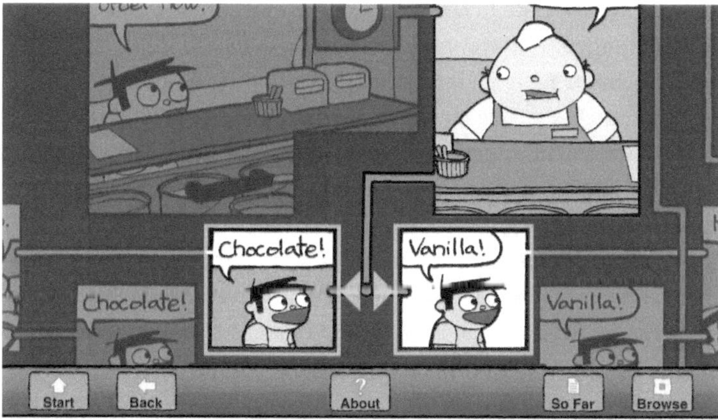

FIGURE 5.9. The iOS app version of *Meanwhile.*

which publishes other wildly successful children's graphic novels like Jeff Kinney's *Diary of a Wimpy Kid* series and Cece Bell's *El Deafo.* Shiga has done numerous events promoting *Meanwhile* at schools and children's bookstores. By contrast, because the *Meanwhile* app is available via the app store, it does not seem to be specifically targeted to children. In the App store, it appears in the "Books" category, which is not further subdivided into book-related apps for adults and children. It is distributed by Zarfhome Software Consulting, whose other offerings consist mostly of Plotkin's highly literary and experimental works of interactive fiction, and it generally seems relevant to gamers or aficionados of electronic literature.

Thus, the digital version of *Meanwhile* does not precisely replicate the print version, but that is precisely what makes it an effective digital translation or adaptation of *Meanwhile,* rather than a precise copy. The iOS *Meanwhile* does not work in the same way as the print version, but it works. It allows the reader to experience the content of the print version in a way that makes sense on an iOS device. A simple scan of the print *Meanwhile* in .cbr or .pdf format would be completely unreadable, as it would be impossible to follow trails from one page to another. Plotkin's version of *Meanwhile* does not seek to literally reproduce the print version in this way; indeed, it radically alters the text's visual structure and functionality. This, however, is necessary in order for *Meanwhile* to work properly in iOS form. As Walter Benjamin explains in "The Task of the Translator," translation is not about producing a literal copy of the original text in the target language; instead, an effective translation seeks to replicate the affective meaning of the original in a way appropriate to the context of the target language. The example of *Meanwhile* suggests that it may be more effective to think about the digitization of printed texts in terms of translation or adaptation rather than simple copying. *Meanwhile* works in digital form because it is not a simple copy but a thoughtful adaptation resulting from a productive collaboration between the original author and a highly experienced programmer who deeply understood the goals of the original text.

Meanwhile suggests a model of digital and print synergy where comics could simultaneously be produced in print and digital form but with significant differences between the two. A step beyond this would be to imagine a comic that exploited both print and digital platforms at once, requiring both media to be used in tandem in order to unlock its meaning. The leading current example of such a text is not a comic at all but an artist's book: Amaranth Borsuk and Brad Bouse's *Between Page and Screen.*

FROM *BETWEEN PAGE AND SCREEN* TO BETWEEN PANEL AND SCREEN

To end this chapter with *Between Page and Screen* is somewhat counterintuitive since it is not a comic but an artist's book. It does not employ sequential art and is primarily marketed toward readers of poetry rather than comics fans. However, *Between Page and Screen* meditates on an issue that has historically been of great concern to comics artists and readers: the ontological status of a two-dimensional page that represents a three-dimensional world. To explore this question, moreover, it employs strategies of verbal-visual blending that are more characteristic of comics than word-based literature. Therefore, *Between Page and Screen* can be read as a proof-of-concept demonstration of where comics and books in general are going, and if other artists explore the possibilities that Borsuk and Bouse's book opens up, they will have to learn from comics.

Between Page and Screen initially appears to be unreadable; each of its right-hand pages is blank except for a square black-and-white geometric design (see figure 5.10). To read the book, the reader has to use the web app located at www.betweenpageandscreen.com. When the reader visits this website and holds the book in front of her computer's webcam, words and illustrations appear as if by magic on top of the black squares. On using the web app, the reader discovers that the book consists of a series of poetic, punning letters between P and S, metaphorical representations of the titular page and screen. Interspersed between the letters are three-dimensional

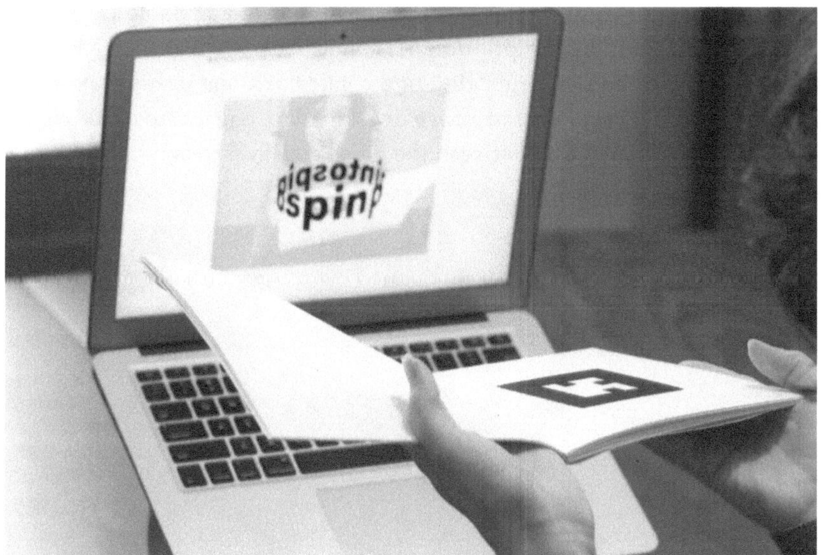

FIGURE 5.10. *Between Page and Screen.* Photo by Brad Bouse.

concrete poems. For example, one of these poems depicts a rotating rectangular column composed of the letters PALE, PAWL, PEEL, and POLE, while another depicts a pig whose body is made out of various permutations of the letters in the word *charcuterie.*

Between Page and Screen is the perfect example of a book that exists interstitially between print and the digital, and the metaphor of a love story between P and S—who are different but complementary, P being more interested in connection and S more interested in division—is a metaphor for the harmonious relationship that Bouse and Borsuk seek to create between print and screen cultures. The book presents certain practical access difficulties: it intentionally cannot be read at all without access to a computer with Adobe Flash, and even then it requires an environment with a sufficient level of ambient light. Like many online role-playing games, the book may eventually become unreadable when the server supporting the webcam is taken down. Still, *Between Page and Screen* represents the current state of the art in terms of combining the modes of materiality characteristic of print and digital books.

Between Page and Screen is not a comic book—its authors don't identify it as such, nor does it meet most definitions of comics. However, it is *almost* a comic book, to the extent that it uses multimodal rhetoric and visual storytelling in ways that are typical of comics. Perhaps more importantly, it offers a model of print/digital synergy that is easily adaptable to comics. We might imagine a hybrid print/digital comic book where some panels are available online and others in print, or a comic book that uses QR codes in the same way *Between Page and Screen* does. Perhaps the future of the comic book might lie somewhere between the panel and the screen.

CONCLUSION

APPLICATIONS FOR STUDYING AND TEACHING COMICS

IN THIS BOOK, I've sought to demonstrate that comics are a useful test case for discussions of the future of the book because of their unique relationship to materiality. Thanks to their tendency to use their own material properties for expressive purposes, comics make the rhetorical effects of materiality visible, in ways that printed books rarely do. I've also tried to suggest that making comics is a holistic design practice, in which lettering, coloring, and publication design are not incidental features but integral elements of the text. How does an understanding of the impact of materiality on comics get translated into pedagogical and scholarly practice? More broadly, how does a materiality-based perspective on comics influence the way we think about textuality and materiality in the digital age?

Let's begin with a question I've avoided throughout this book: What *is* "comics"? This question has been the cause of massive and often unproductive debate because it's typically asked in order to delimit the field of comics.[1] Standard definitions like McCloud's "juxtaposed pictorial and other

Some of the material in this chapter is based on Aaron Kashtan, "ENGL 1102: Literature and Composition: Handwriting and Typography," *Composition Studies*, vol. 43, no. 1 (2015): 147–69.

1. On the history of attempts at defining comics, see Meskin.

images in deliberate sequence" (1994, 9) or Groensteen's "relational play of a plurality of independent images" (128) emphasize the primacy of elements that separate comics from other visual media. The political purpose of such definitions is to prove that comics is a separate field from illustrated literature, painting, and so on, with the further implication that comics studies therefore deserves to be a field on its own. My favorite definition, however, instead emphasizes the commonality between comics and other media. In Dylan Horrocks's graphic novel *Hicksville,* a character named after the author has the following conversation with Emil Kopen, a cartoonist from the fictional land of Cornucopia:

> HORROCKS: Okay, how are *piktorii* [i.e., comics] like maps?
>
> KOPEN: They are the same thing: using *all* of language—not only words or pictures.
>
> HORROCKS: But some *piktorii* have *no* words.
>
> KOPEN: And some have no pictures. When we speak, we do not always use our whole vocabulary . . .
>
> HORROCKS: So it's still a comic even with no pictures?
>
> KOPEN: Perhaps. It is still a map. Why not? I have seen maps made entirely of text. (n.p., emphasis in original, first ellipsis in original)

Horrocks's radical insight is that *everything* is a comic, ranging from a painting to an un-illustrated novel. In Horrocks's definition, making comics is not a specific and clearly definable craft but a way of thinking, a mentality that recognizes words and images as opposite ends of a single spectrum. For Horrocks,[2] images can be semiotic and words can be visual, as well as vice versa. Even when we compose a text that seemingly includes no pictures, for example, pictures are still part of the vocabulary we draw upon. Composing such a text is a visual activity, in the same way that painting is a semiotic activity.

What might a comic (or map) "made entirely of text" look like? It might simply be a written composition in which the visual and other sensory properties of text serve as means of generating meaning and in which any

---

2. Of course this definition is provided by the fictional character Emil Kopen and should not necessarily be taken as representative of Horrocks's actual views. However, in his essay "Inventing Comics," Horrocks critiques McCloud's definition of comics in terms somewhat similar to those he places in Kopen's mouth. For example, Horrocks criticizes McCloud's "logophobia" and the essentializing nature of his definition, and concludes by mentioning possible connections between comics and cartography (Horrocks 2001).

change in the visual arrangement of text produces a corresponding change in meaning. In that sense, *any* text that pays careful attention to its own material and physical properties can be viewed as a comic, whether or not it uses pictures. Comics (in the narrow sense) are thus different from other types of texts, such as prose texts, only insofar as their use of document design is more visible and deliberate. Reading and making comics is a process of what Horrocks calls using our whole vocabulary, where *whole* is understood in the same sense in which Kathleen Blake Yancey uses this word to describe multimodal composition:

> The ways we write aren't quite shifting, however; we *aren't* abandoning one medium for another. Rather, the layered literacies Cynthia Selfe (1989) described have become textured in interesting ways: Print and digital overlap, intersect, become *intertextual.*
>
> And key to these new ways of writing, these new literacies, these new textures, I'll argue, is *composition,* a composition made whole by a new kind of coherence. If we are to value this new composition—text that is created on the screen and that in finished form is also mediated by the screen—we will need to invent a language that allows us to speak to those new values. Without a new language, we will be held hostage to the values informing print. . . . (89–90)

For both Horrocks and Yancey, the word *whole* denotes an expansive approach to composition, an approach in which writing practices that are traditionally kept separate (respectively, writing and drawing, and print and digital composing) are seen as different modalities of a single activity.

In a book that takes Yancey's phrase "toward a composition made whole" as its title, Jody Shipka observes that this approach applies equally to digital and nondigital composing, despite the frequent assumption that multimodal composition and digital composition are synonymous. Shipka opens her book by describing a student project that consisted of "a pair of pink ballet shoes . . . on which a student had transcribed by hand a research-based essay" (2). Subsequently, she quotes the same statement by Yancey that I quoted above and asks:

> I cannot help wondering where the "new composition" that Yancey describes leaves the composer of the ballet shoes. How might it position, whether rhetorically, materially, or technologically, texts that explore how print, speech, still images, video, sounds, scents, live performance, textures (for example, glass, cloth, paper attached to plastic), and other

> three-dimensional objects come together, intersect, or overlap in innovative and compelling ways? . . . There is nothing in the definition of composition Yancey offers at the end of her piece to suggest that this "new composition" should be limited to a consideration of screen-mediated texts. (9)

For Shipka, the key point in Yancey's "composition made whole" is not that print-based methods of composing need to be replaced by digital-based methods, but that students need to learn to show awareness of the material parameters of writing practices, whether those writing practices are print, digital, both, or neither:

> What matters is not simply that students learn to produce specific kinds of texts—whether linear, print-based, digital, object- or performance-based texts, or some combination thereof. Rather, what is crucial is that students leave our courses exhibiting a more nuanced awareness of the various choices they make, or even fail to make, throughout the process of producing a text and to carefully consider the effect those choices might have on others. (84–85)

If digital technology has increased the importance of such attentiveness of the materiality of writing practices, the reason is simply that it has made writers aware of material parameters of writing, which were previously invisible. As Anne Wysocki points out, "Writing is always changing . . . but part of what has changed the warp and woof that used to seem so steady underneath us is precisely that we are now aware of the warp and woof, that we are aware of the complex weaves of writing as a material practice" (Wysocki, et al. 2), thanks to the coexistence of two radically different modes of writing (i.e., print and digital).

All of these statements ultimately suggest that awareness of materiality plays a key role in contemporary writing practices, and this is one reason why asking students to read and create comics can be a useful means of teaching multimodal composition. This argument may seem to contradict Shipka's statement that "what matters is not simply that students learn to produce specific kinds of texts," but I'm not arguing that students should make comics simply for the sake of doing so; rather, I suggest that making comics is one useful means of helping students develop an awareness of materiality that can apply to other writing technologies as well. This is true because, as I've suggested throughout this book, material awareness is necessary for the effective creation of comics. We might modify Jeet Heer's statement that "all cartoonists . . . have to be thinking in spatial terms" by observing that cartoonists cannot avoid thinking about the design of their work and the way in which it interacts with its physical and material form, whether that work is optimized for one specific material form (like *MIND MGMT*) or is intended to be distributed in several forms (like *Peanuts* or *Bandette*). Awareness of materiality is a necessary skill for cartoonists, and the most successful works discussed in this book—*Fun Home, MIND MGMT,* "Click and Drag," *Bandette, Building Stories, Meanwhile,* and others—are works where physical form intersects with semiotic meaning in interesting ways. Of course this is not exclusively true of comics—as I've also repeatedly suggested, awareness of materiality is also important in the creation of print texts—but the useful property of comics is that they make materiality visible, whereas prose texts frequently render it invisible. Therefore, comics can be a useful pedagogical tool for promoting awareness of materiality. In this conclusion, I will offer, first, some concrete suggestions for how comics can be used in this way and, second, additional speculative ideas about how comics can be used to model the importance of awareness of materiality in scholarship as well as in teaching.

From 2011 to 2014, I worked as a Marion L. Brittain Postdoctoral Fellow at Georgia Tech, primarily teaching ENGL 1102, the second half of the Georgia university system's mandatory first-year writing sequence. The Georgia Tech Writing and Communication Program is unique in its focus on multimodal pedagogy. As of 2007, each ENGL 1101 and 1102 course must incorporate assignments covering four specific rhetorical modes: written, visual, electronic, and oral/nonverbal (summarized by the acronym WOVEN). In lieu of a final exam, each ENGL 1101 and 1102 course culminates in a reflective portfolio in which students select artifacts published over the course of the semester that fit into each of the WOVEN categories; then they write reflective essays analyzing the process of composing each of these artifacts. Beyond that, Brittain Fellows are encouraged to teach their ENGL 1101 and 1102 classes on any topic within their area of expertise as long as it meets these and other requirements. Comics are a natural fit with the WOVEN approach because they inherently incorporate the written and visual modes of communication and, increasingly, the electronic mode. Therefore, in each of my ENGL 1101 and 1102 courses, I had my students read comics, and I used comics as examples of multimodal synergy. In addition, the assignments in each course were inspired by what comics have taught me about multimodality and materiality. In my *Composition Studies* course design article, I describe one such course whose topic was handwriting and typography. Another course I taught that used comics in ways more directly relevant to this book's topic was my fall 2013 course, "The Future of the Book." I taught a similar course at Miami University in spring 2015, using *Building Stories* and J. J. Abrams and Doug Dorst's S. as textbooks.

The course description for this course explored topics similar to those of the present book:

> New technologies like the Kindle and iPad, as well as new means of book distribution like Amazon.com, are radically changing both the physical nature of books and the ways in which we use and circulate them. Many now mourn (or celebrate) the impending death of the printed book, and yet books still retain an unparalleled power over our imaginations. In this course we'll survey the history and the present state of the book in order to predict its future. Readings will consist of literary works that do interesting things with the physical properties of books. In your assignments you will learn firsthand about the changing nature of the book by producing books of your own.

Readings included *Talisman* and *Meanwhile,* both discussed elsewhere in this book, as well as three works of text-based literature (Italo Calvino's *If on a Winter's Night a Traveler,* Theresa Hak Kyung Cha's *Dictée,* and Garth Risk Hallberg's *A Field Guide to the North American Family*) and one artist's book (Tom Phillips's *A Humument*). I also showed my students *Building Stories,* which was published during the semester, and my colleague John Harkey, a poet and book artist, gave a guest lecture in which he showed the students some examples from his collection of artists' books.

Overall, the readings for the class asked the students to think about books not simply as vehicles for text but also as artistically or rhetorically designed objects, whose meanings emerge from the combination of their textual content with their material rhetoric. The written assignments in the class asked students to manipulate the material rhetoric of the texts they produced, in the same way (albeit on a smaller scale) as artists like Jason Shiga and Tom Phillips have done. The first project for the course asked the students to "choose a book you have read or used and discuss how the experience of purchasing and reading this book affected your understanding of it," while the second project asked the students to "choose any book and discuss how its physical and material properties affect the experience of reading it." For both projects, I asked the students to format their essays *as* books, using the material properties of their essays to remind the reader of the experience of reading the books they discussed. This project resulted in a variety of creative submissions—most memorably, one student wrote a paper about *The Hunger Games* which was submitted as a foam quiver containing toy arrows, each of which had a page of the paper wrapped around it. In the final project, students collaboratively produced essays that predicted the future of the book and that were designed as examples of the "book of the future." Many of these essays combined print and digital modes of textuality, often through the use of QR codes.

Not every book that we read in my "Future of the Book" course was a comic, and few if any of the students' projects took the form of comics. Yet the entire course was inspired by the ways of understanding books that I've learned from comics. This book (especially the first chapter) has sought to demonstrate that in a comic, every feature of the book is important—the book is not just a container for the narrative, but an artifact whose physical and material properties affect the reader's interpretation of it. And reading comics allows us to see how this is true not just of comics but of books in general. In order to succeed in the class, my students had to develop the sort of awareness of the materiality of the book that comics readers instinctively acquire. I taught a similar "Future of the Book" course in spring 2016, and in this course I explicitly used comics as a way of modeling awareness of materiality, by using *Building Stories* as one of the textbooks.

My argument here is that sensitivity to material rhetoric is important for twenty-first-century writers and that in our capacity as writing teachers, we can use comics to develop such sensitivity in ourselves and to teach it to our students. I want to conclude by suggesting, more speculatively, that we should also try to show awareness of materiality in the ways we produce and distribute our research in comics studies. Most published works of comics scholarship are traditional prose essays that use images only as illustrations, if at all. This book is no exception—it doesn't have the same level of material complexity as the texts it discusses (though the section on Shiga is under review elsewhere in a format that incorporates Choose Your Own Adventure functionality). Cartoonists themselves have been producing works of comics theory that incorporate or consist entirely of comics at least since Will Eisner's *Comics and Sequential Art* (1985). Yet the use of comics as a medium for academic comics studies is still unusual. The 2015 publication of Nick Sousanis's groundbreaking *Unflattening*, by a very prestigious academic press (Harvard University Press), suggests that comics are becoming widely accepted as a medium for scholarly inquiry. Yet anecdotal evidence suggests that scholars who attempt to publish academic work in comics form sometimes encounter resistance from publishers and external reviewers, even though scholarly texts that employ creative and innovative publication formats are becoming widely accepted in other academic fields.

Kairos, one of the most respected online journals in rhetoric and composition, declares in its mission statement: "Since its first issue in January of 1996, the mission of *Kairos* has been to publish scholarship that examines digital and multimodal composing practices, promoting work that enacts its scholarly argument through rhetorical and innovative uses of new media. [. . .] We publish 'webtexts,' which are texts authored specifically for publication on the World Wide Web" ("What Is Kairos?"). In film studies, the newly founded journal *[in]Transition* describes itself as

> the first peer-reviewed academic journal of videographic film and moving image studies.
>
> Practitioners of these forms (which include, *inter alia,* the "video essay," "audiovisual essay," and "visual essay" formats) explore the ways in which digital technologies afford a new mode of carrying out and presenting film and moving image research. The full range of digital technologies now enables film and media scholars to write using the very materials that constitute their objects of study: moving images and sounds. ("About *[in]Transition*")

Notably, one of the founders of *[in]Transition,* Drew Morton, is also a comics scholar. Both *Kairos* and *[in]Transition* may be seen as examples of a growing trend toward what has variously been called "practice-based research" or "critical making." Theorists like Alexander Galloway, Jussi Parikka, Matt Ratto, and Garnet Hertz have recently called for scholarly practices that use media to theorize themselves and that engage in design and making as critical activities. For Ratto, "critical making"

> focuses . . . on making practices themselves as processes of material and conceptual exploration. The ultimate goal of critical making experiences is not the evocative or pedagogical object intended to be experienced by others, but rather the creation of novel understandings by the makers themselves. Neither objects nor services are the currency of critical making. For me, it is the making experience that must be shared. (205)

As I've argued throughout this book, we as comics scholars are effectively positioned to embrace this sort of production-based approach to scholarship, because the experience of reading comics teaches us to pay attention to materiality and to be aware of the rhetorical effects of design choices. Moreover, our field is centrally concerned with questions of artistic practice and technique, and many of us even give our students assignments that incorporate artistic practice. (For example, one of my standard assignments is to ask my students to choose a particular comics page, draw it again in a different style, and then analyze the rhetorical decisions the artist made in drawing the original page. Ideally, each student's analysis of her chosen page will be enriched by the practical knowledge she will have gained through redrawing it.) Therefore, it's unfortunate that we have fallen behind other fields in terms of our promotion of production-based scholarship. Perhaps the time is ripe for a comics version of *[in]Transition,* a journal that would devote itself to works of comics theory executed in comics form.

Unfortunately, the present book is not an example of that sort of comics theory. This book is open to the same critique I leveled at Carla Speed McNeil in chapter 2, in that it doesn't take effective advantage of its own material features, and it can be read in either print or digital form without significantly changing the writing experience. As mentioned above, in other work I've tried to do a better job of practicing what I preach; for example, another version of the Jason Shiga material in chapter 5 was written as a *Choose Your Own Adventure* story, and I have another article that uses comics to theorize the importance of materiality in comics studies. It's because of my own lack of expertise in this area that I hesitate to offer more than general recommendations for how comics studies can show greater attentiveness to materiality. The point here is simply that as scholars and teachers of comics, we need to be more sensitive to issues of materiality in our pedagogy. Comics studies can be a means not only of understanding but also of helping to model both the future of the book and the book of the future.

WORKS CITED

"1110: Click and Drag." *explainxkcd*, 19 Sept 2012, www.explainxkcd.com/wiki/index.php/1110:_Click_and_Drag.

Aarseth, Espen. *Cybertext: Perspectives on Ergodic Literature.* Johns Hopkins UP, 1997.

"About." *Monkeybrain Comics*, n.d., web.archive.org/web/20150512094911/http://www.monkeybraincomics.com/about/.

"About *[in]Transition.*" *[in]Transition: A Media Commons/Cinema Journal Project*, n.d., mediacommons.futureofthebook.org/intransition/about-intransition.

Adams, Richard. "Amazon's ebook Sales Eclipse Paperbacks for the First Time." *The Guardian*, 27 Jan 2011, www.theguardian.com/world/richard-adams-blog/2011/jan/28/amazon-kindle-ebook-paperback-sales.

Allen, Amanda. "Yep—Same Reasons as Aaron [. . .]." *Facebook*, 1 July 2015, 1:18 p.m.

Alverson, Brigid. "Unbound: Webcomics in Print." *Robot 6, Comic Book Resources*, 27 Feb 2010, www.cbr.com/unbound-webcomics-in-print/.

Banita, Georgiana. "Chris Ware and the Pursuit of Slowness." *The Comics of Chris Ware: Drawing Is a Way of Thinking.* Ed. David M. Ball and Martha B. Kuhlman. UP of Mississippi, 2010. 177–90.

——. "The Silent Sublime." *The Comics Journal*, 2 Nov 2012, www.tcj.com/the-silent-sublime/.

Barry, Lynda. *Picture This: The Near-Sighted Monkey Book.* Drawn & Quarterly Publications, 2010, http://thenearsightedmonkey.tumblr.com.

——. *Syllabus: Notes from an Accidental Professor.* Drawn & Quarterly Publications, 2014.

——. *What It Is.* Jonathan Cape, 2009.

Beaty, Bart. *Unpopular Culture: Transforming the European Comic Book in the 1990s.* U of Toronto P, 2007.

Benjamin, Walter. *Illuminations.* Harcourt, Brace & World, 1968.

Bechdel, Alison. *Fun Home: A Family Tragicomic.* Mariner Books, 2007.

——. "Thank you, Eva!" Comment to Blog Post "Working." *Alison Bechdel*, 14 Aug 2011, dykestowatchoutfor.com/working.

Berlatsky, Noah. "The Promise—and the Danger—of Comparing Comic Books to Poetry." *The Atlantic,* 7 Aug 2013, www.theatlantic.com/entertainment/archive/2013/08/the-promise-and-the-danger-of-comparing-comic-books-to-poetry/278430/.

"Best Sellers—Paperback Graphic Books." *The New York Times,* 17 May 2015, www.nytimes.com/books/best-sellers/2015/05/17/paperback-graphic-books/.

Birkerts, Sven. *The Gutenberg Elegies: The Fate of Reading in an Electronic Age.* Faber & Faber, 2006.

Bolter, Jay David. *Writing Space: Computers, Hypertext, and the Remediation of Print.* Routledge, 2001.

Bolter, Jay David, and Richard Grusin. *Remediation: Understanding New Media.* The MIT Press, 2000.

"Bookplate." *Wikipedia, the Free Encyclopedia,* 16 July 2015, en.wikipedia.org/wiki/Bookplate.

Borsuk, Amaranth, and Brad Bouse. *Between Page and Screen.* SpringGun Press, 2016.

Bradley, Drew. "Minding *MIND MGMT:* Issue #1." Multiversity Comics, 16 Apr 2013, http://www.multiversitycomics.com/annotations/minding-mind-mgmt-issue-1/.

———. "Minding *MIND MGMT*: The io9 strips and Dark Horse Presents #19." *Multiversity Comics,* 8 Jan 2013, http://www.multiversitycomics.com/annotations/minding-mind-mgmt-the-io9-strips-and-dark-horse-presents-19/.

Burchby, Casey. "The Life Cycle of the Cartoonist: An Interview with Chris Ware." *Los Angeles Review of Books,* 25 Oct 2012, https://lareviewofbooks.org/article/the-life-cycle-of-the-cartoonist-an-interview-with-chris-ware/.

Carr, Nicholas. *The Shallows: What the Internet Is Doing to Our Brains.* W. W. Norton, 2011.

Carrión, Ulises. "The New Art of Making Books." *Kontexts,* vols. 6–7 (1975), http://www.arts.ucsb.edu/faculty/reese/classes/artistsbooks/Ulises%20Carrion,%20The%20New%20Art%20of%20Making%20Books.pdf.

Cepeda, Esther. "Stephen King Clings to Paper, and I'm Right There With Him." *Milwaukee Journal-Sentinel,* 8 June 2013, http://archive.jsonline.com/news/opinion/stephen-king-clings-to-paper-and-im-right-there-with-him-b99287322z1-210660881.html/?page=1.

Chabani, Karim. "Double Trajectories: Crossing Lines in *Fun Home,*" *GRAAT,* vol. 1, no. 1 (2007), www.graat.fr/bechdel001aaaa.pdf.

Chabon, Michael. Untitled Keynote Address. July 2004, San Diego, Comic-Con International, Eisner Awards.

Chute, Hillary L. *Graphic Women: Life Narrative and Contemporary Comics.* Columbia UP, 2010.

———. "Materializing Memory: Lynda Barry's *One Hundred Demons." Graphic Subjects: Critical Essays on Autobiography and Graphic Novels.* Ed. Michael Chaney. U of Wisconsin P, 2011. 282–309.

———. "Secret Labor." *Poetry* magazine, July/Aug 2013, www.poetryfoundation.org/poetrymagazine/articles/detail/70022.

Chute, Hillary L., and Patrick Jagoda. "Special Issue: Comics & Media." *Critical Inquiry,* vol. 40, no. 3 (Spring 2014): 1–10.

Clark, Joe. Comment on "Kindle-Proof Your Book in Seven Easy Steps!" *The Millions*, 31 May 2011, 12 June 2011, 3:52 pm, http://themillions.com/2011/05/kindle-proof-your-book-in-seven-easy-steps.html.

ComiXology (Tumblr account). "How Do You Do the Guided View?" Tumblr, *ComiXology Unbound: Taking Comics Further*, 26 July 2013, http://comixology.tumblr.com/post/56520607885/how-do-you-do-the-guided-view-is-their-a-team.

ComiXology (Twitter account). "Batman #5 contains upside-down and sideways pages. To maximize the reading experience you may want to lock the orientation on your device." *Twitter*, 18 Jan 2012, 12:38 p.m., twitter.com/comixology/status/159736319856218113.

"Commonplace Book." *Wikipedia, the Free Encyclopedia*, 28 Aug 2015, en.wikipedia.org/wiki/Commonplace book.

Cope, Ashley. *Unsounded Volume 1*. Kickstarter, 19 Sept 2012, www.kickstarter.com/projects/502093706/unsounded-comic-volume-1.

Crary, Jonathan. *24/7: Late Capitalism and the Ends of Sleep*. Verso, 2013.

Crilley, Mark. *Mastering Manga with Mark Crilley: 30 Drawing Lessons from the Creator of* Akiko. IMPACT Books, 2012.

Deegan, Marilyn, and Kathryn Sutherland. *Transferred Illusions: Digital Technology and the Forms of Print*. Ashgate, 2009.

Dickinson, Emily. *The Complete Poems of Emily Dickinson*. Little, Brown, 1976.

Dimock, Wai Chee. "Deep Time: American Literature and World History." *American Literary History*, vol. 13, no. 4 (2001): 755–75.

D'Orazio, Dante. "ComiXology Removes in-app Purchases to Avoid Paying Fees to Apple." *The Verge*, 26 Apr 2014, www.theverge.com/2014/4/26/5656468/comixology-ios-update-removes-in-app-purchases.

Drucker, Johanna. *The Visible Word: Experimental Typography and Modern Art, 1909–1923*. U of Chicago P, 1997.

———. "What Is Graphic about Graphic Novels?" *English Language Notes*, vol. 46, no. 2 (Fall/Winter 2008): 39–56.

Duncan, Randy, Matthew J. Smith, and Paul Levitz. *The Power of Comics: History, Form, and Culture*. Bloomsbury, 2015.

DuPont, Alexandra. "AICN COMICS EXCLUSIVE! Alexandra DuPont Interviews *BONE* Creator Jeff Smith!! PART TWO!!" *Ain't It Cool News*, 10 July 2003, www.aintitcool.com/node/15612.

Edidin, Jay. "*Finder* for Beginners." *Dark Horse Comics*, 12 Nov 2010, http://www.darkhorse.com/Blog/168/finder-beginners.

Ehrenreich, Ben. "The Death of the Book." *Los Angeles Review of Books*, 18 Apr 2011, lareviewofbooks.org/article/the-death-of-the-book/.

Emerson, Lori. *Reading Writing Interfaces: From the Digital to the Bookbound*. U of Minnesota P, 2014.

Engel, Joel. "Graphology at Home—Lesson 14—The Letters J–L." *eZine @rticles*, 22 Apr 2008, 8 Sept 2015, ezinearticles.com/?Graphology-at-Home—Lesson-14—The-Letters-J-L&id=1127468.

Evans, Karin. "Re: Question about a Particular Type of Notebook." E-mail to WPA-L, 3 Dec 2014.

Fattor, Hannah, "Manifesting Stories: The Progression of Comics from Print to Web to Print." *Summer Research Paper* 178 (2013), soundideas.pugetsound.edu/summer_research/178/.

Flacy, Mike. "Study: Why Facebook Is Making People Sad." *Digital Trends,* 22 Jan 2012, www.digitaltrends.com/social-media/study-why-facebook-is-making-people-sad/.

Gabilliet, Jean-Paul. *Of Comics and Men: A Cultural History of American Comic Books.* UP of Mississippi, 2009.

Gardner, Jared. *Projections: Comics and the History of Twenty-First-Century Storytelling.* Stanford UP, 2012.

Gioia, Dana. Preface. *Reading at Risk: A Survey of Literary Reading in America.* Ed. Tom Bradshaw and Bonnie Nichols. National Endowment for the Arts, 2004. vii.

Gitelman, Lisa. *Scripts, Grooves, and Writing Machines: Representing Technology in the Edison Era.* Stanford UP, 1999.

Grant, Steven. "*Masters of the Obvious: Issue #3.*" *Comic Book Resources,* 18 Aug 1999, www.cbr.com/issue-3-14/.

Gravett, Paul. *Manga: Sixty Years of Japanese Comics.* Harper Design, 2004.

Green, Justin. *Binky Brown Sampler.* Last Gasp, 1995.

Greg, Walter W. "The Rationale of Copy-Text." *Studies in Bibliography,* vol. 3 (1950): 19–36.

Groensteen, Thierry. *The System of Comics.* Trans. Bart Beaty and Nick Nguyen. UP of Mississippi, 2009.

Hague, Ian. *Comics and the Senses: A Multisensory Approach to Comics and Graphic Novels.* Routledge, 2014.

Hallberg, Garth Risk. "Kindle-Proof Your Book in Seven Easy Steps!" *The Millions,* 31 May 2011.

Harpold, Terry. *Ex-Foliations: Reading Machines and the Upgrade Path.* U of Minnesota P, 2009.

Hassler-Forest, Dan. *Capitalist Superheroes: Caped Crusaders in the Neoliberal Age.* Zero, 2012.

Hatfield, Charles. *Alternative Comics: An Emerging Literature.* UP of Mississippi, 2005.

Hayles, Katherine. *Electronic Literature: New Horizons for the Literary.* U of Notre Dame P, 2008.

——. "Flickering Connectivities in Shelley Jackson's *Patchwork Girl*: The Importance of Media-Specific Analysis." *Postmodern Culture,* vol. 10, no. 2 (Jan 2000), muse.jhu.edu/article/27720/summary.

——. *My Mother Was a Computer: Digital Subjects and Literary Texts.* U of Chicago P, 2005.

——. "Print Is Flat, Code Is Deep: The Importance of Media-Specific Analysis." *Poetics Today,* vol. 25, no. 1 (2004): 67–90.

——. *Writing Machines.* MIT P, 2002.

Heddings, Lowell. "The *xkcd* Alt Text Extension Takes Half the Fun Out of Reading *xkcd.*" *How to Geek,* 6 Sept 2010, www.howtogeek.com/89829/the-xkcd-alt-text-extension-takes-half-the-fun-out-of-reading-xkcd/.

Heer, Jeet. "Re: Comics and Poetry." E-mail to comixscholars-l, 7 Aug 2013.

Heller, Steven. "Jonathan Safran Foer's Book as Art Object." *The New York Times,* 24 Nov 2010. artsbeat.blogs.nytimes.com/2010/11/24/jonathan-safran-foers-book-as-art -object/.

Hirsch, Marianne. "Family Pictures: *Maus,* Mourning, and Post-Memory." *Discourse,* vol. 15, no. 2 (Winter 1992–93): 3–29.

"History of Scanlation." *Fanlore Wiki,* 12 Dec 2012, https://fanlore.org/wiki/History_of _Scanlation.

Hoffman, Eric, and Dominick Grace, eds. *Dave Sim: Conversations.* UP of Mississippi, 2013.

Horrocks, Dylan. *Hicksville: A Comic Book.* Drawn & Quarterly, 2002.

———. "Inventing Comics: Scott McCloud's Definition of Comics." *The Comics Journal,* no. 234 (June 2001): 29–39.

Hussie, Andrew. *Homestuck Book One.* Self-published, 2011.

Indvik, Lauren. "Why Amazon Won't Give You Free Digital Copies of Your Movies and Books." *Mashable,* 10 Jan 2013, mashable.com/2013/01/10/amazon-free-movies-books/.

Irving, Christopher. "Chris Ware on Building a Better Comic Book." *Graphic NYC,* 6 Mar 2012, www.nycgraphicnovelists.com/2012/03/chris-ware-on-building-better-comic .html.

Jenkins, Henry. "Transmedia Storytelling 101." *Confessions of an Aca-Fan: The Official Weblog of Henry Jenkins,* 22 Mar 2007, henryjenkins.org/2007/03/transmedia _storytelling_101.html.

Johnston, Paddy. "Going Digital: Chris Ware's *Touch Sensitive.*" *Comics and the Multimodal World,* 15 June 2013, Douglas College, New Westminster, BC, Conference Presentation.

Johnston, Rich. "Barnes & Noble Pulls *Watchmen, Sandman,* and 100 DC Graphic Novels from Their Shelves over Amazon Kindle Fire Deal." *Bleeding Cool,* 7 Oct 2011, www .bleedingcool.com/2011/10/07/barnes-noble-pulls-watchmen-sandman-and-100-dc -graphic-novels-from-their-shelves-over-amazon-kindle-fire-deal/.

———. "DC Announces Digital Print Combo Packs for Batman and Action Comics Too." *Bleeding Cool,* 13 Oct 2011, www.bleedingcool.com/2011/10/13/dc-announce-digital -print-combo-packs-for-batman-and-action-comics-too/.

Kashtan, Aaron. "My Mother Was a Typewriter: *Fun Home* and the Importance of Materiality in Comics Studies." *Journal of Graphic Novels and Comics,* vol. 4, no. 1 (2013): 92–116.

———. "Nostalgia for Handwriting: The Rhetoric of Comics Lettering." *Type Matters: The Rhetoricity of Letterforms.* Ed. C. S. Wyatt and Danièle Nicole DeVoss. Parlor Press, 2017.

———. "Preliminary Observations on Using the Kindle Fire to Read Comics." *The Ogre's Feathers,* 29 Nov 2012, ogresfeathers.wordpress.com/2012/11/29/preliminary -observations-on-using-the-kindle-fire-to-read-comics/.

———. "Talismans: Using Graphic Novels to Teach Materiality." *Class, Please Open Your Comics: Essays on Teaching with Graphic Narratives.* Ed. Matthew L. Miller. McFarland Press, 2015. 103–16.

———. "This Living Hand: Fantasies of Handwriting in the Comics of Kevin Huizenga." *Forum for World Literature Studies,* vol. 3, no. 1 (2011): 94–106.

Katz, Demian. "Frequently Asked Questions." *Demian's Gamebook Web Page*, n.d., gamebooks.org/faq.htm.

Keim, Brandon. "Why the Smart Reading Device of the Future May Be . . . Paper." *WIRED*, 1 May 2014, www.wired.com/2014/05/reading-on-screen-versus-paper/.

Kelly, Kevin. "Scan This Book!" *The New York Times*, 14 May 2006, www.nytimes.com/2006/05/14/magazine/14publishing.html.

Khouri, Andy. "ComiXology Ends 2010 with 1 Million Downloads and over 5,000 Comics." ComicsAlliance, 29 Dec 2010, comicsalliance.com/comixology-1-million-downloads/.

Kindt, Matt. *MIND MGMT*, no. 16, Dark Horse, October 2013.

Kindt, Matt. *MIND MGMT*, no. 19, Dark Horse, February 2014.

Kirschenbaum, Matthew G. *Mechanisms: New Media and the Forensic Imagination*. MIT P, 2008.

Kirtley, Susan E. *Lynda Barry: Girlhood through the Looking Glass*. UP of Mississippi, 2012.

Kittler, Friedrich A. *Gramophone, Film, Typewriter*. Stanford UP, 1999.

Kosturski, Karen. "New York Comic-Con Days 3 and 4: Of Censorship and (Digital) Content." *American Libraries Magazine*, 17 Oct 2012, americanlibrariesmagazine.org/blogs/the-scoop/new-york-comic-con-days-3-and-4-of-censorship-and-digital-content/.

"Laid-Back Company Allows Employees To Work From Home After 6 P.M." *The Onion*, vol. 50, no. 44 (4 Nov 2014), http://www.theonion.com/article/laid-back-company-allows-employees-to-work-from-ho-37358.

Landow, George P. *Hypertext: The Convergence of Contemporary Critical Theory and Technology*. Johns Hopkins UP, 1992.

Lanier, Jaron. *You Are Not a Gadget: A Manifesto*. Alfred A. Knopf, 2010.

Larimer, Kevin. "The Color and the Shape of Memory: An Interview with Chris Ware." *Poets & Writers*, 31 Oct 2012, www.pw.org/content/the_color_and_the_shape_of_memory_an_interview_with_chris_ware.

Lefebvre, Pascal. "The Importance of Being 'Published.' A Comparative Study of Different Comics Formats." *Comics & Culture: Analytical and Theoretical Approaches to Comics*. Ed. Anne Magnussen and Hans-Christian Christiansen, Museum Tusculanum P, 2000. 91–106.

Lidl, Bruce. "*Bandette*'s Coover and Tobin Talk about Digital Comics Going into Print." *The Comics Beat*, 3 Mar 2014, www.comicsbeat.com/bandettes-coover-and-tobin-talk-about-digital-comics-going-into-print-interview/.

Lombard-Cook, Kat. "Jason Shiga's *Meanwhile* and Digital Adaptability of Non-Traditional Narratives in Comics." *Journal of Graphic Novels and Comics* vol. 6, no. 1 (2015): 15–30.

MacDonald, Heidi. "Breaking News: The Comics Industry Is Not Dying." *The Beat*, 12 June 2013, www.comicsbeat.com/breaking-news-the-comics-industry-is-not-dying/.

——. "ComiXology Was the #1 Grossing Non-Game App on iPad in 2013 with Four Billion Comics Pages Served." *The Comics Beat*, 13 Jan 2014, www.comicsbeat.com/comixology-was-the-1-grossing-non-game-app-on-ipad-in-2013-with-four-billion-comics-pages-served/.

———. "Marvel to Include Digital Copy with all $3.99 Comics." *The Comics Beat,* 9 Mar 2012, www.comicsbeat.com/marvel-to-include-digital-copy-with-all-3–99-comics/.

Mangen, Anne. "Hypertext Fiction Reading: Haptics and Immersion." *Journal of Research in Reading,* vol. 31, no. 4 (2008): 404–19.

Manguel, Alberto. *A History of Reading.* Penguin, 2014.

Marks, Laura. *Touch: Sensuous Theory and Multisensory Media.* U of Minnesota P, 2002.

Massey, Heather. "Are Comic Books Dying?" *Tor.com,* 21 Jan 2009, www.tor.com/2009/01/21/comicsdying/.

Mathisen, Ralph W. "Palaeography and Codicology." *The Oxford Handbook of Early Christian Studies.* Ed. Susan Ashbrook Harvey and David G. Hunter. Oxford UP, 2010. 140–66.

McCloud, Scott. "I Can't Stop Thinking! #4." *Scott McCloud.com,* Fall/Winter 2000, scottmccloud.com/1-webcomics/icst/icst-4/icst-4.html.

———. *Reinventing Comics: How Imagination and Technology Are Revolutionizing an Art Form.* HarperCollins, 2000.

———. *Understanding Comics: The Invisible Art.* William Morrow Paperbacks, 1994.

McDonald, Peter D., and Michael Felix Suarez, eds. *Making Meaning: Printers of the Mind and Other Essays.* By Donald F. McKenzie. Amherst: U of Massachusetts P, 2002.

McGann, Jerome J. *The Textual Condition.* Princeton UP, 1991.

McMillan, Graeme. "ComiXology Tops Apple's 2013 iPad Highest-Grossing Non-Game App Chart." *The Hollywood Reporter,* 13 Jan 2014, www.hollywoodreporter.com/heat-vision/comixology-tops-apples-2013-ipad-670549.

McNeil, Carla Speed. *Talisman. Finder Library Volume 1.* Dark Horse, 2011.

Meskin, Aaron. "Defining Comics?" *The Journal of Aesthetics and Art Criticism,* vol. 65, no. 4 (2007): 369–79.

Michel, Lincoln. "The Future of the Future of Books." *Buzzfeed,* 17 Sept 2014, www.buzzfeed.com/lincolnmichel/the-future-is-never?utm_term=.scLQBx5Gm#.atNzr3NEK.

Mitchell, Adrielle. "Spectral Memory, Sexuality and Inversion: An Arthrological Study of Alison Bechdel's *Fun Home*: A Family Tragicomic." *ImageTexT: Interdisciplinary Comics Studies* vol. 4, no. 3 (2009), www.english.ufl.edu/imagetext/archives/v4_3/mitchell/.

Mitchell, Dan. "In Online World, Pocket Change Is Not Easily Spent." *The New York Times,* 27 Aug 2007, www.nytimes.com/2007/08/27/technology/27micro.html.

Mitchell, W. J. T. *Picture Theory: Essays on Verbal and Visual Representation.* U of Chicago P, 1995.

Montfort, Nick, and Noah Wardrip-Fruin. "Acid-Free Bits: Recommendations for Long-Lasting Electronic Literature." *Electronic Literature Organization,* 14 June 2004, eliterature.org/pad/afb.html.

Moody, Rick. "Fugue for Centrifuges: On Chris Ware's Building Stories." *Los Angeles Review of Books,* 25 Oct 2012, lareviewofbooks.org/article/fugue-for-centrifuges-on-chris-wares-building-stories/.

Morton, Drew. "The Unfortunates: Towards a History and Definition of the Motion Comic." *Journal of Graphic Novels and Comics,* vol. 6, no. 4 (2015): 347–66.

Munroe, Randall. "Beer." *xkcd,* 5 June 2015, xkcd.com/1534/.

——. "Click and Drag." *xkcd,* 19 Sept 2012, www.xkcd.com/1110/.

Murray, Noel. "Reading Comics on Cell Phones Changes the Way the Medium Works." A. V. Club, 21 July 2015, www.avclub.com/article/reading-comics-cell-phones-changes-way-medium-work-222218.

O'Donnell, James J., et al. "Do You Like Your E-Reader?" *The Chronicle of Higher Education,* 13 June 2010, www.chronicle.com/article/Do-You-Like-Your-E-Reader-/65840/.

Packard, Edward. *Inside UFO 54–40.* Bantam, 1982.

Parisi, David. "Fingerbombing, or 'Touching is Good': The Cultural Construction of Technologized Touch." *Senses & Society,* vol. 3, no. 3 (Nov 2008): 307–27.

Parkin, J. K., moderator. "Digital and Print: Friends or Foes?" 19 July 2013, San Diego, Comic-Con International. Panel discussion.

Pearce, Christopher. "Thrift Store Finds: A Parcel of *Peanuts* Paperbacks." *Teachable Moments: A Comics Journal by Chris Pearce,* 5 Mar 2011, chrispearce.wordpress.com/2011/03/05/thrift-store-finds-a-parcel-of-peanuts-collections/.

Phegley, Kiel. "EXCLUSIVE: Matt Kindt Expands 'MIND MGMT' for Readers & Retailers." *Comic Book Resources,* 13 Nov 2012, www.cbr.com/exclusive-matt-kindt-expands-mind-mgmt-for-readers-retailers/.

Piper, Andrew. *Book Was There: Reading in Electronic Times.* U of Chicago P, 2013.

Pratt, Henry John. "Narrative in Comics." *Journal of Aesthetics and Art Criticism,* vol. 67, no. 1 (2009): 107–17.

"Print Dead at 1,803." *The Onion,* vol. 49, no. 3 (25 July 2013), www.theonion.com/articles/print-dead-at-1803,33244/.

Pustz, Matthew. *Comic Book Culture: Fanboys and True Believers.* UP of Mississippi, 1999.

Raley, Rita. "Reveal Codes: Hypertext and Performance." *Postmodern Culture,* vol. 12, no. 1 (Sept 2001), muse.jhu.edu/article/27750.

Raskin, Jef. "Recollections of the Macintosh project." Articles from Jef Raskin about the history of the Macintosh, n.d., drbobtechblog.com/articles-from-jef-raskin-about-the-history-of-the-macintosh/.

Ratto, Matt. "Critical Making." *Open Design Now: Why Design Cannot Remain Exclusive.* Ed. Bas van Abel, et al., BIS, 2011, opendesignnow.org/index.html%3Fp=434.html.

Reid, Calvin. "A Life in A Box: Invention, Clarity and Meaning in Chris Ware's 'Building Stories.'" *Publishers Weekly,* 28 Sept 2012, www.publishersweekly.com/pw/by-topic/industry-news/comics/article/54154-a-life-in-a-box-invention-clarity-and-meaning-in-chris-ware-s-building-stories.html.

Renear, Allen H. "Text Encoding." *A Companion to Digital Humanities.* Ed. Susan Schreibman, Ray Siemens, and John Unsworth. Blackwell, 2004. 218–39.

Rhoades, Shirrel. *Comic Books: How the Industry Works.* Peter Lang, 2008.

Robinson, Alex. *Box Office Poison.* Top Shelf, 2001.

Rogers, Vaneta. "So . . . Who IS COMIXOLOGY, the Digital Comics Leader?" *Newsarama,* 24 June 2010, www.newsarama.com/5517-so-who-is-comixology-the-digital-comics-leader.html.

Ryan, Marie-Laure. *Narrative as Virtual Reality: Immersion and Interactivity in Literature and Electronic Media.* Johns Hopkins UP, 2003.

Salkowitz, Rob. *Comic-Con and the Business of Pop Culture: What the World's Wildest Trade Show Can Tell Us about the Future of Entertainment.* McGraw-Hill Education, 2012.

Sattler, Peter. "Building Memories: Mine, Hers, and Ours." *The Comics Journal,* 2 Nov 2012, www.tcj.com/building-memories-mine-hers-and-ours/.

Schappell, Elissa. "A Conversation with Lynda Barry." *Tin House,* vol. 29 (Fall 2006): 50–57.

Schodt, Frederik L. *Manga! Manga! The World of Japanese Comics.* Kodansha USA, 1986.

Schulz, Charles. "National Dog Month." *Peanuts.* 22 Sept 1960.

Selzer, Jack. "Habeas Corpus: An Introduction." *Rhetorical Bodies.* Ed. Jack Selzer and Sharon Crowley. U of Wisconsin P, 1999. 3–15.

Shiga, Jason. *Meanwhile: Pick Any Path. 3,856 Story Possibilities.* Harry N. Abrams, 2010.

———. "Upcoming Depravity in *Demon.*" Shigabooks, 23 July 2014, www.shigabooks.com/wordpress/?p=508.

Shipka, Jody. *Toward a Composition Made Whole.* U of Pittsburgh P, 2011.

Shirky, Clay. "Why I Just Asked My Students to Put Their Laptops Away." *Medium,* 9 Sept 2014, medium.com/@cshirky/why-i-just-asked-my-students-to-put-their-laptops-away-7f5f7c50f368.

Simons, Gideon. "UX is Not Usability." *Medium.com,* 8 Jan 2015, medium.com/@papasimons/ux-is-not-usability-a9f82e4a60ba.

Slott, Dan (writer) and Mike Allred (artist). "Never After." *Silver Surfer #11,* Marvel Comics, June 2015.

Spurgeon, Tom. "CR Newsmaker: Sammy Harkham." *The Comics Reporter,* 27 Aug 2008, www.comicsreporter.com/index.php/cr_newsmaker_sammy_harkham/.

Stewart, Susan. *On Longing: Narratives of the Miniature, the Gigantic, the Souvenir, the Collection.* Duke UP, 1984.

Szalavitz, Maia. "Do E-Books Make It Harder to Remember What You Just Read?" *Time* magazine, 14 Mar 2012, healthland.time.com/2012/03/14/do-e-books-impair-memory/.

Tenner, Edward. "The Prestigious Inconvenience of Print." *The Chronicle of Higher Education,* 9 Mar 2007, www.chronicle.com/article/The-Prestigious-Inconvenience/30771.

Thomas, Joseph T. *Poetry's Playground: The Culture of Contemporary American Children's Poetry.* Wayne State UP, 2007.

Thornton, Tamara Plakins. *Handwriting in America: A Cultural History.* Yale UP, 1996.

Tinker, Emma. "Manuscript in Print: The Materiality of Alternative Comics." *Literature Compass,* vol. 4, no. 4 (2007): 1169–182.

Tobin, Paul, and Colleen Coover. *Bandette Volume 1: Presto!* Dark Horse, 2013.

———. *Bandette Volume 2: Stealers Keepers!* Dark Horse, 2015.

Turkle, Sherry. *Alone Together: Why We Expect More from Technology and Less from Each Other.* Basic Books, 2012.

Updike, John. "The End of Authorship." *The New York Times,* 25 June 2006, www.nytimes.com/2006/06/25/books/review/25updike.html.

Versaci, Rocco. *This Book Contains Graphic Language: Comics as Literature.* Continuum, 2007.

Walsh, John A. "Comic Book Markup Language: An Introduction and Rationale." *Digital Humanities Quarterly*, vol. 6, no. 1 (2012), www.digitalhumanities.org/dhq/vol/6/1/000117/000117.html.

Walton, Saige. "Baroque Mutants in the 21st Century? Rethinking Genre through the Superhero." *The Contemporary Comic Book Superhero*. Ed. Angela Ndalianis. Routledge, 2009. 86–106.

Warde, Beatrice. "The Crystal Goblet, or Printing Should Be Invisible." *The Crystal Goblet: Sixteen Essays on Typography*. Sylvan, 1955. 11–17.

Ware, Chris. *Building Stories*. Pantheon, 2012.

Watson, Julia. "Autobiographic Disclosures and Genealogies of Desire in Alison Bechdel's *Fun Home*." *Graphic Subjects: Critical Essays on Autobiography and Graphic Novels*. Ed. Michael Chaney. U of Wisconsin P, 2011. 123–56.

Weiner, Zach. "SCIENCE: Ruining Everything since 1543 (an SMBC Collection)." *Kickstarter*, 23 Jan 2013, www.kickstarter.com/projects/weiner/science-ruining-everything-since-1543-an-smbc-coll.

Weiss, Jennifer. "Second Act for Some Independent Bookstores." *The Wall Street Journal*, 9 Apr 2013, blogs.wsj.com/metropolis/2013/04/09/second-act-for-some-independent-bookstores/.

Weissmann, Jordan. "The Decline of the American Book Lover." *The Atlantic*, 21 Jan 2014, www.theatlantic.com/business/archive/2014/01/the-decline-of-the-american-book-lover/283222/.

Wershler-Henry, Darren. "Digital Comics, Circulation, and the Importance of Being Eric Sluis." *Cinema Journal*, vol. 50, no. 3 (2011): 127–34.

———. *The Iron Whim: A Fragmented History of Typewriting*. McClelland & Stewart, 2005.

"What Is Kairos?" *Kairos: A Journal of Rhetoric, Technology, and Pedagogy*, n.d., kairos.technorhetoric.net/about.html.

Whitbrook, James. "Here's What It Really Looks Like When Classic Comics Get Recolored." *io9*, 7 Apr 2015, io9.gizmodo.com/heres-what-it-really-looks-like-when-classic-comics-get-1696313219.

Whitman, Walt. *Leaves of Grass*. Rees Welsh, 1882.

Wilkins, Peter. "#155 Color in Comics: The Case of Matt Kindt." *Graphixia*, 18 Feb 2014, archive.is/iHDmK.

Wurth, Kiene Brillenburg. Introduction. Between Page and Screen: *Remaking Literature through Cinema and Cyberspace*. Ed. Kiene Brillenburg Wurth. Fordham UP, 2012. 1–23.

Wysocki, Anne Frances, et al. *Writing New Media: Theory and Applications for Expanding the Teaching of Composition*. Utah State UP, 2004.

Yancey, Kathleen Blake. "Looking for Sources of Coherence in a Fragmented World: Notes toward a New Assessment Design." *Computers and Composition*, vol. 21, no. 1 (2004): 89–102.

Young, Victoria. "Strategic UX: The Art of Reducing Friction." 10 Feb 2015, www.dtelepathy.com/blog/business/strategic-ux-the-art-of-reducing-friction.

INDEX

STUDIES IN COMICS AND CARTOONS

Jared Gardner and Charles Hatfield, Series Editors
Lucy Shelton Caswell, Founding Editor Emerita

Books published in Studies in Comics and Cartoons focus exclusively on comics and graphic literature, highlighting their relation to literary studies. The series includes monographs and edited collections that cover the history of comics and cartoons from the editorial cartoon and early sequential comics of the nineteenth century through webcomics of the twenty-first. Studies that focus on international comics are also considered.

Between Pen and Pixel: Comics, Materiality, and the Book of the Future
AARON KASHTAN

Ethics in the Gutter: Empathy and Historical Fiction in Comics
KATE POLAK

Drawing the Line: Comics Studies and INKS, *1994–1997*
EDITED BY LUCY SHELTON CASWELL AND JARED GARDNER

The Humours of Parliament: Harry Furniss's View of Late-Victorian Political Culture
EDITED AND WITH AN INTRODUCTION BY GARETH CORDERY AND JOSEPH S. MEISEL

Redrawing French Empire in Comics
MARK MCKINNEY

www.ingramcontent.com/pod-product-compliance
Lightning Source LLC
LaVergne TN
LVHW091053080826
845145LV00002B/735

* 9 7 8 0 8 1 4 2 5 4 7 0 7 *